ROUTLEDGE LIBRARY EDITIONS:
SMALL BUSINESS

Volume 4

SMALL FIRMS IN URBAN AND RURAL LOCATIONS

SMALL FIRMS IN URBAN AND RURAL LOCATIONS

Edited by
JAMES CURRAN AND DAVID J. STOREY

Routledge
Taylor & Francis Group

LONDON AND NEW YORK

First published in 1993 by Routledge

This edition first published in 2016
by Routledge
2 Park Square, Milton Park, Abingdon, Oxon OX14 4RN

and by Routledge
711 Third Avenue, New York, NY 10017

Routledge is an imprint of the Taylor & Francis Group, an informa business

© 1993 James Curran and David Storey

British Library Cataloguing in Publication Data
A catalogue record for this book is available from the British Library

ISBN: 978-1-138-67308-3 (Set)
ISBN: 978-1-315-54266-9 (Set) (ebk)
ISBN: 978-1-138-68235-1 (Volume 4) (hbk)
ISBN: 978-1-138-68237-5 (Volume 4) (pbk)
ISBN: 978-1-315-54524-0 (Volume 4) (ebk)

Small Firms in Urban and Rural Locations

Edited by
James Curran and David Storey

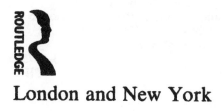

London and New York

First published 1993
by Routledge
11 New Fetter Lane, London EC4P 4EE

Simultaneously published in the USA and Canada
by Routledge
29 West 35th Street, New York, NY 10001

© 1993 James Curran and David Storey

Typeset in Times by J&L Composition Ltd, Filey, North Yorkshire
Printed and bound in Great Britain by L. Mackays of Chatham PLC,
Chatham, Kent

British Library Cataloguing in Publication Data
A catalogue record for this book is available from the British Library

Library of Congress Cataloging in Publication Data
Small firms in urban and rural locations / edited by James Curran and
   David Storey.
      p.   cm. — (Small business series)
   Includes bibliographical references and index.
   1. Small business—Great Britain—Location.   2. Rural Industries—
Great Britain.   3. New business enterprises—Great Britain.
4. Rural-urban migration—Great Britain.   5. Great Britain—Economic
conditions—1945– I. Curran, James, 1936–   . II. Storey, D.J.
III. Series: Small business series (London, England)
HD2346.G7S643   1993   93–18756
338.6'42'0941—dc20   CIP

ISBN 0–415–10037–2

Contents

Figures

Tables

Contributors

Robert A. Blackburn is Midland Bank Research Fellow and Senior Lecturer in the Small Business Research Centre at Kingston University. He was a Senior Scholar in the ESRC Centre for Research on Small Service Sector Enterprises set up under the ESRC Small Business Research Initiative, 1989–92. His special interest is small firms and subcontracting, but he has also carried out research on other small business topics, most recently on the ethnic small business. With James Curran he edited *Paths of Enterprise, The Future of the Small Business*, Routledge, 1991.

James Curran is Midland Bank Professor of Small Business Studies and Director of the Small Business Research Centre at Kingston University. He directed the ESRC Centre for Research on Small Service Sector Enterprises set up for the ESRC Small Business Research Initiative, 1989–92. He has written on a wide range of aspects of the small enterprise and with Robert A. Blackburn edited *Paths of Enterprise, The Future of the Small Business*, Routledge, 1991.

Richard Harrison is Professor of Management Development in the Centre for Executive Development, Ulster Business School, University of Ulster at Jordanstown. He has previously held research and lecturing posts in Economics and Business Development at both the Queen's University of Belfast and the University of Ulster at Jordanstown. He is a founding member of the International Informal Venture Capital Research Council, the International Association for Entrepreneurship Development and of the editorial board of the journal *Research on International and Comparative Entrepreneurship*.

David Keeble is a Lecturer in Economic Geography and Fellow of St Catharine's College, Cambridge. He has published extensively on the geography of new firm formation and small business growth in Britain and the European Community with special reference to business services, high technology industry, and rural entrepreneurship.

Roger Leigh is a Reader in Geography and member of the Centre for Enterprise and Economic Development Research at Middlesex University. He has published widely on a range of economic development issues and he has a particular interest in inward investment policy and in local technology policies. He has undertaken a number of sector studies for local economic development agencies.

Karl Mallalieu is a Research Associate previously at the Economics Research Centre, University of East Anglia. He is at present conducting research into, and writing about, Micro Enterprises and Small Businesses and Entrepreneurship.

Colin Mason is a Senior Lecturer in Economic Geography and a Director of the Urban Policy Research unit at the University of Southampton. He has written extensively on such topics as the new firm formation process, the geography of new firm formation and growth, the role of small firms in regional development, regional variations in the impact of small firms policy. He is an editor of three recently published books: *Towards the 21st Century: The Challenge for Small Business*, *Small Enterprise Development: Policy and Practice in Action* and *New Direction in Small Business Research*.

David North is Principal Lecturer in Geography and member of the Centre for Enterprise and Economic Development Research at Middlesex University. His research over the last 20 years has been in the fields of industrial location analysis and urban and regional economic development policy, involving work for government departments and for local economic development agencies. Much of this work has focused on the contribution of small and medium sized firms to local economic development.

David Smallbone is Head of the Centre for Enterprise and Economic Development Research at Middlesex University. His research interests are focused on small and medium sized firms and he has undertaken studies of both new and established SMEs. Particular themes include the characteristics and strategies of high growth companies and the support needs of different types of SME. He has also undertaken research on local enterprise agencies and small business policy.

David Storey is Director of the Small and Medium Sized Enterprise Centre at the Warwick Business School and is Co-ordinator of the ESRC Programme of Research on Small Business. He has published widely on the subject of small firms and has co-edited a number of books in the Routledge ESRC series including *Employment and Small Firms*, *Financing Small Firms* and *Urban and Rural Small Firms*.

Peter M. Townroe is Professor of Urban and Regional Studies and Director of the School of Urban and Regional Studies at Sheffield Hallam University. He has studied issues related to urban and regional development in the United Kingdom, in member states of the European Community and in a number of Third World nations. He has published on the themes of industrial location, regional economic development policy, urban growth, problems of urban transport, and local labour markets, as well as on entrepreneurship and local policies of support for small businesses.

Preface

This volume reports the results of research supported by the Economic and Social Research Council's Small Business Research Programme. Additional support for the programme has been provided by Barclays Bank, the Commission of the European Communities (DG XXIII), the Department of Trade and Industry and the Rural Development Commission. This support is gratefully acknowledged, although the views expressed do not necessarily reflect those of the sponsoring organisations.

At a personal level the research has benefited from the active participation of the co-sponsors notably John Martin from Barclays Bank, Martin Harvey from the Commission of the European Communities, Keith Lievesley from the Rural Development Commission, and Cliff Baker from the Department of Trade and Industry.

David Storey
Small business series editor

1 The location of small and medium enterprises: are there urban-rural differences?

James Curran and David Storey

INTRODUCTION

For perhaps two centuries or more until the 1960s the United Kingdom experienced continuous urbanisation. Towns and cities provided a home for an increasing proportion of the British population, and the countryside experienced net out-migration. This was particularly the case in the South of England and in Wales, with the impact being somewhat weaker in Scotland and the North of England. David Keeble (1976) was one of the first to point to the remarkable reversal in this trend which began some time in the 1960s. A number of explanations for this were put forward by Keeble, and subsequently by other authors, most notably Fothergill and Gudgin (1982). The Keeble (1976; 1986) explanations have tended to focus upon the amenities and quality of life provided by the countryside, which act as a powerful magnet to individuals to live in such areas; in these cases the individuals then have to create their own jobs. The alternative arguments put forward by Fothergill and Gudgin were that the urban environment was hostile to enterprise – particularly smaller enterprise. They argued that the simple physical constraints of urban location meant that the conduct of business was difficult, with rents being high, premises being difficult to obtain and expansion on an existing site being almost impossible. In addition some cities in the 1960s and 1970s such as London, were implementing active policies to move industry away from city areas partly on the grounds that they were unsuitable neighbours for a residential population.

The latter explanations, focusing directly on economic issues, are of particular interest in the discussion of small and medium-sized enterprises (SMEs). The Fothergill and Gudgin approach, however, like so much other discussion of its period, over-emphasised manufacturing activities. In fact, a very substantial proportion of SMEs are in the service sector which since the early 1970s, has become responsible for the largest share of gross national product (GNP) and jobs in the UK economy (Graham *et al.* 1989; Ball *et al.* 1989; Daly 1990). Moreover, as value added tax (VAT) data and other research has demonstrated, it was not in the mainly rural areas that the greatest net increase in business registrations took place during the 1980s but in the South East and Greater London. The rural areas did do well – there was a large net increase, for instance, in East Anglia – but this was not simply a straightforward urban-rural shift (Daly, 1991).

The other point emerging in the above and worth stressing, is that the small enterprise itself also staged a remarkable comeback over the same period. By the early 1970s, the small business had been in a long-term decline in the UK. The influential Bolton Report (1971: 342) which examined the role of the small business in the UK economy in the late 1960s, concluded that it could find few reasons to suggest how this decline might be reversed. Yet since 1971 the number of small firms (defined crudely as employing less than 200 people) has been increasing sharply. Thus in 1971 one estimate suggests that there were 71,000 small enterprises in manufacturing responsible for 21 per cent of manufacturing employment but by 1988 the total had risen to 133,000 responsible for over 31 per cent of total manufacturing employment (Stanworth and Gray, 1991: tables 1.1 and 1.2). Similarly, data on self-employment also shows a rapid increase, though this appears to have started rather later. In 1971 there were about 2 m self-employed and by 1983 this had risen to 2.2 m, but between 1983 and 1990 self-employment rose to 3.3 m with an overall increase of 73 per cent over the period 1971–90 (Department of Employment, 1992: 46). In other words, accompanying the population shift from the larger cities to small towns and rural areas was an equally remarkable resurgence in the SME in the UK economy. The two sets of phenomena are, of course, likely to be connected but the precise links are not that easily revealed. This book focuses upon these issues.

As pointed out by a number of authors, by the standards of North America or even continental Europe, the UK is a highly urbanised economy. Very few places in England are not within an hours' drive of a town with a population of 50,000 people, although Scotland and Wales are much more rural. Even so, there has clearly been a marked shift of population and employment, mainly from urban to rural areas, over the last twenty years. Agencies such as the Rural Development Commission are concerned to understand these developments in order to implement appropriate policy to assist smaller businesses in the countryside. Since the main movement is from urban to rural areas the main focus of this book is on rural businesses. It is the need to understand the motivations for starting and developing these businesses, the problems which they experience, and the extent to which these problems can be overcome by appropriate public policies that is our purpose here.

The individual chapters concentrate on non-agricultural activities in rural areas. On conventional views of rurality this might appear slightly odd. However, rural economic activities – food production, food processing and associated activities and forestry – are now very much minority sources of employment even in some of what are called 'remote rural areas'. These activities have been in strong decline at least since the 1950s as the data cited by Keeble, and Townroe and Mallalieu in their chapters show clearly. Alternative types of economic activities in manufacturing and services have been replacing traditional economic activities and these newer activities are becoming the real base of economic support in rural areas as well as their hope for the future (Champion and Watkins, 1991: 9–11).

In these chapters the main focus is upon the individual firm. Much has been written at an aggregate level about the movement of population into the countryside. Champion and his co-authors have extensively documented this development (Champion and Watkins, 1991). Furthermore, Daly has also shown that within the United Kingdom there are very substantial geographical differences in new form formation rates (Daly, 1990). This work has been developed by Keeble, Walker and Robson (1992) who show that over the decade of the 1980s some administrative counties had new firm formation rates approximately three times that of others. Figures 1.1 and 1.2, taken from Keeble, Walker and Robson (1992) clearly demonstrate these spatial variations.

However, it should be noted that these figures are based on VAT data which have certain deficiencies in relation to the urban-rural comparison of new firm formation rates. It is likely, for instance, that VAT derived data understates new business formation rates in rural areas because, as the data in the other chapters in this volume show, businesses in rural areas tend to be smaller than those in urban areas and are therefore less likely to be registered for VAT. (One estimate (Jennings, 1991) for instance, suggests that up to a half of all small businesses are not registered and these are likely to be predominantly 'small' small businesses.)

Our purpose in this book then is to go beyond this aggregate data.

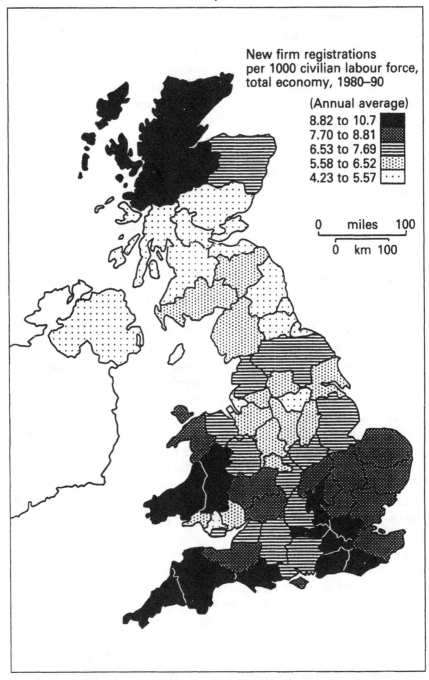

New firm registrations
per 1000 civilian labour force,
total economy, 1980–90

(Annual average)
8.82 to 10.7
7.70 to 8.81
6.53 to 7.69
5.58 to 6.52
4.23 to 5.57

0   miles   100

0   km   100

Figure 1.1   New firm formation rates in the total economy, 1980–90 (labour force based)
Source: Keeble, Walker and Robson (1992)

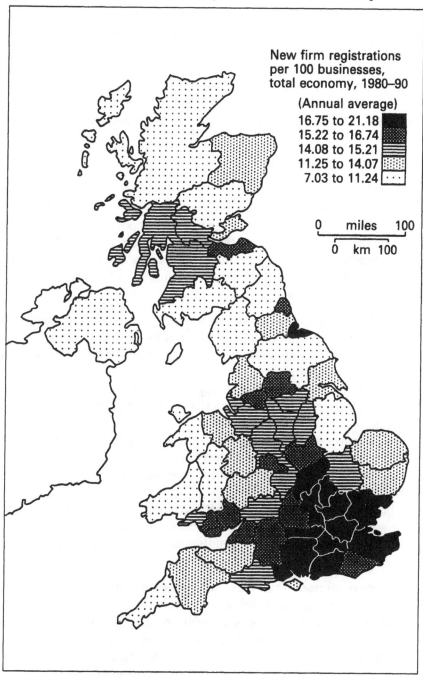

Figure 1.2   New firm formation rates in the total economy, 1980–90
(business stock based)
Source: Keeble, Walker and Robson (1992)

The research reported here in all but Chapter 2, makes a comparison between small enterprises in rural areas and broadly similar firms located in towns and cities. The purpose of Chapter 2 is to provide insights which can only be derived from dialogue with entrepreneurs on the merits and demerits of a rural location.

The current chapter provides both a context for the individual essays, and also some form of overview of the results obtained.

PREVIOUS RESEARCH

Whilst the individual chapters were in preparation Keeble, Tyler, Broom and Lewis published their report *Business Success in the Countryside* (1992). This is the major UK report of this topic and is referred to by most of the other authors here. Its agenda corresponded closely to several of the essay contributors to this volume, and so it is appropriate to provide a brief overview of the key findings as follows:

1 Rural business founders are much more likely to be in-migrants to their local area than founders of urban businesses.
2 Employment has grown faster in recent years in rural small firms than in urban firms.
3 Rural firms are somewhat younger than urban firms, suggesting that the birth rate of firms in rural areas is higher than that in urban areas.
4 Rural firms occupy specific market niches which differ from urban firms, and which they have successfully exploited. Firms in accessible rural areas are significantly more likely to be exporting than those in urban areas.
5 There seems to be evidence that the rural firms, particularly those in accessible rural locations, are more innovative.
6 Overall, businesses in the countryside appear to be happier with their location than those in urban areas.

The report stresses that there are important differences between small firms in remote rural areas and those in rural areas more accessible to major centres of population. It suggests new initiatives to help firms in remote areas. Such firms would benefit particularly from targeted advice on innovation, marketing and other business skills. It is also suggested that greater shortages of skilled labour and the inadequate supply of larger local premises for such firms places them at a comparative disadvantage.

What the individual chapters in this volume do is to add considerably to the detail offered by Keeble and colleagues and to demonstrate the heterogeneity of small enterprise in rural areas. The latter is worth emphasising since the processes involved in the changing economic character of these areas are highly complex.

KEY THEMES

In this section we review a number of the topics discussed in the book. It should not be assumed that there is a consensus amongst the authors on the issues addressed. In part this reflects the different approaches of the researchers.

Instead of providing a synopsis of each of the chapters in turn, our approach has been to identify five key themes which emerge from several of them. We highlight the similarities of the findings, and where appropriate, point to differences in results and interpretation.

Formation rates

As noted earlier, the VAT based statistics suggest that formation rates of business have been higher in United Kingdom rural areas than in urban areas. Support for this is found in the work of Keeble in his essay, supporting the earlier work of Keeble *et al.* (1992a), using a rather different data base. Indirect support for the Keeble findings is also provided by Smallbone and colleagues in their chapter on mature manufacturing firms. They show that the firms in the rural areas are, on balance, younger than those in the urban areas. Blackburn and Curran, however, in their study of service sector firms in North-East Suffolk, do not find any evidence that these firms are any younger than those in the other more urban labour markets which they study, Guildford, Nottingham, Doncaster and the London borough of Islington.

This is one example of a difference in findings which almost certainly arise from the different approaches adopted by the researchers together with the fact that the Curran and Blackburn sample contains a larger proportion of both smaller and urban firms than the samples of the other researchers.

Formation 'types'

There are two major issues addressed here: the first is whether businesses established in the rural areas have a different sectoral composition from those established in urban areas. The second is whether the motivations of people establishing businesses in rural areas differs from those in urban areas.

The evidence presented in these chapters suggests that there are indeed differences in the sectoral composition of urban and rural firms. At the most obvious level the rural areas are characterised by very small-scale enterprise. This precludes many large capital intensive manufacturing establishments. The differences are neatly illustrated by Smallbone and colleagues who attempted to obtain an identical sectoral composition of firms in both London and their rural areas of Cumbria, North Lancashire and North Yorkshire, together with Midland rural areas of Derbyshire and Lincolnshire. They found that in several sectors the rural firms were drawn from a much narrower range of sub-sectors than the London firms. This was particularly true for the furniture and printing sectors. Conversely, they found that in the clothing sector it was the London based firms which were much more likely to be sub-sectorally concentrated, whereas the rural firms were more likely to be spread over a wider variety of sub-sectors.

Given that much of the research indicates that the urban-rural shift has been primarily in the manufacturing sector, it is not surprising that several of the researchers found that manufacturing is of greater relative importance in rural, than in urban, areas. For example, Keeble shows that within a national SME sample equally divided between manufacturing and professional and business service sector firms, only 35 per cent of firms surveyed in rural areas were in professional and business services, compared with 53 per cent in the conurbations. Mason and Harrison, in their survey of attitudes to equity investment, indicate that manufacturing firms are of the greatest significance in the rural areas of the UK.

Overall, these findings suggest that there are significant differences between the manufacturing and the service sector composition of firms in urban and rural areas. It also suggests that differences may exist at a sub-sectoral level, with the rural areas being more likely to have a preponderance of craft based firms, for example.

The second major issue here relates to the motivations of individuals starting businesses in urban, as compared to rural areas. The Keeble *et al.* (1992a) argument is that many of the individuals establishing new small businesses in rural areas are attracted by environmental considerations. They are more likely to be in-migrants than in urban areas and to see self-employment or business formation as a way of achieving this objective. However the majority of in-migrant entrepreneurs had some employment in a rural area before starting a business. In Chapter 3 Keeble links this argument with the finding that 35 per cent of founders of firms in rural areas established their business as a result of actual or potential unemployment, compared with only 26 per cent in the conurbations. He allies this with his finding in Keeble *et al.* (1992a) that 66 per cent of founders of rural businesses were in-migrants to the area, compared with only 35 per cent of founders of urban businesses.

These issues are most comprehensively examined in Chapter 2, by Townroe and Mallalieu, where the motivations of business founders in the countryside are explored. When asked about the reasons why they established businesses the dominant influence was a desire for independence. In this sense, as Blackburn and Curran point out in their chapter, rural entrepreneurs are no different from those in urban areas. The insight which the Townroe and Mallalieu chapter provides, however, is that it relates these motivations to a categorisation of business types which would only be appropriate in the countryside. They identify a total of seven categories of business start: off-farm diversification (6 per cent), arts and crafts (21 per cent), early retirement (4 per cent), mid-life switchers (17 per cent), spin out from previous employment (31 per cent), rebuilding earlier businesses (10 per cent), and an 'other' category (10 per cent), with the per cent in parenthesis constituting the proportion of firms in their large sample which were established in rural areas in each of these categories.

This is a particularly helpful categorisation since, although some categories would be common to both rural and urban business formations, some are either irrelevant – off-farm diversification, or hugely more important in rural areas than in urban areas – arts and crafts for example. The value of the categorisation is that the motivation in forming the business is related to the type of business. Thus although the desire for independence is consistently important in all categories, apart from the early retirers, other motivations do vary according to the type of business. Thus arts and crafts based businesses are strongly motivated by the desire of the owner to use particular skills which he or she has. They also appear to be strongly motivated by a desire to achieve a secure (but not necessarily a high) income. Interestingly, the off-farm diversifiers and the arts and crafts based owners are the least likely to point to being motivated by the threat of unemployment.

Finally, the contribution of Blackburn and Curran suggests that in their mainly rural area of North East Suffolk individuals are less likely to state that they were motivated by the prospects of making money than comparable businesses in the urban area of Islington.

Overall the individual chapters point to differences in motivations for starting a business in urban and rural areas. In part, these reflect the differences in the types of businesses established, with a preponderance of small manufacturing, arts and crafts, and farm-related businesses in rural areas. They also reflect a higher proportion of people moving into rural areas and seeking employment opportunities. Given these differences, the results are compatible with a view that the people establishing such businesses in rural areas place a greater emphasis upon 'life style' than those in urban areas. The urban area businesses appear to be more likely to be established by people seeking wealth as a prime objective. Nevertheless, as Blackburn and Curran point out, it is extremely difficult to categorise motivation in a single, or even a composite index. They also point out that the greatest similarity in their results on service sector firms is between entrepreneurs in Doncaster and North East Suffolk. Yet Doncaster is an urban, unprosperous area; the implication is that motivations may be more related to the level of prosperity in the area than to its urban-rural categorisation.

Problems facing urban-rural firms

A priori there are a number of reasons for believing that the problems facing urban and rural firms will differ. It might be expected that rural firms would suffer problems of distance from customers, distance from suppliers, a lack of access to formal and informal networks of advice such as accountants and solicitors, and perhaps a lack of credibility with some customers in the sense of being viewed as 'out in the sticks'. Smaller and more dispersed labour markets may make labour recruitment more difficult. On the other hand, urban firms might be thought likely to have problems in being able to recruit labour because of higher wages and greater local competition, of high rents for premises in urban areas, or of a lack of space both to conduct current operations and to expand into.

The findings in these chapters about the problems facing small firms suggest that these differences are nowhere near as clear cut as indicated above. For example, Mason and Harrison are unable from either the existing literature or their own survey, to point to clear differences in the UK in the financing of urban as opposed to rural small business. Smallbone and colleagues, in their study of long-established businesses, examined the types of adjustments made by firms in response to the various problems and opportunities facing firms in urban and regional environments. Whilst there will be little difference overall in the nature and extent of the adjustments made by urban and rural firms, there was evidence that rural firms needed to be more active in terms of market adjustments, because of more limited market opportunities. Townroe and Mallalieu, in their extensive questioning of rural entrepreneurs, also come to the conclusion that locating in a rural area had mixed benefits. For example in their survey 29 per cent of respondents indicated that they thought there were no advantages from a rural location. Of those who did indicate location benefits, the most frequently identified were related to cheaper overheads.

Keeble addresses these issues in a somewhat different way by asking about the constraints to growth experienced by urban and rural firms. Again the most striking feature of his analysis is the similarity of response between the two groups. Out of the 11 factors identified, in four cases these are slightly more important for rural firms than in urban firms, in three of them they are more important for urban firms and in the remaining four they are identical. The only significant difference is the fact that rural firms did feel themselves more constrained in terms of finance, whilst they also gave a slightly higher rating to the problems of skilled labour shortages. Most urban-rural differences are not, however, significant.

Overall, the chapters suggest that the problems facing business people in urban and rural areas are broadly similar. Differences do exist, but certainly not on the scale which suggest major location advantages for either urban or rural businesses. It also suggests, as Townroe and Mallalieu point out, that such differences as do exist are more likely to reflect the character of businesses and their founders in the two localities – such as the preponderance of craft based businesses in rural areas.

Performance of urban-rural firms

Most prior empirical work on this topic has been concerned with investigating the hypothesis that urban manufacturing firms experience a disadvantage in the sense that their costs are higher than comparable firms located elsewhere. These cost differences are those of land and premises as reflected in higher rents, less space and poor access and higher wage and salary costs (Tyler, Moore and Rhodes, 1988). Yet empirical work on the profitability of inner city manufacturing firms, compared with manufacturing firms located elsewhere, has suggested that there is no significant difference between the two locations. A study by Bayldon, Woods and Zafaris (1984) for example compared the profitability of small manufacturing firms in Inner London locations with those in New Towns and found no significant difference in profitability in the two locations. They did, however, find that whilst trading profits were identical, profit retention, i.e. that ploughed back into the business for reinvestment purposes, was much lower in urban locations than in the New Towns. Confirmation of this finding is provided in a study of Northern England by Coombes *et al.* (1991). The significance of these findings is that it has been shown by Storey *et al.* (1987) that it is retained profits, rather than trading profits, which are the prime factor influencing employment creation in small firms. Simply expressed, it would appear that trading conditions do not seem to vary between urban and non-urban areas. What seems to vary is the willingness of small entrepreneurs to reinvest in their business, with a greater reluctance being shown by the urban entrepreneur.

Given these prior findings it is not surprising that a number of the essays in this volume point to more rapid employment growth in firms in rural than in urban areas. In Chapter 3, Keeble shows that median employment growth between 1987 and 1990 was lowest in the conurbations (22.5 per cent) and highest in the rural areas (33.3 per cent) for firms surveyed. In their work on business success in the countryside, Keeble *et al.* (1992a) find that rural firms grew by four jobs per firm between 1988 and 1991 whereas urban firms declined by an average of 1.7 jobs per firm. Smallbone and colleagues in their chapter on long-established manufacturing firms, also point to a slightly better performance in terms of employment creation by rural, as opposed to urban, firms. Examining their London panel over the 1979–90 period, and comparing it with their rural panel, they find that the mean number of additional employees in the London panel is two per firm, compared with seven for the rural panel. This is significantly influenced by a relatively small number of rural firms which experienced quite significant job creation during the 1980s. What is very interesting, when related to earlier research, is that these differences in employment growth *do* appear to be reflected in the profitability of the rural sample compared with the London sample. Thus, 69 per cent of rural firms reported rates of profit in excess of 5 per cent, compared with only 21 per cent of the London panel during the year 1987. It is, of course, appropriate to point to the normal caveats in obtaining data on profitability, that firms are both reluctant to provide it and that the definitions of 'profits' used vary. Using pre-tax profits as a percentage of sales turnover, Smallbone and colleagues show that the profitability of the London firms in their survey is generally lower than that of firms in the remote rural areas. This is in contrast to the Bayldon and colleagues results, and may reflect more recent trading conditions in London.

The Blackburn and Curran chapter, which concentrates exclusively on service sector businesses, suggests that firms in the more rural location of North East Suffolk have been less influenced by the recession than those in urban areas. Over the 1990–2 period fewer Suffolk service sector businesses reported declines in turnover and employment reduction than those in the other urban areas studied.

Overall the pattern which seems to emerge is that manufacturing firms located in rural areas have *both* higher rates of profitability and higher rates of employment growth than manufacturing firms located in urban areas. The study of service small firms by Blackburn and Curran also suggests that during the current recession firms in rural Suffolk have been less severely affected than those in urban areas.

Policies

All the chapters, in their different ways, make some assessment of the implications of their results for policy. Most of the policy recommendations are directed at the public sector, although Mason and Harrison are also interested in the implications for private sector providers of finance. In this brief review it will not be our purpose to repeat all of the policy recommendations. Instead we will concentrate upon three topics addressed by several of the chapters: training, premises and the provision of finance.

The subject of training is of considerable interest to Townroe and Mallalieu. They clearly report significant dissatisfaction with the nature of training currently provided for small business owners in rural areas. They point to the fact that it is the young and female business founders who are most likely to take advantage of training, even though in rural areas businesses are much more likely to be established by older founders and by males. They also show that those individuals who have been in business previously are *less* likely to attend for training, even though it could be argued that it is those individuals who could benefit most from training. The direct policy implications of these findings are not clear since it is possible to argue that the lack of take up of training reflects the poor quality of the training provided, or the unique 'mind-set' of the entrepreneur who wishes to learn only from his or her own experiences. The Keeble chapter shows that this is a matter of policy concern since rural firms were the least likely to use any form of external advice. Of course, the availability of help needs to be taken into account: in less populated areas it may be more thinly spread. As Keeble points out, since the use of external advice is positively correlated with business performance, it suggests that more extensive utilisation of advice by rural firms could lead to significant improvements in performance.

The differences observed by Keeble do not seem to be picked up in the work by Blackburn and Curran on service sector businesses. The latter show that there is little difference between firms in North East Suffolk and the urban areas in the extent to which they have used the Small Firms Service of the Department of Employment, although there is a difference in their use of the local Enterprise Agencies – with urban firms being twice as likely as those in North East Suffolk to use the Agencies.

Overall, these findings suggest that rural firms are less likely to make use of formal training and external advice than urban firms. It is also suggested that, since there appears to be an association between utilisation of advice and training and business performance, even greater efforts should be made to improve access to this training and to advice for firms in rural areas. Unfortunately, it is unclear whether this lack of take up reflects the poor quality of the training provided or whether it is simply a reflection of the costs in terms of the entrepreneur's time, in obtaining access to training.

A number of the studies also address the question of premises. One of the interesting, and perhaps surprising, findings shown by Keeble *et al.* (1992a) is that premises constitute a very minor constraint upon the ability of a business to grow. For the small services businesses studied by Curran and Blackburn, the problem appeared to be even less serious since over half of their firms owned their own premises compared to about a third of the urban firms. It is also interesting to note that there appears to be no difference in the importance of this constraint between conurbations and rural areas. One particularly interesting finding provided by Smallbone and colleagues is that the firms in rural areas which relocated moved significantly shorter distances than those in the London area. They infer that rural firms are much more strongly tied to local conditions, and that the challenge for policy makers in rural areas is to provide premises which enable expansion of firms to take place within the same immediate locality. By this we mean the firm may only be able to grow if alternative premises are provided within the same village or even hamlet. It may be this need to stay in the locality which explains the higher dissatisfaction which remote rural firms expressed about the lack of larger local premises to enable growth in the Keeble *et al.* (1992a) study.

The third policy area relates to the provision of finance. Mason and Harrison show there is no evidence of rural firms being disadvantaged in the raising of equity. They also show that the aversion to the use of equity, so characteristic of British firms, is if anything lower amongst rural firms than those in the urban areas. This they take to indicate a latent demand for equity provision in rural areas. This could be accomplished by a public sector initiative to provide a 'matchmaking service' for 'business angels' – individuals willing to provide sums of equity on an *ad hoc* basis through private businesses. Mason and Harrison argue that there exists an information gap between suppliers and demanders of equity. Thus wealthy individuals prepared to be business angels are ill-informed about business opportunities, and the businesses themselves are unaware of the individuals seeking to make equity investments. Hence some form of marriage bureau or information service which brings the parties together, could be mutually beneficial.

The importance of financial constraints upon the development of businesses in both rural and urban areas is reflected in the survey results reported by Keeble. He shows that cost and availability of finance and access to overdraft finance are the single most important constraints upon business growth. He also shows that these are rated as being even more important by rural firms than by urban firms. As was pointed out earlier, we do not have any objective evidence that for example, rural firms are more likely to have been refused finance or are charged higher rates for finance than firms in urban areas. Nor can we assume rural businesses are always more growth minded. Curran and Blackburn, for instance, found a lower level of desire for growth among their rural businesses than their urban businesses. Nevertheless, it is the perception of these firms that differences exist and that they are a significant constraint upon the development of businesses which wish to grow.

OVERALL

The majority of chapters in this volume indicate that there are some differences between small businesses established in urban locations, and those established in rural areas. However the authors have been at pains to point out that the United Kingdom is essentially an urban economy and that problems of rurality are not on a comparable scale to those in many European or North American countries. They have also stressed that many of the problems of operating a business are the same irrespective of location and that the urban-rural dichotomy should not be too sharply drawn.

The general pattern which emerges is that for manufacturing businesses in particular, rural settings pose no disadvantages to the business. If anything the advantages appear to outweigh the disadvantages, with this being reflected in recent years in the faster employment growth, higher rates of profitability and higher birth rates of firms in rural areas. The findings are somewhat less clear cut for the service sector.

Nevertheless the types of business and the motivations for starting businesses also appear to differ. The entrepreneur in the rural area appears to be more likely to be establishing a business for reasons of life style and to be establishing a craft or very specialised type of business. He or she appears to be more likely to be occupying a growing market niche than the urban business and perhaps for this reason has experienced relatively buoyant demand for the product or service. This buoyancy may well be a reflection of the ability to provide one-off or specialised products or services, rather than mass-produced products, which appear to be more in demand as incomes rise over time.

However, whether this situation is holding as the present recession continues is another matter. Businesses established to meet the wants of affluent consumers through craft production, for instance, are likely to suffer badly as consumers cut back on less basic spending. A recent indication is that it is those businesses started by in-migrants to rural areas which have suffered most (*The Guardian*, 27 November 1992).

If these differences between urban and rural areas exist on any scale then the challenge for public policy makers appears to target their activities. Public policy seeks to support the economic vitality of rural areas as activities directly related to agriculture decline in significance. Public sector agencies need policies to enable entrepreneurs in rural areas to benefit on a more extensive scale from the provision of additional training and advice, to ensure that adequate premises are available for them to expand into, and to ensure that they are not in any way disadvantaged in their access to finance.

2 Founding a new business in the countryside

Peter Townroe and Karl Mallalieu

1 INTRODUCTION[1]

The United Kingdom is a very urban nation. Indeed, an independent England would be the most densely populated country in Europe. Socially it is now difficult to distinguish rural society from urban society in Britain, in its outlook and values and in most of its social activity. Rural living is now the prerogative of a relatively small minority of the population, and that living is both functionally and culturally closely tied in with the dominant fabric of urban Britain.

In economic terms also, rural Britain is not just linked to urban Britain but in most of the relevant characteristics it is a continuation of urban Britain but at a lower density. Electricity, water, sewerage, telephones, the basic infrastructure services, are available everywhere; and, for England, there is now no rural corner that is more than two hours driving time away from an urban centre which is large enough to provide necessary public sector and private sector business services. Post and parcel services complement the telecommunication system in linking in firms to their input and output networks.

Given this urban nature of the British countryside in so many respects, is establishing a new small business any different in a rural area than in an urban area? Are there significant handicaps? Are there indeed some advantages? What do the relevant small business support agencies whose remit extends into rural areas need to be especially aware of? Should there be a rural dimension to small business support policy? Is there a rural entrepreneurship?

A detailed answer to these questions has to be based on the experience of new small businesses in rural areas; and it is this experience which the research behind this contribution draws upon, by a postal survey, stretching across four English counties.[2] The research builds upon a particular conceptual framework, characterising the business founders as entrepreneurs who come to their task with varied mixtures of skills and abilities as well as motivations. The entrepreneurial competencies are viewed in terms of a quasi-market, with both a manifest and a latent dimension on the demand side and with a wide portfolio of both public sector and private sector training and advice forming the supply side. The resulting 'market place' in competencies can then be examined in terms of 'prices' and 'quantities', building on the assumption that supply and demand will rarely be in equilibrium. However the interaction over time will strengthen the economic base of rural areas, to remain competitive with urban areas where this is possible. The public sector agencies concerned have a key role in this.

The public sector concern here can be seen as coming from five directions. The first wells up from a deep British emotional attachment to the countryside and to 'village life', even when the majority of the population can experience it only on holidays or weekends or at second hand through the media. The emotion involved has not obscured the understanding that what is valued needs to rest upon a firm economic base, and that base can no longer be provided by agriculture alone. A second source of concern arises from the structural adjustments in recent decades in the agricultural labour market, and now coming in the scale and mix of the product range of food production. There is a standard argument here for government intervention, to ease the transition and to protect the losers from the changes. One form of intervention is to encourage alternative economic activities to food production by farmers.

A third concern comes from a desire to keep unemployment and under-employment at a minimum, both for the individuals concerned and also to maintain the population base of rural areas. A further hope from support to new small businesses is that the social mix and outlook in rural areas will widen, as the tie to a single industry is loosened. The public sector has also taken a role in the promotion of UK based tourism, and there is a clear rural dimension to this.

This chapter has four main sections. Section 2 extends this introduction by offering a brief discussion of changes in the countryside in Great Britain, identifying employment change, the reduced role of agriculture, and the surge of new small businesses formed in the 1980s. Most country areas now have all of the infrastructures necessary to establish a new business, as noted above: electricity, telephones, water supply and sewerage, good road connections to urban centres, a potential workforce, largely with its own transport, etc. Public sector agencies which seek to promote new business activity in rural areas can concentrate therefore on training and advice to the new owner managers, supported in some areas by elements of financial subsidy.

Findings from the two postal surveys, undertaken in four English counties, are presented in sections 3 and 4. Section 3 focuses on the characteristics of the owner managers, using a seven-way categorisation of the businesses in terms of its origins ('Spin-Out', 'Early Retirement Move', etc.). The motivations involved for establishing the new business are considered in the second part of section 3; and the links between the choice of a rural location and both the characteristics and motivations of the founder in the third part. A number of logit equations clarify important relationships.

Findings on the themes of skills, competencies and training needs follow in section 4, again with the help of some logit equations. The survey found that only a small proportion of respondents had participated in training courses designed to raise their business expertise, and many of those in receipt of external advice found it confusing. The respondents were then asked to provide their own assessment of their competencies, building on their achieved levels of formal education and their previous business experience. In general, it was respondents from slow growing businesses who acknowledged one or more areas of competency weakness, and an associated need for training. The final part of this section notes that business failure can be a learning experience. It is not necessarily the result of a lack of capability of the owner-manager in question, but may result from changed external circumstances (e.g. the business failure of one or more major customers).

All entrepreneurs are endowed with a particular mix of skills and abilities. No given mix ensures business success, given the variety of contexts and constraints operating on firms in one sector of economic activity compared with another; but the survey results reported on here point to a significant proportion of the entrepreneurs involved putting aspects of rural living and the quality of life ahead of business success in terms of profit and growth in their motivations. This poses a problem for the public sector agencies charged with supporting small businesses in rural areas. They may be encouraging firms to grow which do not want to grow. There is therefore a need for selectivity in support, with an advance appreciation of both those new small businesses which can grow and those which want to grow. There are issues here which are picked up in section 5, the conclusions.

2 ECONOMIC ACTIVITY IN THE COUNTRYSIDE

Of the 49 million residents of England and Wales recorded in the 1981 Census of Population, 3.3. million, or just under 7 per cent, could be regarded as living in wholly rural areas (OPCS, 1987). Britain has been more urban than rural since 1851 and it is therefore a common perception to associate all economic activity other than agriculture and local village services with urban environments. And yet it is clear to any Sunday afternoon car tourist that more is going on in the British countryside than tilling the fields and pulling pints in the village pub. However, demonstrating the full scale and nature of economic activity in rural areas proves to be problematic.

The term 'rural' covers many different categories of countryside environments. The Rural Development Commission for example has distinguished five types of area: remote upland areas, remote lowland areas, less remote areas, the urban fringe, and areas of industrial dereliction. The nature of economic activity to be found in these different kinds of rural areas must be expected to be rather different, in its nature and its intensity, relative to the size and density of local settlements.

The 1981 Census recorded the following types of employment in Great Britain and in rural areas as percentages of the total:

	GB	*Rural mean*
Agriculture	2.2	10.3
Energy and water	2.1	2.8
Manufacturing	27.0	13.7
Construction	7.0	7.9
Distribution and catering	19.2	17.7
Transport	6.5	5.0
Other services	34.0	31.9

These figures reflect the relative unimportance of agriculture as a source of employment, even in the rural areas of Britain. And they stress the important role that manufacturing plays in rural areas, as well as the many categories of service based jobs. Unemployment has tended to be somwhat lower in rural areas than in urban areas over the past two decades, although there may be a degree of disguised under-employment.

The number of jobs in agriculture in the United Kingdom as a whole has been falling continuously throughout the period since the Second World War. For example, the total number of workers (including family) hired by farmers was 788,000 in 1955, but only

289,000 in 1988 (Strak, 1989). In the 1980s, between 1980 and 1988, this category of worker was declining in numbers by 2.3 per cent per annum. The number of full-time farmers, their employers, has also been falling, by 0.98 per cent per annum over the same period; although the number of part-time farmers in contrast has been increasing, at 1 per cent per annum. This trend to part-time farming is found in many of the more developed parts of Western Europe; with a clear linkage to the development of new businesses in rural areas.

The forecast trends to the year 2000 foresee a further decline in agricultural employment. The fall will be encouraged by further gains in the productivity of the labour force, but also by a reduction in the production incentives offered by agricultural policy, especially changes in the Common Agricultural Policy of the European Economic Community. It has been estimated that between 10 and 15 per cent of the agricultural land in England and Wales may need to be taken out of the production of food over the next ten years or so (NEDO, 1989).

Any decline in the value of agricultural output can be expected to have a knock-on effect on to related industries. A 1986 estimate, on the basis of 1984 full-time equivalent employment figures, suggested that jobs in agriculture and horticulture directly support about the same number of jobs again in industries providing inputs of goods and services, i.e. industries purchasing the outputs, and in related public sector activities (Errington, 1986). Not all of these knock-on effects will be felt within the rural areas but many would be.

One result of the pressure on farm incomes has been the involvement of farming households in Other Gainful Activities (OGAs). Some households will have gone down this route by choice of course, establishing their farming on a part-time basis, but others will have been pushed into a search for further sources of income. One estimate puts almost one third of all farm households as combining OGAs with their farming (Gasson, 1988). The distribution of the OGAs is put as:

Work on other farms	18%
Other employment off the farm	49%
Farm-based activity	16%
Other business situated on the farm	17%

Farmers often have considerable business and commercial expertise and can be expected to be an important group of prospective entrepreneurs in establishing new businesses in rural areas.

The survey at the core of this study focused in on new small businesses in the rural parts of four English counties: Derbyshire, Devon, Norfolk and Northumberland. The population of these four counties in 1988 was 924,000, 1,021,000, 744,000 and 301,000. Through the 1980s Derbyshire and Northumberland grew very little, but between 1981 and 1988, Devon gained 5.7 per cent more residents, and Norfolk experienced an increase of 6.1 per cent. All of the counties experienced an increase in the number of local businesses. While it is not possible to separate out the increases for the rural parts of these counties alone, the statistics on registrations and de-registrations for valued added tax (VAT) provide a picture of strong growth, stronger than the national average.

Over a nine-year period to the end of 1988 there was a growth of between 14 per cent and 21 per cent of the total number of businesses registered for VAT. The importance of this growth, given changing criteria for registration over time, lies in the relative growth across different sectors. Three sectors have been in relative decline in terms of numbers of businesses across the four counties: agriculture, retailing and catering (except in Northumberland). The motor trades sector has grown somewhat, while all other sectors have grown strongly. Growth was stronger in Derbyshire and Norfolk than in Devon and Northumberland.

This growth reflects an entrepreneurial buoyancy in four rural counties in England in the 1980s. What it does not reflect is the detail of the emergence of new small businesses in the countryside. The survey described in sections 3 and 4 found that most new businesses initially fall below the gross turnover threshold for VAT registration (£27,000 at the time of the survey). This is particularly true of small businesses in the arts and crafts sector, many of which are single male or female entrepreneurs, with no employees.

Very little of the countryside in England and Wales can really be regarded as 'remote', certainly by the standards of other large European nations. Improved road links have made access to the largest metropolitan markets relatively easy for any rural business seeking to sell its products to more than local customers; while increased visitor activity from urban centres has supported rural services of many kinds. At the same time, the ubiquity of mains electricity supplies has provided power where needed, and many new rural businesses have benefited by the employment of well trained ex-agricultural workers. Suitable property has not been available everywhere, but the lead of county councils, district councils and the Rural Development Commission working with English Estates in the

1980s has resulted in many successful conversion projects of old industrial and agricultural buildings in the countryside as well as a range of new workshop and small factory projects. Private developers have tentatively followed this lead in some areas.

The prerequisites for establishing a new small business now exist in most country areas. Many of these areas have also been benefiting from a growth in population, as part of the 'urban-rural shift', or 'counter-urbanisation' movement in population distribution (Champion *et al.*, 1987) over the past two decades. While much of this relative strength of population growth in proportional terms has been in small towns, as opposed to cities and metropolitan areas, there has been population pressure on villages and rural settlements also. To the extent that planning policies have allowed development in these areas, this growth has provided local business opportunities in local services to counter the loss of services brought about by economies of scale in retailing, entertainment, education, health care, etc. (Moseley, 1979).

The findings of Keeble *et al.* (1992) in a survey of over 1100 small firms in remote rural, accessible rural and urban areas, using a matching of company type technique and focusing primarily on the manufacturing sector, reflected a vigorous process of formation of new locally based and independent enterprises in rural England in the 1980s. The survey found that an environmentally attractive residential setting for the founders (and their families) of significant minorities of the rural new firms was an important part of the decision both to establish a new enterprise and to locate the enterprise in a rural area. Company relocation was a secondary influence.

It is against this background that this study has been undertaken. The objective was to reach a deeper understanding of entrepreneurial behaviour as exhibited in the establishment of a new small business and as experienced in a rural environment. The rural dimension here is a context only and is not likely to influence entrepreneurial qualities or skills per se; but the rural environment does exercise certain constraints and certain attractions for the would-be founder of a new business. Understanding these constraints and attractions is important for those agencies concerned with promoting and support-ing new economic activity in rural areas. These include those already referred to in connection with property (the county and district councils and the Rural Development Commission), but will also include the Ministry of Agriculture, Fisheries and Food, local enterprise agencies, the Small Firms Service of the Department of Employment; and related private sector interests, such as solicitors, accountants and the clearing banks. The issue of policy relevance is returned to in following sections.

3 THE FOUNDERS OF THE BUSINESS

Characteristics

As noted in the introduction, the emphasis in the two postal questionnaires used was different, although they used a common core. Results from the 'B' questionnaire are used in section 4. The questioning there built on the themes of entrepreneurial competence, training and skills, and problems of growth. The questions in the 'A' questionnaire were focused on the rural environment as one context for the new small business. The discussion in this section concerns the characteristics of the sample, the motivations of the new owners

Table 2.1 Characteristics of the founders of new small businesses in Derbyshire, Devon, Norfolk and Northumberland

Characteristics	(Percentages)	
	'A' sample (n = 329)	*'B' sample (n = 230)*
1. Formed within last five years	59	51
2. Age of founder: 20–29	24	29
30–39	38	37
40–49	25	26
50–59	10	7
60 plus	2	1
3. Gender: female	21	20
4. Two or less employees	48	48
5. Sectors:		
Manufacturing	24	21
Construction and motor trade	15	16
Retail and wholesale	9	10
Tourism and related	11	14
Agriculture and marine	11	13
Arts and crafts	22	20
Miscellaneous	5	7
6. Nature of Ownership:		
Limited company	26	23
Partnership	27	35
Co-operative	–	1
Sole trader	46	41
Response rates	27.4	23.3

Source: 1990 survey

in forming the new business, and the reasons for the choice of a rural location as a base for the business.

The general characteristics of both the 'A' and the 'B' samples are given in Table 2.1. As shown in the table, well over half of the sampled firms were established within the five years before receiving the questionnaire, and very nearly half were very small, with two employees or less. Only one quarter were limited companies, and just under a quarter only were involved in manufacturing: both categories being more familiar targets of small business research.

Table 2.1 is reassuring in respect of sample bias, with very similar patterns of characteristics emerging from the two samples. The sectoral spread is wide but is not wildly out of line with the rural employment distribution referred to in section 2. The main exception in both samples is the stronger representation in the area which attracts many into self-employment: 'arts and crafts'. The age distribution of the founders is of interest because it varies with the category of business and the motivation for forming the business, as shown in the logit equations below. Seven categories or types of business were used in the survey. The range of activity covered is wider than has been usual in surveys of rural small businesses (e.g. Keeble *et al.*, 1992: 9).

The distribution of the respondents to the 'A' and 'B' question-naire was:

	Percentage	
	'A'	*'B'*
Off-farm diversification from farming	6	6
Arts and crafts based	21	21
Early retirement move	3	5
Mid-life switch of direction	19	15
Spin out from previous employment	28	34
Rebuilding an earlier business	12	9
Other	12	9

The main surprise here was the small number of early retirement moves (19) in the total, against a prior expectation of respondents from village shops and sub-Post Offices and other small retail outlets. This is a category of business on which the Rural Development Commission lays particular stress in its support and training. However that category may well overlap with the 'spin out' category. Female founders, a minority of 21 per cent in the total sample here against their male counterparts, were relatively more strongly represented in the first three categories.

How well equipped were the respondents for the challenges of establishing a new business? The answer to this question can be taken in two parts: by an inference from the past work history of the respondents, and from information on their educational background and the elements of training received while launching the new firm.

Of the 329 respondents to questionnaire 'A' across the four counties, 196 (or 60 per cent) had been in full or part-time employment. Some 36 (11 per cent) came out of unemployment (although not necessarily registered unemployment) while a further 5 per cent classified themselves as housewives and another 5 per cent as students. This left just over 17 per cent, 57 of the 329, who had been self-employed and in that sense had a degree of previous business experience.

Just over half of the 242 respondents for whom the question was relevant had been involved in an occupation (while they were previously either employed or self-employed) which involved similar skills to those required on the production side of their new business. They were capitalising on their experience.

In a different way, a surprisingly high number, 149 or 45 per cent of the sample, had had experience previously either owning (110), or running (42) a business, although not necessarily immediately previously. Other small business research has pointed to the fact that many new businesses arise out of the ashes of a previous business, and these ashes do not necessarily involve failure and bankruptcy. The new start can arise from a sell out, or a refinancing and a new direction, or from a change in personal circumstances such as a divorce. Or from a change in life style, such as a desire to live in the country.

For 64 (41 per cent) of these 149, their previous business had involved a similar product or service to the new business; and two thirds of the previous businesses were located in a rural rather than an urban area. The pool of experience here was considerable, a further two thirds of this group having owned or run a business previously for more than five years.

Turning to the educational background of the business founders, the survey revealed what might be regarded as a surprisingly well-educated and well-qualified group of people (although it has to be recognised that there may be a sample response bias here). The answers below are cumulative, because the question asked was: 'What educational qualifications do you possess? (Please tick more than one as appropriate.)'

Apprenticeship	24%	School Certificate	7%
City and Guilds	20%	CSEs	12%
OND	7%	'O' Levels	54%
HND	10%	'A' Levels	32%
Professional	24%	Degree	28%
None	12%		

There were two non-respondents among the 329. What is perhaps noteworthy here is the high proportion holding a degree and/or a professional qualification, and the small number with no recorded qualification. This accords with data from the Labour Force Survey which shows that the proportion of the self-employed in the United Kingdom with no qualifications has fallen from 40 per cent to 25 per cent between 1981 and 1990.

This level of education may explain why, previous business experience notwithstanding, one quarter (83) of this group of business founders attended some sort of training course in connection with the setting up of the business. Ideally, of course, it should probably be a higher proportion, but this figure was higher than that expected on the basis of prior conversations with those involved in supporting and advising new small businesses. (A slightly lower proportion of the questionnaire 'B' respondents also attended a course, 51 of 231, or 22 per cent.)

The nature of the new business seems to have some relationship with the growth rate in turnover that is achieved but very little with whether a desire for a rural life style (as opposed to more profit orientated factors) was a key consideration in the choice of location for the new business. These relationships are examined in the logit equations in Table 2.2.

The first logit equation in Table 2.2. takes the different categories of new business as independent variables against a dependent variable of fast as opposed to slow growth, using the 'B' sample. The bivariate dependent variable was extracted from a question where respondents had been asked to indicate their levels of turnover in seven categories, for each of six years. Growth could therefore be seen, but not measured as a continuous variable, by the movement over the years from turnover category to turnover category. The compromise in the form of the question in order to yield a response reduces the resulting detail (and 21 respondents still refused to answer). The variable used also had to allow for different years of start-up.

The definition used was: the growth variable takes a value of 1 when the difference between the turnover category in 1985, or in the

Table 2.2 Logit estimates of the probability of fast growth rather than slow growth, and of a rural life style factor in locating the new business, by the nature of the new firm

Nature of the new firm	Distribution No.	(%)	Growth rate[2]	Rural life style factor[3]
Off-farm diversification	A 11	(6)	−1.204	0.619
	B 14	(6)	(−1.829)*	(1.320)
Arts and crafts based	A 71	(21)	−1.186	−0.198
	B 49	(21)	(−3.441)*	(−0.829)
Early retirement move	A 8	(3)	−1.946	1.099
	B 11	(5)	(−1.820)*	(1.346)
Mid-life switch	A 63	(19)	−0.511	−0.095
	B 36	(15)	(−1.399)	(−0.378)
Spin out	A 92	(28)	−0.111	−0.534
	B 79	(34)	(−0.471)	(−2.473)*
Rebuilding	A 36	(12)	−0.368	0.000
	B 22	(9)	(−0.848)	(0.000)
Other	A 39	(12)		−0.211
	B 20	(9)		(−0.648)
Log-likelihood			−132.66	−222.29
Chi-squared			9.79*	8.95
Iterations			5	5

Note: See notes (2) and (3).

start-up year, and the category achieved in 1990, was a jump of at least two categories in the lower bands (under £10 K, £10 K–£25 K, £25 K–£50 K, and £50 K–£100 K); and of at least one category in the higher bands (£100 K–£500 K, £500 K–£1 m, over £1 m). Of the 210 respondents, 76 then fell into a 'fast growth' category.

The first equation in Table 2.2. shows that knowledge of the nature of the new small business does not yield a significant association with the probability of fast growth. However, there is a significant association with the fast growth *not* happening for the first three types of new firm: the off-farm diversification, the arts and crafts based new business (strong significance), and the early retirement mover. This pattern is as expected. It does stress the distinction in performance terms between these three types of firm and the other categories (the mid-life switch, spin-out, rebuilding and other), each of which has perhaps a stronger 'business success' orientation to be found among their owners. This theme wil be returned to below. The second equation in Table 2.2. is very inconclusive, with a hint, in terms of signs and weak statistical significance, that as may be expected the rural life style factor is important for the early retirement moves and the off-farm diversifications but is unimportant for the spin-outs. The negative signs in the mid-life switch and arts and crafts based categories are surprising.

Motivations

The respondents were asked to indicate the top three factors lying behind their intention or motivation to form their new business, from a list of ten factors. Table 2.3 sets the replies to this question against the categorisation of the new businesses. The presentation in this table offers the number in each cell of the table scoring 1, against the number scoring 1, 2 or 3. Since this procedure would mean that each factor would receive a score of $(329 \times 3 \div 10) = 99$ on an even distribution basis for at least a mention (a rating of 1, 2 or 3), the immediate result from the answers that stands out is the fact that 202 ranked 'To achieve independence', with 103 placing this as the first factor. Also noteworthy is the high first ranking of 'To achieve a secure income', seen particularly in the arts and crafts based businesses and in the 'Rebuilding an earlier business' category. 'Interest in the field of activity' and 'Use of artistic and manual skills' come through relatively strongly as secondary factors. 'To avoid unemployment' was important for those citing it, with 26 of the 49 answers placing it as a '1'.

The question of motivation is closely linked with the criteria which an individual entrepreneur applies in judging his or her business success. In Table 2.4 replies to six alternative success criteria are presented on the same basis as the replies in Table 2.3, again with a scoring of 1, 2 or 3. Since this time an even distribution would yield $(329 \times 3 \div 6) = 165$ as a norm for the right hand figure in the total row, the criteria of 'High quality of product or service' stands out very strongly, with also a particularly high proportion of '1' scores. Every other criteria is very subsidiary to that, with only 'Profitability on capital employed' coming close to the even distribution norm. The quality factor is especially noticeable for the spin-out category of business. This pattern of response matches that found from a similar question in the Keeble and colleages survey, although here respondents were asked for the criteria by which they would judge success, whereas in the Keeble survey respondents were asked what they regarded as the crucial factors 'underlying and explaining the successful development of your business' (1992: 19).

Rurality, profit and life style

Respondents to the 'A' questionnaire were asked to indicate both the competitive advantages and the competitive disadvantages from the

Table 2.3 The intention or motivation in forming the new business*

Type of new business	Achieve a secure income	Increase personal wealth	Achieve independence	Hobby into a business	Interest in field of activity	Achieve an ambition	Work from home	Make most of commercial opportunity	Use artistic or manual skills	Avoid unemployment
Off-farm diversification from farming	3/9	1/5	3/6	0/1	0/6	2/4	0/8	4/5	1/3	3/7
Arts or craft skill based business	9/16	4/7	21/42	4/14	6/27	2/15	4/13	1/7	17/51	3/9
An early retirement move	2/3	–	0/3	2/3	–	2/2	1/7	–	0/2	1/1
A mid-life switch in direction	7/17	3/20	21/43	2/9	7/18	4/14	3/11	6/15	2/14	6/11
A direct spin-out from previous employment	11/31	8/30	37/66	1/5	4/31	10/28	0/12	8/28	4/22	8/13
Rebuilding an earlier business	9/14	1/14	10/22	1/3	2/10	2/8	0/6	5/12	3/9	2/4
Other	5/14	5/11	10/19	1/2	1/10	4/8	1/8	5/11	0/8	3/4
Total	46/104	22/87	103/202	11/38	20/103	26/79	9/65	29/78	27/109	26/49
Missing observations	225	242	127	291	226	250	264	251	220	280

Notes: (n = 329)
* Respondents scored 1, 2 or 3. Replies in each cell give the numbers of '1s and '1, 2 or 3s'.
Source: Questionnaire 'A', Rural Entrepreneurs Survey

Table 2.4 Criteria for judging business success*

Type of new business	Male founder	Previous experience	Of which, similar product	Rural setting	High quality of product or service	Simple survival	Standard of living achieved	Profitability on capital employed	Growth in sales achieved	Provision of employment
Off-farm diversification from farming	12/20	11/20	1/11	13/19	12/16	1/5	2/8	4/11	0/10	1/7
Arts or craft skill based business	48/71	21/71	9/21	32/70	40/66	8/28	4/25	8/24	5/34	1/17
An early retirement move	5/8	0/8	–	6/6	4/6	0/2	0/5	12/5	0/2	1/1
A mid-life switch in direction	47/62	27/63	3/27	30/62	25/50	3/8	7/26	20/35	2/39	1/15
A direct spin-out from previous employment	84/92	38/92	16/38	34/92	53/79	4/14	3/33	17/46	7/53	7/36
Rebuilding an earlier business	31/36	29/36	25/30	18/36	21/32	2/8	1/12	9/19	1/17	2/15
Other	31/39	23/38	10/26	17/38	18/31	3/11	6/16	5/12	2/16	2/15
Total	258/328	149/329	64/153	150/323	173/281	21/76	23/126	65/152	18/172	15/106
Missing observations	1	0	176	6	48	253	203	177	157	223

Notes: (n = 329).
* Respondents scored 1, 2 or 3. Replies in each cell give the numbers of '1s' and '1, 2 or 3s'.
Source: Questionnaire 'A': Rural Entrepreneurs Survey

rural setting of their businesses. The replies, predictably perhaps, very much revolved around aspects of distance and access. While 26 respondents to the disadvantage question referred to 'Getting supplies' and 38 to 'Defining a market', 113 or just over one third of the total offered general replies of distance to market and access to customers. Further problems coming out of the answers had to do with infrastructure and services (48), shortages of skilled labour (26), capacity to expand (20), and an 'Other' category which included comments such as 'Docility of the local community'. These replies are similar to those found by the Keeble *et al.* (1992) study. Interestingly, it was repondents from the retail and wholesale and the agriculturally related businesses who cited access and distance as problems, more so than the manufacturing and tourist and service related businesses. However, 85 replies were firm that there were no competitive disadvantages from the rural location.

On competitive advantages, 97 (or 29 per cent of the 329 respondents) thought that there were none arising from their rural location. Of the advantages cited, accessibility was offered by 32 respondents, normally referring to access to a principal supplier or customer (e.g. in food processing). Other advantages noted were cheaper overheads (66), relation to customers (44), market image (42), quality of life (oddly, 34), less competition (31), local supplies (23), space for expansion (17) and land availability (6). A number of respondents also argued that low rates on premises had been an advantage, but that this advantage for those working from home had been reduced by the switch to the Community Charge, and for those with factory of office premises by the switch to the Uniform Business Rate.

Two further factors came through in this area of questioning. One was the feeling that the rural setting of the business offered benefits from the local sense of community and the local business culture. The contact with customers was a personal one, with a sense of community loyalty. However, similar sentiments may be found from entrepreneurs based in more urban environments when asked about local links.

The second finding refers to the importance of the rural location for the market image or market position of the products or services of many businesses in the countryside. The rural location was seen as enhancing their market position in the face of competition for over one third (35 per cent) of all of the business participating in the survey. This seems to be a surprisingly high proportion.

What is clear from the rather generalised overall figures is that a rural location per se can often be a distinct advantage to a new small company, both in terms of its cost base and its market image; but that it is rarely a major handicap. (Of course if the handicap were fundamental the new firm would lack competitiveness and quickly go out of business.) The pros and cons will vary by sector and the respondents here are a heterogeneous mix. What is not clear from these answers is how far the difficulties of a rural as opposed to an urban location (e.g. in obtaining supplies, access to markets, recruiting skilled and experienced labour) were anticipated as the new business was being established or were run into later, emerging as surprise problems once the firm was launched.

Were the new owner-managers looking for a rural life style first, and a business location second (as found for significant minorities in the Keeble *et al.* (1992) study)? Half of the 'A' sample replied that 'Desire for a rural surrounding' was one factor in influencing the rural location of the new business; and one sixth (52 respondents) placed it as their number one factor. A further 51 listed 'Quality of family life' as the prime factor. A further 42 placed 'Personal satisfaction' as the number one locational choice factor. This may or may not have a rural dimension. The full pattern of replies to this question is given in the first column of Table 2.6. These rural life style factors in locational choice, as expected, come through particularly strongly for the arts and crafts based businesses.

If a rural family life style was an important element in either starting up a new small business in the countryside, or in the decision to locate the business in a rural location once the commitment to start up had been made, or both, then arguably that is a non-profit factor which might detract from possible growth and expansion. While it is not possible to test that proposition directly across the two samples, it is possible to link the rural choice factor across to other location factors, to stated motivations behind the formation of the business in general, and to some of the characteristics of the founder.

The three equations in Table 2.5 take three age bands of firm founders: 30–39, 40–49, and 50–59, together covering 73 per cent of the 'A' sample. The dependent variable here is the same as in the second equation in Table 2.2. 'Small firm' among the independent variables is two or less employees. And 'Previous experience' indicates a positive response to the question: 'Had you owned or had previous experience at running a business before the current business?'

The coefficients on the age variables are not significant, but the negative sign for the forties age group is an interesting contrast to the thirties and the fifties. The female owner factor is consistent,

Table 2.5 Logit estimates of the probability of a rural life style factor in locating the new business by characteristics of business founder

Characteristics	'Younger'	'Older'	'Older again'
Age 30–39	0.065 (0.281)		
Age 40–49		−1.146 (−0.559)	
Age 50–59			0.019 (0.051)
Female	0.425 (1.551)*	0.422 (1.340)*	0.421 (1.530)*
Small firm	0.349 (1.533)*	0.345 (1.526)	0.352 (1.555)*
Previous experience	0.349 (1.541)*	0.367 (1.600)*	0.345 (1.508)
Intercept	−0.623 (−2.809)*	−0.566 (−2.693)*	−0.598 (−2.955)*
Log-likelihood	−223.18	−223.06	−223.22
Chi-squared	7.17	7.41	7.10
Iterations	4	4	4

Note: See note (3).

suggesting a particular attraction of the countryside for many of the 70 female entrepreneurs in this sample, together with a factor (with the causation running both ways) of the kind of activity many women owners get involved in. However, this last factor is not clear cut from these results. Women head up more than proportionately of the arts and crafts based businesses as might be expected, but also of the off-farm diversifications and the early retirement moves. There may be an 'empty nester' effect at work here. This cannot be tested however, as questions about children and marital status were not asked.

The signs on the small firm variable are positive as expected, and significant at 10 per cent or close to it. That is not a surprise, but the positive sign on the previous experience does not fit with the a priori hypothesis. It was thought that past experience of owning or running a company would lead to a fairly straight commercial location decision in most cases, with life style factors taking second place, and hence a low positive or negative coefficient. In fact of course much of the previous experience was gained in other *rural* based businesses, small and large. The significant intercept term here invites inclusion of further relevant entrepreneurial characteristics were the data to exist. Many variables may in fact have to do with life history (location of childhood, source of spouse, current occupation of spouse, etc.), but these details were not collected.

The follow-up question in the questionnaire to the 'A' sample to the question about rural life style asked respondents to rank 1, 2 or 3 the three top factors (from a choice of ten) lying behind their decision to locate their business in a rural area. 306 respondents replied. The pattern of the responses is given in the first column of Table 2.6, where the first figure is the number recording the factor as '1' and the second figure is the number offering the factor as '1, 2 or 3', as in Tables 2.3 and 2.4.

Table 2.6 Logit estimates of the probability of a rural life style factor in locating the new business and of having owned or run a business by reasons for choosing a rural area

Choice reasons	Response pattern	Rural life style factor (n = 306)	Previously owned or run a business (n = 306)	'Changers' (n = 71)	'Experienced' (n = 128)
Personal satisfaction	42/132	1.618 (2.050)*	0.116 (0.304)	−0.170 (−0.109)	17.474 (0.006)
Quality of family life	51/144	2.213 (3.807)*	0.338 (1.067)	2.843 (1.779)*	19.494 (0.207)
Health related factors	10/27	−4.338 (−4.426)*	−0.467 (−0.931)	−3.244 (−1.426)*	−37.606 (−0.009)
Desire for a rural surrounding	52/157	0.925 (1.993)*	−0.110 (−0.453)	0.886 (0.916)	0.081 (0.082)
Links to other business activities	18/42	0.685 (1.797)*	−0.020 (−0.091)	0.262 (0.313)	1.798 (2.830)*
Use of local suppliers	8/31	−0.472 (−0.720)	0.278 (0.639)	0.727 (−0.481)	−2.830 (−1.468)*
Local market for the product or service	34/82	1.740 (3.986)*	−0.227 (−0.991)	2.996 (2.412)*	3.933 (2.598)*
Land and factory availability	15/36	−0.547 (−0.873)	0.736 (2.113)*	−1.695 (−0.984)	−2.856 (−1.508)*
Accessibility to main markets	6/32	−1.421 (−1.857)*	0.142 (0.317)	−2.328 (−1.348)	−0.168 (−0.095)
Factory space availability	48/96	−0.206 (−0.434)	−0.644 (−2.182)*	−1.810 (−1.586)*	0.084 (0.093)
Log-likelihood		−80.06	−221.00	−18.03	−18.27
Chi-squared		293.40*	11.17	62.34*	136.38*
Iterations		7	4	10	10

Note: See note (3).

The two rural locational choice reasons of 'Quality of family life' and 'Desire for a rural surrounding' are given first preference by one sixth of the respondents and are chosen 1, 2 or 3 by half, overlapping, obviously, with the 47 per cent offering a 'Yes' to the previous rural life style question. 'Personal satisfaction' is also picked out by a high proportion of respondents. The 'Local supplies' factor and the 'Accessibility to main markets' factor are much less important to the group as a whole than 'Local markets', although they stand as of prime importance for 8 and 6 of the firms. 'Lack of availability', as may be expected with very small firms, is not important to as many as 'Factory space availability'. Links to other local businesses are important to a large minority (14 per cent); while on a personal basis health related factors were cited by 27 respondents.

All ten rural locational choice factors have been used as independent variables in the four equations of Table 2.6, with the strong assumption of independence, conceptually and statistically, from one another. They score 1 when given a rating of 1 or 2 by respondents, and otherwise score 0.

In the first equation with the rural life style factor as the dependent variable, signs and significance are as expected for 'Personal satisfaction', 'Quality of family life', 'Desire for a rural surrounding', and 'Accessibility to main markets'. More surprising is to see the 'Links to other businesses' and the 'Local market' reasons come through. 'Use of local suppliers', and 'Land and factory availability' have negative signs as might be expected but not with significant coefficients. The health factor is significant and negative, against expectations.

The third and fourth columns here take the same dependent variable as the first equation but for two sub samples. The 'Changers' are the 'Mid-life switchers' and the 'Early retirement moves', both groups for whom the rural factor might be thought to be especially strong and significant. The overall equation is stronger statistically than the first equation, but with fewer variables reaching the 10 per cent significance test. Signs do not change, except for the 'Personal satisfaction' reason for the choice of a rural area. For this group of new businesses, 'Desire for a rural surrounding', 'Links to other businesses', and 'Accessibility to main markets' drop out of significance (although the last one only just); while the 'Factory space availability' factor comes in significant and negative, as might be expected.

The 'Factory space availability' factor is not significant in the fourth column equation, which is more surprising. Here the 'Experienced' sub-sample combines the spin-outs and the rebuilding group. As expected, the equation brings out the significance of the directly business-related reasons (links and local markets positively and local supplies and land availability negatively), and loses the significance of the rural life style factors as a group. However, the fact that the signs on these ('Personal satisfaction', 'Quality of family life' and 'Desire for a rural surrounding') do not turn negative for this group indicates that a minority of members of this group voting for the rural life style locational choice factors did translate that into the prime factor in their location, as indicated by the dependent variable.

The second equation in Table 2.6 which uses a 'Yes' response to the question on previously having owned or run a business as the dependent variable offers a rather different cut to the locational choice factors. The results are weak, with significance on only two factors : land availability (positive) and factory space (negative), which is an interesting conjunction. The sign on the 'Desire for a rural surrounding' factor goes negative but the 'Quality of family life' stays positive. No clear pattern emerges from which one would be able to predict previous experience from the rural locational choice answers.

A similar question to that posed for the rural location factors listed in Table 2.6 was posed to respondents in respect of their 'intention or motivation to form this company', with a 1, 2 or 3 answer requested against ten possible answers. The pattern of replies from the 329 respondents is given in the first column of Table 2.7, in a similar manner to that offered in Table 2.6: the number of '1s', and the number of '1, 2 or 3s'.

The pattern of replies is interesting, as was seen in Table 2.3. On the first choices 'To Achieve Independence' (and be one's own boss) stands out, for nearly one third of the sample. Half that number quote 'To achieve a secure income'; and half of that half (7 per cent – 10 per cent) ticked 'To increase wealth', 'Interest in field of activity', 'To achieve an ambition', 'To exploit an opportunity', 'To use manual or artistic skills' or 'To avoid unemployment'. 'To develop a hobby' and 'To work at home' were ranked first by only 11 and 9 of the respondents.

The pattern with second and third choices included is similar, except for a relative increase in the wealth, work at home, and interest in the field motivations.

The first logit equation given in Table 2.7, with a similar recording of independent variables as 1 or 0 as before, suggests a positive and significant association with the rural life style factor dependent variable from the independent variable Work at Home, and negative and significant with Hobbies, and Ambition and Exploiting an opportunity. There is no evidence of 'rural linkage' in these various motivations.

Table 2.7 Logit estimates of the probability of a rural life style factor in locating the new business and of having owned or run a business by the intention and motivation behind the formation of the business

Motivations	Response pattern	Rural life style factor (n = 306)	Previously owned or run a business (n = 306)	'Changers' (n = 71)	'Experienced' (n = 128)
Secure income	46/104	−0.174 (−0.734)	0.275 (−1.149)	−0.405 (−0.717)	−0.351 (−0.885)
Increase wealth	22/87	−0.050 (−0.169)	−0.160 (0.541)	1.772 (2.356)*	0.031 (0.067)
Achieve independence	103/202	0.107 (0.578)	−0.366 (−1.953)*	−0.563 (−1.299)	0.359 (1.169)
Develop a hobby	11/38	−1.027 (−2.017)*	−0.682 (−1.367)	0.311 (0.371)	−0.852 (−0.944)
Interest in field of activity	20/103	−0.214 (−0.812)	0.050 (0.191)	0.222 (0.391)	−0.681 (−1.470)*
Achieve an ambition	26/79	−0.454 (−1.566)*	−0.349 (−1.184)	0.459 (0.606)	−1.426 (−2.653)*
Work at home	9/65	0.893 (2.405)*	−0.003 (0.009)	0.490 (0.682)	1.133 (1.336)
Exploit opportunity	29/78	−0.533 (−1.797)*	0.885 (2.932)*	−1.005 (−1.177)	−0.644 (−1.487)*
Use manual or artistic skills	27/109	0.343 (1.308)	−0.250 (−0.943)	0.750 (0.970)	0.985 (1.784)*
Avoid unemployment	26/49	−0.347 (−0.857)	0.766 (1.891)*	−0.555 (−0.729)	−1.276 (−1.527)*
Log-likelihood		−217.19	−215.4	−43.48	−77.25
Chi-squared		19.14*	22.2	11.45	18.411*
Iterations		4	4	9	9

Note: See note (3).

The same is broadly true of the two sub-samples, in the third and fourth equation in Table 2.7. However, the sign changes against the wealth, independence, hobby, field of interest, and ambition factors are noteworthy for the 'Changers' group of entrepreneurs. For the 'Experienced group', the motivation to use manual or artistic skills has a positive and significant coefficient, and interestingly the wealth coefficient contrasts directly with that in the Changers equation.

The second equation in Table 2.7 again uses the previous experience dependent variable. It is perhaps surprising that the independence motivation has a negative (and significant) sign; while it is less surprising that 'Exploiting an opportunity' and 'Avoiding unemployment' are positive and significant. The financial motivations are not good predictors here, perhaps reflecting the wisdom and insight gained by experience.

The fortunes of very small new firms are the product of both internal and external forces. The forces of the market place, of other competitors, of changes in the price of loan finance, of a switch in allegiance of a dominant customer, etc., can easily take the decision of exist, grow or die out of the hands of the owner entrepreneur. He or she has more influence over the internal forces however. Depending upon the line of business, factors such as energy, stamina, drive and force of personality are maybe what yield the necessary competitive edge; or certainly the commitment to survive in a hostile commercial environment. However, skills and knowledge, over and above personality traits, have their place. The theme of skills and training is picked up in the next section.

4 SKILLS AND TRAINING NEEDS

Identifying training needs

The fact that so few entrepreneurs who start up in business actually commit themselves to any type of pre-business or on-the-job training highlights one of the major problems faced by those espousing the virtues of formal training as a major key to business success. Many programmes on offer to the small business clientele tend to cater for only a fraction of the total needs of the entrepreneur and at charges per hour or per day many view as excessive. Needs may be highly specific and specialist in nature; and the support programmes made available are often too generalist, meeting requirements of start-ups only. This criticism is reflected in the results of research conducted by David Smallbone (1990) for example. He noted that a large proportion of the time and effort devoted by small business support initiatives was concentrated on the early formation aspects of business skills enhancement. These include the formulation of business plans, cash balances, administrative know how, paperwork procedures and general knowledge of commercial legislative requirements relating to tax, capital, labour, etc. As an illustration of public sector moves to assist start ups, between 1982 and 1988 more than 340,000 individuals had received government assistance through its Enterprise Allowance Scheme (Keeble, 1990). The Rural Development Commission had a client base of some 34,000 firms by 1988, the majority of these being very small start-up enterprises.

Despite these impressive figures, specific technical assistance and training is often in short supply and at some cost (in time as well as cash outlay) to the entrepreneur. Local availability of assistance and training is one problem. Business skills which are specific to an industrial sector form another. These tend to have been drawn from experience, either from a past employer, or from a previous attempt to run a business. Many authors have noted the accepted view that founders tend to establish businesses in the activities in which they were previously employed. Access to relevant training, to built up competency in unfamiliar areas, is a particular problem in rural areas, given distances to urban centres and the very wide variety of new business activity.

Only 193 (or 53 per cent) of the 329 respondents in the 'A' survey had been in full-time employment prior to the formation of their business; 36 (or 11 per cent) of the founders had been unemployed while a further 57 (17 per cent) were self-employed. There were 83 (or 25 per cent) founders who had attended some kind of training programme, the largest number (37) of these involved in management and marketing. A further 32 were involved in various specialist courses of a technical nature. The distribution of those who had and who had not experienced training is given in Table 2.8 according to their previous situation.

Table 2.8 Previous situation and training experience

Previous situation	Training experience			
	Yes	No	Total	(%)
Full-time employment	40	133	173	53
Part-time employment	6	17	23	7
Self-employed	12	45	57	17
Unemployed	10	26	36	11
Housewife	6	12	18	5
Student	8	12	20	7

Proportionately, the ex-unemployed, the ex-students and the ex-housewives were somewhat more likely to have been involved in a training programme. The equations in Table 2.9 suggest that the probability of attending a training course is higher (and positive) for younger entrepreneurs and for female entrepreneurs; but that the probability is negative and significant for the very small firms. The significant intercept here is indicative of an underspecified equation. The negative, but non-significant, coefficient for the forties age group may reflect a widespread attitude of the current middle-aged towards training.

The training received by the 83 new business owners in this group was only one or two days at most. This may reflect what was on offer in terms of accessible courses. It may reflect the publicity and marketing of those courses. It may reflect the circumstances of the new owners in the time period immediately before the launch of the new business. And, from comments received, both from this questionnaire and from later interviews, the limited take-up of courses reflects two further factors. One is the word-of-mouth reputation of courses. The other is the high opportunity cost of time (and possibly energy) for new entrepreneurs. Any time away from direct involvement in the business is regarded as a great sacrifice.

Table 2.9 Probability of attending a training course by characteristics of business founder

Characteristics	'Younger'	'Older'
Age 30–39	0.414	
	(1.569)*	
Age 40–49		−0.118
		(−0.389)
Female	0.540	0.514
	(1.815)*	(1.737)*
Small firm	−1.108	−1.089
	(−2.414)*	(−2.377)*
Previous experience	−0.264	−0.264
	(−0.995)	(−0.988)
Intercept	−1.127	0.927
	(−5.083)*	(−4.682)*
Log-likelihood	−178.38	−179.53
Chi-squared	14.89*	12.59*
Iterations	5	5

Note: See note (3).

The respondents in this survey who had received training echoed answers given by the respondents who had received professional advice. The contention was made that providers of training and advice tend to assume the prior existence of a base line of skills. They assume familiarity with the language and terminology of business by the would-be entrepreneur. And, if one adviser perceives a deficiency in another area (e.g. a banker in talking about issues of legal status or the intricacies of liability for value added tax), recipients are referred on, to what they perceive as a quagmire of expensive and inaccessible sources of assistance. For example, the views expressed by dissatisfied respondents in the rural entrepreneurs survey included statements like, 'for most advice I got I didn't have the experience to apply it', 'both accountant and solicitor assumed that I had knowledge which I didn't have' or 'the accounting systems on offer were not compatible with the specialist needs of my business'. In particular criticism was laid at the way in which advice is communicated to recipients, making the assumption that recipients are capable of understanding technical knowledge.

Further criticisms came from the survey about the nature and inability of advisers to cater for the longer term training needs of small businesses. The needs of a business may change over time as fundamental skills become enhanced and give way to other needs, such as the development of new products, or services, or the expansion of credit arrangements, etc.

A further problem relating to the identification of training needs from the point of view of the entrepreneur who is setting up in business is the confusion expressed by the sheer number of opportunities for training and advice offered. For example, quotes from the interview survey included statements such as: 'all advice is available if you know where to look for it', and: 'I have approached all small business advice services . . . they don't seem to liaise with each other, they didn't seem to know about each others' schemes/grants . . . . This has wasted a lot of time and caused a lot of problems . . . I eventually got it but through luck'.

This is partly a consequence of policies aimed at injecting incentives into institutional support, and from deregulation from above to the localised level. Sources of financial aid and advice include the major clearing banks, accountants, solicitors, Enterprise Agencies,[4] local government, industrial development officers, the Department of Employment (Small Firms Service), the Rural Development Commission, Ministry of Agriculture, Fisheries and Food and the local and regional Tourist Boards. Other sources include family, friends and business associates and would-be investors of various kinds. The major new players in this arena are the Training and Enterprise Councils. There have been 74 TECs established in England and Wales throughout 1990 and 1991, with a variant in Scotland.[5]

Founders were asked about the various kinds of financial aid which came with the advice they had received and why they sought it. There were 30 per cent of the 231 founders in the 'B' sample who sought no aid at all: only six of these attended a training programme. Looked at in terms of age, a high proportion of the founders aged between 20 and 30 had some form of training experience. There were

65 in this age range, and 19 received training. The proportion of those who had sought training experience generally declined with increasing age; with only 10 per cent of those aged between 40 and 50 years.

Although 15 per cent of the sample of 231 sought financial assistance (including specific grant aid), most respondents had sought help with selling and marketing, with 16 per cent in this category. Help with financial management came next with 12 per cent of the responses, followed by help with 'paperwork and administration' with 9 per cent.

When asked whether they were charged a fee for this service, 59 out of 165 respondents that sought external advice said 'yes'. Most of these were with an accountant (22) followed by the Rural Development Commission with 13, and solicitors with 12. Only 45 (or 27 per cent) thought that advice was confusing or different from one source to the next. The most common explanation being that it was mixed, unsound and 'a waste of time', with 22 responses.

Although the choice of sources of advice and training in the United Kingdom may have dramatically increased over the last decade, the fact that various sources supply virtually the same kind of support has created a market incentive for some institutions to compete for clients. New forms of institutional competition (both public and private), induced by both cash and bureaucratic incentives to attract potential clients, may thus adversely affect the standard and quality of advice supplied. For example one respondent in the survey here noted that they would like 'unbiased financial advice – i.e. not from someone who wants you to buy their services or lend you their money'. One cannot therefore assume that all advice received is complementary to the needs of the recipient entrepreneur. Clients seeking advice are faced with a price for information for which they have no preconception of value with respect to its content and usefulness. Founders of small businesses are more likely to be receptive to advice at start-up if they feel they really need it. Consequently the demand for advice at this stage of a firm's life is high, and institutions will supply a wide range of services catering for it. However, charging for advice may deter potential clients in need of assistance and may fail to cater for needs which are not in general demand. Some respondents in the survey here expressed quite negative views such as, 'advice tends to be too negative and too general. . . . I cannot foresee anyone providing relevant information'.

Many respondents argued that those administering advice and training should have at least some form of past experience of business as part of their recruitment credentials. The most common view expressed about the way in which advice was delivered was the fact that those administering it seemed to be 'out of touch' with the day-to-day real-life experiences of business. For example, 'Advice should be available to those starting out from people with the experience necessary to give it, i.e. ex-businessmen.'

A difficult problem associated with the identification of training needs is the criteria used to assess the success potential of a business. The most common reason expressed in the literature for business failures is demand deficiency. Many new starters fail simply because they do not recognise the fact that without a sufficient market a business cannot succeed; and they do not possess the planning and marketing skills to deal with such a deficiency. The success potential of a business requires a market to aim at. Many small businesses are supply driven and so fail for lack of demand.

The extent to which business failure rates are due to lack of foresight or lack of post start-up training could be significantly reduced if the quality of business start-ups were improved. Ganguly (1983), and Storey and Johnson (1987) have shown that approximately 40 per cent of businesses fail within the first three years of operation and that only a fraction actually succeed and grow. This proportion is higher in times of recession.

In the Smallbone (1990) survey only seven out of 33 respondents received pre-business training. The proportion of those attending pre-business training in the rural entrepreneurs survey was slightly higher, at around 25 per cent. The most common reason for those who do not follow any course of training in the rural entrepreneurs survey was that they saw no need for it or simply did not have the time. It seemed that the majority of founders had not fully investigated training because they perceived that it was not likely to be an important influence on their ability to succeed. There was no real desire for training.

The desire for training

The low level of recognition by the founders of small businesses of the potential contribution of an investment in time spent developing entrepreneurial skills directed at the future success of their business may, in part, be associated with the original motivation for striking out as an owner manager in the first place.

The 'A' survey results show that two thirds, or 205 in the sample of 329, said that their decision was made on the basis of achieving a sense of 'independence' or to be 'their own boss', as shown in Table

2.2. Many authors have noted the high degree of importance associated with the desire of a founder for independence and its relationship to business formation. For example, Demarche and Dupont (1985) suggest that one of the reasons why so few founders gain experience of training is 'their desire for entrepreneurship stemming from a motive of individuality'. This correlates well with a need to escape from red tape and a rejection of external intervention. This stance tends to re-inforce those entrepreneurial models which attempt to explain the origins of entrepreneurship in terms of the social or family experiences of the founder; highlighting cases of parental neglect, social misfits and poor educational attainment. For example, Kets de Vries (1977), in building an explanation of the characteristics of the entrepreneur, cites entrepreneurial behaviour as the outcome of specific childhood experiences and as a result the entrepreneur is driven by ambition and a strong need for independence. These views are also similar to those expressed by the report of the Bolton Committee on Small Firms (Bolton Report, 1971) which characterises entrepreneurship in terms of poor educational qualifications, but also tends to draw a stereotypical image of the entrepreneur. However, the results obtained from the rural entrepreneurs survey tend to suggest a rather more intricate picture, with a high number of highly qualified 'independent' individuals.

Large proportions of the respondents in the 'A' survey had achieved high levels of formal education, as shown in the last section; 178 had 'O' levels, 105 'A' levels and 92 (28 per cent) had a degree. Only 39 founders (or 12 per cent) had no formal educational qualifications. Only two of these had attended a pre-business training programme. Intuition suggests that good formal educational qualifications aids successful entrepreneurship. For Mark Casson (1982) formal education is advantageous but not an essential ingredient. Busir ?ss skills are not essential to the entrepreneur provided that he knows how to delegate to other (hired) professionals and how to motivate those he employs.

Other studies have demonstrated that new business successes are associated with managerial experience and high educational standards. For example, Cross (1981) and Barkham (1987). Barkham's study of regional differences in the quality of entrepreneurship focused attention on the personal characteristics of founders. His study noted the high formation rates of business in the South East, East Anglia and West Midlands, emphasising that these founders, like those in our sample and others, often start up in the same sector or sub-sector in which they were previously employed. Firm formation rates can be significantly affected by the localised rates of profit, variation in accessibility to capital, industrial structure, inconsistent demand, etc. Barkham (p. 27) also explains that the 'higher the proportion of the population with high levels of education or managerial experience . . . the higher the pool of potentially successful entrepreneurs'. Barkham explains the South Eastern bias in formation rates in terms of educational levels 'the larger turnover and profitability in the South East seems to indicate that entrepreneurs in the South East are better qualified in terms of experience and information to achieve growth'. He also cites that there is a higher proportion of in-migration into this region which may reflect an outflow of talent in other areas; 'the more dynamic, highly qualified managerial talent is drawn to the prosperity and high rewards available in the South East . . . where there are more entrepreneurs with higher levels of educational attainment than elsewhere'.

Previous business experience is clearly an important asset in establishing a new business. Such experience might also, it may be suggested, lead to a greater understanding to the potential pay-off of relevant training. However, the converse appears to be the case.

There were 152 respondents who had previous business management experience of some nature in the sample, which includes those who had previously owned a business or had part-ownership. We would expect that these founders were less likely to attend pre-business training than those who had no previous business experience. Of the 83 respondents that had been involved in some kind of business training programme, 25 had owned or had part-ownership of a business before. The remaining 58 had no business experience but had attended a training programme (i.e. 70 per cent of attenders had no previous experience compared to 30 per cent of those with experience). In absolute terms, however, 246 did not attend any training programme and 177 had no previous business experience: 69 (or 21 per cent) founders had neither. The fact that 70 per cent of founders who attended a training programme of some sort had no business experience reflects the point expressed above: that those with such experience are less likely to be attenders.

In terms of their own classification there were 36 founders who had re-built an earlier business: only three of these underwent any form of training; 30 were the sole owners, but 17 said that it was not entirely similar. There were also 92 founders who had developed a business as a direct spin-off from their previous employment: only 15 of these received training, 56 revealing that their previous employment was similar to their present business and 38 saying that they had past experience of business. Another interesting categorisation included 63 respondents who had defined their move as a 'mid-life switch in direction': 27 of whom had gained previous experience of business, but only 16 received training.

A further factor which may well influence entrepreneurial competence is the previous occupation of the founder. One would expect that a previous occupation which is similar in some way to their present business involvement would result in a smaller proportion of those with these credentials attending a training course. There were 126 (or 36 per cent of questionnaire 'A') founders who said that their previous occupation was similar to their present business; 24 of these had attended a training programme. Meanwhile 34 of the 115 who said their previous occupation was in no way similar also attended a training programme. The proposition is therefore supported. There were slightly fewer founders attending a training programme whose previous occupation was similar. Of the remaining 88 founders who felt that this question was not relevant, 25 had experienced a training programme.

These figures suggest an obvious gap in 'potential' entrepreneurial competence, with 44 respondents in our sample having had no previous experience of business, no pre-business training and had set up in a business which was in no way similar to their previous occupation.

As noted earlier, founders are also helped with advice and with forms of 'informal' training from friends, relatives and other contemporaries. This is an attribute of the new owner manager which is commonly scrutinised by bank managers; but only with respect to their assessment of the risk averseness relating to loans made to prospective entrepreneurs. The wider social sphere of the entrepreneur may play an important role in the process of acquiring and utilising skills. It is especially important with respect to those with no prior knowledge of business because founders can draw upon the advice or skills of friends and relatives which save time and reduce transactions costs.

In the rural entrepreneurs survey there were 143 (43 per cent) founders who had no peer group influences prior to the formation of their business; only 33 of these, however, had attended a training programme. This is probably the case for some because they either had no opportunities open to them to seek this source of support or they were not aware of it. One recommendation which can be construed from this is the incorporation of the wider use of an entrepreneur's social sphere in the criteria used to judge whether to provide free or low cost advice. However, 66 (or 46 per cent) of the 143 who had no peer group influences at start-up had some degree of pre-business experience, i.e. 43 per cent (66) of those with past experience of business (153) did not turn to their peers for assistance or advice. This leaves a significantly high proportion (57 per cent) of founders who had no informal sources of advice, etc., and no prior business experience.

The survey results point to the important role of advisers of various kinds in prompting a time and cash constrained entrepreneur to take up some form of basic training. However, this leaves unresolved the issues of training in what and from whom. One response to this is to ask the owner managers about their levels of competency in their different entrepreneurial roles. A list of nine competencies is identified in Table 2.10.

Table 2.10 Logit estimates of the probability of fast growth rather than slow growth by competency of owner

Competencies	Full sample (n = 210)	'Changers'[4] (n = 40)	'Experienced'[5] (n = 72)
Risk taking	−0.036 (−0.174)	0.439 (0.500)	0.075 (0.187)
Team building	−0.058 (−0.643)	0.159 (0.632)	−0.060 (−0.319)
Cash flow control	−0.090 (−0.553)	0.453 (0.521)	−0.380 0.516
Production management	0.216 (2.233)*	0.255 (0.411)	0.516 (1.890)*
Quality control	−0.296 (−2.478)*	−2.397 (−1.806)*	−0.233 (−0.833)
Arbitrage	−0.006 (−0.063)	−0.596 (−0.742)	0.072 (0.464)
Marketing	0.090 (0.838)	1.888 (1.552)*	−0.110 (−0.732)
Innovation	−0.086 (−0.103)	0.087 (0.299)	0.011 (0.103)
Application of technology	−0.189 (−2.224)*	−0.367 (−0.584)	−0.212 (−0.990)
Log-likelihood	−129.10	−18.37	−45.42
Chi-squared	16.69*	13.7*	8.54
Iterations	6	9	5

Note: See notes (3) (4) and (5).

Respondents to the 'B' questionnaire were asked to consider this listing of competencies as 'Business tasks and skills'. They were asked to indicate whether they felt they were satisfactorily endowed with these skills, either by dint of personal experience or from attending training courses; or whether their competence could be improved upon. About one third of respondents felt that their competency in each area could be improved upon, with rather higher proportions feeling this way in the three areas of team building, cash flow management and marketing.

Respondents to this question did not vote 'the slate'. There was a lot of variation, with each respondent considering each competency individually. Therefore it was not unexpected that experiments with logit equations, seeking to associate fast and slow growth with a feeling or not of competency in each area, did not produce clear results. However, the significant coefficients in the first equation in Table 2.10 are interesting, being negative for 'Quality control' and for 'Application of technology'.

Competency in 'Product management' offers a probability of fast growth, more so than the other skills. 'Marketing' also has a positive coefficient. The remainder are all negative with low coefficients and so difficult to read much into. The underlying implication for these competencies is that those respondents saying that their skills in that area could be improved upon were not the respondents in the fast growing firms.

The second two equations in Table 2.10 provide something of a contrast in signs on variables. The 'Changers' equation refers to a sub-sample, of early retirement moves and the mid-life switchers. These are groups of start-up entrepreneurs with a strong rural life style factor in their decision to set up a new business. They are often people with limited business experience, particularly in running their own business. The 'Quality control' variable remains significant and negative; while the positive 'Marketing' coefficient says that marketing competency in this group of owner-managers yields a significant probability of fast growth: a possible untapped flair factor, or a skill brought from a previous employment. The positive, but insignificant, coefficients on the first three competencies contrast with the first equation, suggesting a (weak) association between fast growth and the self-evaluation of a satisfactory skill level in those areas.

There may be a degree of optimism in the second equation by the 'Changers' group that dissipates when the 'Experienced' group is considered, in the third equation. This group is made up of new owner-managers who describe themselves as either having been spin-outs from other companies, or as being involved in rebuilding an earlier business. The experience factor is not that strong among the spin-outs in terms of having owned or had experience in running a business before the current business (41 per cent of those replying); but many had broad business experience. In contrast, as expected, 81 per cent of the rebuilders had owning or controlling experience. In this equation only the 'Production management' variable comes through as significant, with otherwise weak results on the other variables.

Competence and failure

There is an apparent paradox between business failure and its assumed relationship to that of deficiencies in entrepreneurial competence. Failure may be exogenous to the present level of capability of the entrepreneur. That is, failure does not result from what can reasonably be regarded as his or her 'fault'. Hudson (1989) points out that potentially successful firms may not be able to find capital to finance their start-up, while those with less chance of success manage to do so. And similarly for weathering an external commercial climate. This point is reinforced by quotes from our sample on past problems such as 'under capitalised to meet growth potential' and other forms of difficulty in obtaining access to capital.

The fact is that a business may succeed where entrepreneurial talents are low and conversely it may fail even though the credentials for entrepreneurial competence have been met. External factors beyond the control of the entrepreneur may adversely affect the potential success of a venture. In the rural entrepreneurs survey a significant number of founders were involved in the reconstruction of an earlier business which had failed: 36 (or 12 per cent) of the first survey and 22 (or 9 per cent) of the second survey. This is an indication of the fact that such individuals may have regarded their previous failure as 'no fault of their own' and that mistakes (if any) will not be made again (or that the risks are worthwhile taking).

Some of the practical difficulties of enhancing entrepreneurial competence are to be found in the attitude and characteristics of founders themselves as well as in institutional and market factors. The so-called gap in entrepreneurial competence referred to here can only go so far in being bridged via institutional methods. Some founders have gone under in the past not through the existence of such a gap but through exogenous factors; as well as from an anti-institutionalist attitude seen in those founders whose prime motivation is that of independence. The scale of the gap in entrepreneurial competence in a new company is seen in the limited duration of business experience, low formal educational qualifications, limited technical knowledge, a poor grasp of the commercial world, and other characteristics seen as undeveloped against the whole population of cometitive small businesses. Most entrepreneurs have certain strengths and certain weaknesses. These yield a certain success potential and would satisfy the attainment of specific aims, but not provide for the ongoing achievement of all objectives.

The successful entrepreneur will frequently be a strong individualist, with an aversion to conformist institutions and a resistance to defined hierarchies. There are therefore psychological barriers to the receipt of training and advice that go beyond an apparent 'provision of the facts'. This points to a role for public policy in recognising the entrepreneurial learning function of experience in failed as well as in successful businesses, and adjusting the financial penalties of failure; and to a role for policy to support small business clubs where experience may be shared. In the more formal training arena, the themes of this study point to the need for training to be linked into other forms of support, and for an individual founder of a small business to be led into a sequence of training experiences rather than a single short course.

The study also demonstrates the (obvious) point that the medium is part of the message when it comes to small business advice. Advisers, whether acting as private professionals, representatives of government agencies or as training instructors, are in need of training themselves to become aware of the limitations of what may be termed the 'learning capability' of the new small business owners to whom they talk.

CONCLUSIONS

Any would-be owner of a successful small firm comes to the task of the initial launch of his or her new business with a portfolio of skills and strengths. The adequacy of his or her particular skills mix for ensuring the ongoing viabilty of the enterprise will rest upon training and education, upon experience, and upon attitude and approach. What will be needed for success will vary, product to product, market to market. For some, technological capability has a premium. For other the skills may lie in promotion and marketing. For others again, they lie in design and in response to a changing market.

To the skills portfolio of the individual entrepreneur may then be brought other strengths, prime among which will be the adequacy of the launch finance, to cover the start-up costs with associated uncertainties. More indirectly, the entrepreneur may then have strengths in his or her own formal and informal advisers, as well as in existing access to suppliers and in openings to customers, and also in having employees (and partners) of a known quality who can be attracted to the new firm.

The research reported upon here, based on empirical work with samples of owner-managers of mostly very small new businesses in four English rural counties, has stresed the significance of different dimensions of skill required for business start-ups: the entrepreneurial competencies. It has shown how relatively few new entrepreneurs undertake training for their new role. In part this is because for a large minority the roles are not entirely new. They have owned or run a business before. For some, a lack of time, or an inadequate realisation of what training could have done for them, has detracted from taking up the possibilities on offer. But for others, many of those looking for a rural life style, the 'rural factor' influences both their choice of location for their new business and their aims and ambitions for their business. The issue for these people, and for their advisers, their financial supporters and their trainers, is how far do they then wish to see themselves led into a business career of potential growth and provision of employment for others? And there is an issue of selectivity in the provision of public sector support and advice.

Prime facie, there is a zero sum game issue here, with an associated danger of a misapplication of public funds. To raise the entrepreneurial capacity of one group of owner-managers and thereby to enhance the survival prospects of their businesses would seem, at first sight, to be at the expense of their weaker competitors. Those owners with a lower all-round level of competence will be pushed out of the market place. However, the view taken here is the conventional one with respect to the benefits of the competitive process to society. Higher levels of entrepreneurial skill will not only increase profit and business longevity for the individual but will also raise the productivity of the capital and labour resources of the economy overall, while in the long run it will result in rejuvenation of markets through innovative developments in both process and product technology. This will be the case with both manufactured goods and the provision of services.

The messages for further research and study into the nature of business start-ups from this research are three-fold. The first is general and probably widely understood by those who have examined new businesses, but it is difficult to set up empirically. That is the importance of the life experience of the entrepreneur, the new owner-manager. Certain objective facts about the past of entrepreneurs are often collected in small business studies: formal educational attainment, occupation pre-start up, industry of that occupation pre-start up, etc. But it is more difficult to collect details of those experiences in the past which have contributed to the skills portfolio the entrepreneur brings to the new enterprise. The relevant experiences may well lie outside a past work history, and certainly lie half-hidden behind occupational descriptions.

A second message from this research is that useful further study could be conducted on the special circumstances of female entrepreneurs, especially those who launch into a business enterprise in middle age, as their children mature and leave home. This is a group which appears to be receptive to the concept of training and which holds many an unfulfilled ambition.

And finally there is an old dilemma for those studying entrepreneurial behaviour: how to diagnose the non-pecuniary and non-growth objectives and motives which lie behind entreprepreneurial actions. For many very small firms these 'life style' factors provide a dominant context for what the new small business will achieve; and they place a disjuncture between past achievements and experiences and future performance. The nature of the linkages here needs further study on the basis of large samples, in order to catch the variance in behaviour.

3 Small firm creation, innovation and growth and the urban-rural shift

David Keeble

THE URBAN-RURAL EMPLOYMENT SHIFT

Ever since the 1960s, the most powerful locational trend in the distribution of employment and economic activity in the United Kingdom has been a shift of firms, output and jobs from the conurbations and big cities to smaller towns and rural areas (Keeble, 1976; 1980; 1984: Fothergill and Gudgin, 1982: Fothergill *et al.*, 1985: Townsend, 1993). Table 3.1, aggregating figures provided by Townsend, reveals that notwithstanding the North–South differences in regional economic performance which attracted so much attention during the 1980s, the period since 1981 has been just as much characterised by a continuing and major urban-rural shift of employment as was the 1970s, when the phenomenon was first recognised. Though the categories used in Table 3.1, derived from a classification of the Office for Population Censuses and Surveys, are by no means ideal, they nonetheless show clearly that it was the rural and less-urbanised areas of Britain which recorded the fastest growth of employment – and the *only* growth of manufacturing employment – during this period, whereas the major cities and large towns experienced decline or only very slow growth. As with the 1970s (Fothergill *et al.*, 1985), there is a striking and consistent gradient in employment performance from the most urbanised, in terms of physical congestion and population density, to the most rural areas of Britain. And Townsend shows that this gradient is equally evident in both northern and southern Britain.

Table 3.1 also reveals that though spearheaded by manufacturing industry, the urban-rural shift is equally evident for total employment and hence services, which now dominate both structure and trends in total employment. And while the shift undoubtedly includes physical relocation of existing businesses by complete transfer or the

Table 3.1 The urban-rural shift of total and manufacturing employment in Great Britain, 1981–89

	1981 000	Manufacturing employment Change 1981–9 '000	%	1981 '000	Total employment* Change 1981–9 '000	%
London and principal cities	2422	−626.5	−25.9	8707	−239.6	−2.8
Non-metropolitan cities	709	−134.5	−19.0	2825	+118.6	+4.2
Industrial areas	968	−77.6	−8.0	2591	+96.6	+3.7
Districts with new towns	396	−24.2	−6.1	1025	+139.5	+13.6
Resort, port and retirement areas	218	−12.8	−5.9	1037	+120.8	+11.7
Urban and mixed urban-rural	903	−55.3	−6.1	3126	+493.3	+15.8
Remoter, mainly rural	434	+10.7	+1.2	1645	+276.8	+16.8

Note: * Excluding agriculture.
Source: Townsend (1993) tables II and III; from unpublished NOMIS Census of Employment data

Table 3.2 Urban-rural differences in new firm formation and small business growth rates, 1980–90

	Mean new firm formation rates	Mean small business growth rates
Conurbations (8)	64.4	+8.9
More-urbanised counties (14)	76.7	+14.2
Less-urbanised counties (22)	83.3	+20.5
Rural counties (20)	83.2	+15.7

Note: Rates are of new VAT business registrations, and net change in total VAT business registrations, respectively, per 1000 of the civilian labour force 1981. Urban-rural classification from Keeble, 1980.
Source: Unpublished Department of Employment VAT registration statistics. See also Keeble *et al.*, 1993.

establishment of branch units, it also and even more powerfully reflects differential growth and decline of already existing enterprises in urban and rural locations (Fothergill, Kitson and Monk, 1985), together with differences in rates of creation of entirely new firms in favour of rural areas and smaller towns. The latter is illustrated by

Table 3.2, which plots average new enterprise creation and small business growth rates during the 1980s for four categories of counties of the UK, as defined in Keeble (1980). Though undoubtedly crude, the urban-rural grouping adopted does broadly capture the differences in urbanisation level between different counties. The data are derived from unpublished Employment Department value added tax (VAT) business registration statistics for the 11-year period 1980–90 inclusive. Though covering all sizes of businesses, the great majority of VAT-registered businesses are small (Keeble *et al.*, 1993), so that net change rates are in effect measuring changes in the stock of small businesses in different areas. The table shows that there was a significant gradient in new enterprise creation rates from low values in the conurbations to high values in less-urbanised and rural counties during the 1980s, while rates of net growth in numbers of small businesses were over twice as great in less-urbanised counties than in the conurbations. Though lower than in the former, rural county small business growth rates were also appreciably higher than in the two most urbanised categories.

EXPLAINING THE URBAN-RURAL SHIFT

Attempts to explain the urban-rural shift of economic activity have hitherto focused almost solely on manufacturing activity, which has undoubtedly led the way in this spatial restructuring process. Manufacturing based theories of the urban-rural shift include 'constrained location theory' (Fothergill and Gudgin, 1982: Fothergill *et al.*, 1985), which emphasises the role of urban space shortages in the context of increasing capital intensity of manufacturing processes, 'production cost theory' (Tyler, Moore and Rhodes, 1988), which highlights operating cost differences between urban and rural locations, and radical 'capital restructuring theory', which sees rural industrialisation as resulting from large firm restructuring in search of higher profits through new forms of labour exploitation (Keeble *et al.*, 1983: Keeble, 1986, 182–7). However, the evident importance of service industry in the urban-rural shift in the 1980s is not perhaps easily accommodated within these manufacturing inspired perspectives, and these explanations also fail to acknowledge the importance of the parallel and powerful urban-rural shift of *population* which was also taking place during the 1980s, as well as earlier.

Thus   average   annual   population   growth   rates   by   local authority district 1984–8 ranged from a decline of −5 per cent in Britain's principal cities (with −1 per cent in Greater London and −3 per cent in non-metropolitan cities) to a growth of +7 per cent in urban and mixed urban-rural districts, +10 per cent in districts with new towns, and +11 per cent and +12 per cent in remoter, mainly rural districts, and resort, port and retirement districts, respectively (*The Economist*, 1989).

This population migration from urban to rural areas – as migration it is, rather than differences in rates of natural increase – moreover appears more to predate than to follow the shift of employment and economic activity, with Greater London's population, for example, falling for nearly 30 years before its employment growth peaked in 1968 (Keeble, 1986, 179–82). Similarly, population change rates over the *preceding* five-year period have recently been identified as the single most consistently significant predictor of subsequent urban-rural variations in both new firm formation and small business growth in the UK during the 1980s (Keeble *et al.*, 1993). These points and much other evidence combine to suggest that a further major if not dominant explanation for the urban-rural shift of economic activity and employment is that this has been stimulated by a preceding and selective shift of population, which is in turn primarily motivated by powerful environmental and residential amenity/quality of life considerations fuelled by rising real household incomes.

Real household disposable income per head in the UK rose by no less than +73 per cent 1971–90, despite acute recession in the 1970s and early 1980s (Central Statistical Office, 1992, 89). And this in turn has generated both much higher levels of personal mobility via mass car ownership, enabling rural residence, and mass demand for more spacious, owner-occupied housing in visually attractive, less-congested rural and small town environments. The importance of environmental attractiveness, spaciousness and housing quality in determining recent population migration by an increasingly affluent population who are able to afford lower-density living is attested by much survey evidence, from the 1970s Lambeth Inner Area Study (Department of the Environment, 1977) to Costello's recent migration study (1990) for the Building Societies Association. The latter found that by far the main unprompted reasons given by a sample of 2300 households for moving within Britain during the 1980s were broadly environmental, namely 'bigger house' (29 per cent), 'better house' (23 per cent), and 'nicer/better area'

(17 per cent). Job-related reasons in fact came only joint third (17 per cent). Numerous residential perception surveys have also identified a marked urban-rural gradient in the UK in household preferences on grounds of environmental amenity and quality of life, preferences which surveys of rural migrants show clearly to be the single most important reason for such migration, whether to the Scottish Highlands (Jones *et al.*, 1984: Jones *et al.*, 1986) or to rural Devon (Bolton and Chalkley, 1989).

In turn, however, environmentally stimulated population migration has major implications for rural and small town economic and employment growth, particularly since migration tends to be selective, of higher income, more professionally qualified and skilled individuals and their families. Growing population stimulates local economic activity by increasing local market demand for consumer-orientated services and manufacturing. But perhaps even more important, it creates a supply of both labour and potential entrepreneurs, with a significant minority of rural migrants opting either for self-employment (Bolton and Chalkley, 1989) or for entrepreneurship through the establishment of new small businesses.

The latter represents one of the most striking findings of a recent major study of rural business growth in England carried out for the Department of the Environment (Keeble *et al.*, 1992). This study, of over 1000 matched rural and urban firms in manufacturing and business services, shows that while most firms in both urban and rural areas are relatively new (66 per cent set up as new independent businesses since 1970), rural firms are significantly differentiated from urban firms in that a much higher proportion of their founders are in-migrants. Some 58 per cent and 66 per cent of founders of firms in remote and accessible rural areas, respectively, had moved to the particular county from elsewhere either before or when establishing their businesses, compared with only 34 per cent of urban firm founders. And no less than 80 per cent of migrant founders in remote rural areas (74 per cent in accessible rural areas) reported that 'the environment of the area as an attractive place to live' was an 'important' reason for their movement decision, compared with only 59 per cent for urban migrant founders. For migrant founders reporting it as 'of great importance', corresponding figures were 50, 40 and 22 per cent, respectively. These findings, which replicate earlier survey results for new firm founders in East

Anglia (Keeble and Gould, 1985), thus demonstrate unequivocally a close and causal link between population migration, prompted to a considerable degree by environmental and quality of life reasons, and rural new firm formation and small business growth.

The argument and evidence above thus support the view that a major determinant of the urban-rural shift of economic activity and employment, in services as well as manufacturing, is antecedent population migration which has stimulated economic activity by increasing both local demand and the pool of potential entrepreneurs. It has also of course increased the supply of labour, particularly qualified and skilled labour, which local and incoming firms can utilise. This consideration is perhaps particularly important for high technology firms, which Figure 3.1 shows have also contributed significantly to the urban-rural shift during the 1980s. Technologically advanced industry, such as microelectronics, computers, information technology and biotechnology, is inherently research intensive and hence especially sensitive to the local availability of highly qualified scientists, engineers and professionals whose activities are crucial for competitive success in a technologically dynamic environment (Keeble, 1992). These sometimes of course also become 'boffin' entrepreneurs and small firm founders in their own right. The recent growth of small high technology enterprises in rural areas and small towns, noted by other recent studies (Oakey and Cooper, 1989), thus almost certainly reflects the migration to these locations of highly qualified individuals who provide a crucial source of both labour and entrepreneurship in this relatively dynamic sector. This phenomenon is most characteristic, however, of rural areas which are reasonably accessible to big cities such as London or Manchester or major universities such as Cambridge and Oxford (Keeble, 1989), previous work for example identifying a band of less-urbanised southern English counties from East Anglia to Devon as the country's prime focus of new computer firm formation since 1970 (Keeble and Kelly, 1986). The same also applies to new and small business service firms, some of which are now locating in rural areas of southern and north-western England, at or close to the homes of their founders but within reasonable distance of clients in London and Manchester (Wood *et al.*, 1993).

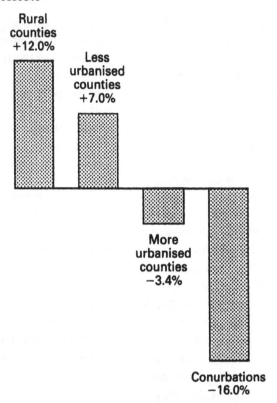

Figure 3.1   The urban–rural shift of high technology employment in the
United Kingdom, 1981–89
Source: Unpublished Census of Employment statistics from NOMIS. For definition of
high technology industry sectors, see Keeble, 1992; for county groups by level of
urbanisation, see Keeble 1980

RURAL AND URBAN SMEs AND THE CAMBRIDGE SBRC SURVEY

The above discussion provides the context for analysis of urban-rural
variations in the pattern of creation, innovation and growth of small
and medium-sized enterprises (SMEs), in Britain, as revealed by the
first full-scale nationwide survey of such firms since the Bolton
Report of 1971. This survey, conducted by the Cambridge University
Small Business Research Centre as a major component of its ESRC-
sponsored research programme, obtained detailed data on the history,
characteristics and performance of nearly 2000 SMEs drawn from
all regions of the country (Cambridge University Small Business
Research Centre (SBRC), 1992). Small and medium-sized enterprises were defined, following the approach adopted by the European

Commission Directorate-General for Enterprise Policy (Commission of the European Communities, 1990), as independent businesses (not establishments) employing less than 500 workers. However, the sample was deliberately designed to be relatively weighted towards medium-sized rather than very small SMEs, given that the former are arguably much more important for national and regional economic growth and job creation. It was also equally divided between manufacturing firms (Standard Industrial Classification or SIC Divisions 2–4) and professional and business service enterprises (primarily SIC Classes 79, 83 and 94). The importance of the latter for national and regional employment and economic growth has recently been highlighted by the work of the Cambridge University SBRC's Business Services project (see Keeble, Bryson and Wood, 1991; 1992; 1993). The service firms included in the present survey cover such activities as management consultancy, advertising, market research, computer services, personnel and public relations agencies, and architects, surveyors, consulting engineers.

The sampling frame of businesses was provided by Dun and Bradstreet, and the combined telephone and postal questionnaire approach adopted achieved a response rate of 33 per cent. Of the final sample of 1978 SMEs, 7.8 per cent employed between 200 and 500 workers, 9.0 per cent between 100 and 199, 54.0 per cent between 10 and 99, and 29.2 per cent less than 10. Some 52.9 per cent were manufacturing firms and 47.1 per cent were service enterprises. The regional coverage is closely similar to that of the total population of such enterprises as recorded by Business Statistics Office VAT records (Cambridge University Small Business Research Centre, 1992, 83–7).

The survey results thus provide an authoritative stock-take of the characteristics of Britain's small and medium-sized firm sector at the beginning of the 1990s. While the survey was of course conducted during a period of deepening recession, it should be noted that rates of change relate to an earlier phase of rapid economic growth, which is unlikely to be repeated in the near future. Amongst other purposes, however, the survey provides a comprehensive picture of differences between SMEs located in Britain's urban and rural settlements. These throw considerable light on some of the issues and questions raised earlier in the discussion of the urban-rural shift. For this analysis, each SME was classified by its precise address to one or other of four types of settlement, defined in terms of physical not administrative boundaries. These are the conurbations (defined as the 1981 built-up areas of Clydeside, Greater London, Manchester,

Merseyside, South Yorkshire, Tyneside, the West Midlands, and West Yorkshire), large towns with resident populations of 150 thousand or more, small towns with populations of between 10,000 and 149,999, and rural areas in which all settlements contain fewer than 10,000 population. The last is the statistical definition employed by the government's official agency for rural areas, the Rural Development Commission. Population totals and built-up area boundaries were taken from the 1981 Population Census volume on *de facto* urban areas. Of the total Cambridge SBRC sample, 40.3 per cent of SMEs were located in the conurbations, 15.9 per cent in large towns, 34.8 per cent in small towns, and 9.0 per cent in rural settlements.

URBAN AND RURAL SME CHARACTERISTICS: SECTOR, SIZE, AGE AND GROWTH

Table 3.3 reveals that defined in this way, the urban and rural SMEs surveyed differ significantly in their sectoral structure, almost certainly in line with similar differences in the total SME population. Over half (53 per cent) of the conurbation sample are business service firms, whereas these make up only 35 per cent of rural SMEs. The dominance of the latter by manufacturing firms (65 per cent) and the relatively low representation of such firms in the conurbation sample (47 per cent) are of course fully consistent with the earlier finding that it is manufacturing industry which has spearheaded the urban-rural shift. These sectoral differences should be borne in mind in considering later results. But it is also true that most of the urban-rural differences identified are equally and separately applicable to both manufacturing and service firms, and are not therefore influenced by the differing sectoral composition of the samples. The urban or rural environment thus operates independently from sectoral affiliation as a significant influence upon SME characteristics.

Urban and rural SMEs also differ, though less strikingly, in terms of size. Median employment size is greatest in large towns and smallest in rural areas (Table 3.4). The latter is entirely logical and explicable in terms of the small size of rural labour markets. In contrast, the relatively small median size of conurbation firms is mainly a reflection of its service sector bias, service firms being on average smaller than manufacturing SMEs. Age differences between the groups (Table 3.4) are chiefly characterised by a significant difference in terms of establishment pre- and post-1970. On this criterion, there is a clear and consistent gradient from the conurbations,

Table 3.3 Urban-rural differences in SME sectoral structure

	Conurbations		Large towns		Small towns		Rural areas	
	No.	%	No.	%	No.	%	No.	%
Metals and chemicals (2)	30	3.8	13	4.1	34	4.9	12	6.7
Engineering vehicles and electronics (3)	152	19.1	83	26.4	168	24.4	44	24.7
Other manufacturing (4)	193	24.2	92	29.2	167	24.3	59	33.1
Professional and business services (7–9)	422	52.9	127	40.3	319	46.4	63	35.4
Total SMEs	797		315		688		178	

Note: The numbers in brackets refers to divisions of the Standard Industrial Classification (1980).
Source: Cambridge University Small Business Research Centre Survey, 1991

Table 3.4 Urban-rural differences in SME size, age and growth

	Conurbations	Large towns	Small towns	Rural areas
Median employment size	22.0	25.0	24.0	18.0
Median employment growth 1987–90 (%)	22.5	25.0	29.8	33.3
Age (%)				
before 1970	29.4	28.2	26.4	23.4
1970–9	22.3	23.9	21.2	29.7
1980–91	48.3	47.9	52.4	46.9

Source: Cambridge University Small Business Research Centre Survey, 1991

which have the highest share of 'old' firms (29.4 per cent) and the lowest share of 'new' (post-1970) firms (70.6 per cent), to the rural areas, which have the lowest share of 'old' firms (23.4 per cent) and the highest share of 'new' firms (76.6 per cent). This difference is consistent with and reflects the recent nature of industrialisation and small business formation in rural and small town Britain. This said, however, it should also be stressed that the largest single group of SMEs by age in all four urbanisation categories are those established since 1980, indicating that all parts of Britain have been experiencing a vigorous process of new and small firm formation in recent years, not just rural areas. The latter's surprisingly low percentage for the 1980s almost certainly reflects not a low rate of new enterprise formation, but the particularly small size of new rural firms and their resultant under-representation in this sample with its deliberate bias towards larger SMEs.

Perhaps the most interesting aspect of Table 3.4, however, is the clear and striking urban-rural gradient it reveals in SME employment growth rates. Median employment growth 1987–90 was lowest in the conurbations (+22.5 per cent), rising to +25.0 per cent in large towns, +29.8 per cent in small towns, and to a peak of +33.3 per cent in rural areas. As with age differences, this finding is entirely consistent with the earlier discussion of the urban-rural shift, and indicates not only that Britain's rural areas have been experiencing high rates of new firm formation, but that the firms thus established have been growing faster than their counterparts in urban areas. This growth rate difference is the more striking in that, as noted above, the rural group contains the lowest percentage of very recent, post-1980, enterprises, which might possibly be expected to exhibit especially high growth rates because of their youthful nature and the mathematics of percentage calculations from small base levels. Interestingly, the difference is equally evident for both manufacturing and service SMEs considered separately, while it reflects both a lower rural proportion of *declining* SMEs (29.0 per cent) relative to the conurbation sample (34.3 per cent) and a higher rural proportion of *fast-growing* SMEs (26.8 per cent over +75 per cent) relative to conurbation firms (22.0 per cent). There is thus a clear general tendency for all SMEs surveyed in rural settlements – and small towns – to record a better employment performance than their conurbation counterparts. This also translates into a somewhat better turnover growth performance, with median values for 1987–90 of +50 per cent for conurbation firms, +51 per cent for firms in large towns, +60 per cent for those in small towns, and +54 per cent for SMEs in rural areas. Again this difference is evident for both manufacturing and service enterprises.

SME ORIGINS AND THE ROLE OF UNEMPLOYMENT

Unlike the recent Department of the Environment study noted earlier, the SBRC survey was not able to investigate SME origins or entrepreneurship in any detail. Two survey findings are nonetheless relevant in this respect. First, Table 3.5 reveals that there are differences between urban and rural SMEs in the nature of the firm formation process, with rural firms recording the highest proportions of all four groups for firms established by 'spin-off from an existing business', by 'management buy-out', and by a 'merger with, or purchase of, existing firm(s)'. The proportion of rural 'completely new start-ups' is thus the lowest of the four groups. The opposite is generally true for conurbation firms, which record the highest proportion of start-ups and the lowest of management buy-outs and merger/purchase cases. For the last two types of originating process, the urban-rural contrast is solely due to manufacturing firms, not to service firms. But urban-rural differences in proportions of spin-offs and new start-ups are common to both sectors. It would thus seem that there is a more active process of spin-out from existing firms, and for manufacturing only, of management buy-outs and acquisition activity, in rural than in urban areas. A speculative explanation for this might be that individuals already working for rural businesses which are facing problems are more likely to pursue strategies – spin-off or management buy-out – which enable them to continue to live and work in such environmentally attractive areas than is the case with their counterparts in struggling urban firms, where there are far more potential job opportunities in other existing companies for them to access. Greater rural acquisition activity may be explained by the better growth record – and hence attractiveness for takeover – of rural firms noted above.

The second and perhaps related finding is that a higher proportion of rural SMEs (34.6 per cent) reported that the business was established as a result of the actual or potential unemployment of the founder(s) than did any other locational group, with conurbation SMEs reporting the lowest percentage (26.4 per cent: the large town figure was 29.2 per cent, with 26.8 per cent for small towns). Again,

Table 3.5 SME origins and the role of unemployment

	Conurbations %	Large towns %	Small towns %	Rural areas %
Mode of origin:				
Spin-off	17.6	16.2	18.9	20.1
Management buyout	4.7	5.5	4.9	5.7
Merger/purchase	3.1	4.5	5.2	7.5
New start-up	74.6	73.8	70.9	66.7
Actual or potential unemployment of founder	26.4	29.2	26.8	34.6

Source: Cambridge University Small Business Research Centre Survey, 1991

this high rural response is equally true for both manufacturing and service enterprises separately. This result is in some ways surprising, given the historically relatively high unemployment rates of most conurbations and large towns other than London. The latter's inclusion certainly does reduce the conurbation figure (London = 22.0 per cent: other conurbations = 29.3 per cent). But this in no way alters the basic result for the rural areas. The latter's explanation may partly be related to the greater proportion of younger firms in rural areas, since the SBRC survey shows not surprisingly that the reported incidence of unemployment as a factor in firm formation is greater for businesses set up since the 1970s than for older firms (Cambridge University SBRC, 1992, 7). But it could also reflect the same argument as that suggested for spin-offs and management buy-outs, namely that individuals already living and working in attractive rural environments who are faced with potential or actual unemployment from their existing employer could well be stimulated to set up their own businesses as the only alternative to migration back to a less attractive urban area, given the dearth of alternative job opportunities in small and dispersed rural labour markets. In urban areas, on the other hand, such individuals can more easily find alternative jobs, resulting in a lower overall urban rate of new business formation because of unemployment. Whatever its cause, however, the higher frequency of the unemployment-push influence on new firm formation amongst rural enterprises does not appear in any way to inhibit their subsequent growth, given the above-average growth performance of rural SMEs identified earlier.

SPECIALISATION, NICHE MARKETS AND THE GROWTH OF RURAL ENTERPRISE

One of the most interesting findings of the Department of the Environment study of rural businesses noted earlier (Keeble *et al.*, 1992) is that while most of the relatively small rural and urban firms surveyed reported that they specialised in particular niche markets, the nature of these markets differed significantly between the different categories. Remote rural firms in particular were relatively specialised in consumer-orientated products or services, demand for which has been growing as a result of rising consumer incomes and preferences for higher quality, more 'customised', items. The results of the present survey support and confirm this finding in two ways.

First, they reveal that rural firms are appreciably more dependent on specialised niche markets than are conurbation and large town firms, as measured indirectly by the number of serious competitors reported by these companies (Table 3.6). Some 55 per cent of the rural SMEs had four or fewer competitors, compared with only 40 per cent of conurbation firms, while 18 per cent of the latter had 20 or more competitors compared with only 11 per cent of rural SMEs. Pratten's recent work (1991) on small firm competitiveness in East Anglia reveals clearly that limited competition directly reflects serving specialised niche markets with distinctive and often sophisticated products. The proliferation of such markets, in both the consumer and business arenas, in the last twenty years is of course arguably a key influence underlying the general growth of Britain's small firm sector over this period (Keeble, 1990: Cambridge University Small Business Research Centre, 1992, ch. 2). But the present survey evidence suggests that this has been especially important for the growth of rural enterprise.

Table 3.6 Urban-rural variations in numbers of serious competitors

	Conurbations %	Large towns %	Small towns %	Rural areas %
4 or less	40.2	43.6	44.2	55.1
5 to 19	41.4	44.7	44.5	34.2
20 and over	18.4	11.7	11.3	10.8
Total SMEs	708	291	600	158

Source: Cambridge University Small Business Research Centre Survey, 1992

Secondly, the SBRC survey further reveals that rural firms more frequently supply consumer or household markets, directly or indirectly through retailers or wholesalers, than do conurbation firms which are more orientated towards serving other businesses. Some 32.2 per cent of rural SME sales are to individual consumers or retailers, compared with only 23.5 per cent for conurbation firms. For sales to 'other firms' (i.e. non-manufacturing firms) the respective mean shares are 24.6 and 30.6 per cent. Manufacturing firms are, however, of equal importance as customers to both rural and conurbation SMEs (30.4 and 30.6 per cent). While these differences in market orientation partly reflect the differing sectoral composition of the urban and rural samples (business service firms naturally predominantly serve businesses), this pattern is also clearly and separately evident within the manufacturing sector on its own. This again mirrors the Department of Environment study finding for remoter rural areas, which links rural small business growth in the

UK to the substantial increase since the 1960s of consumer incomes and demand for specialised and customised goods, in line with some 'flexible specialisation' theoretical arguments (Keeble, 1990). Interestingly, the survey results also show that where rural firms serve other manufacturing and service businesses, these are more frequently small firms (less than 200 employees) unlike urban firms, which more frequently serve large organisations. Rural enterprises are thus more dependent on the fortunes of Britain's small firm sector generally than are urban SMEs. But overall, these results support the Department of Environment study in identifying a clear link between high levels of specialisation on production for distinctive, and quite often consumer-orientated, market niches and the recent formation and growth of rural as opposed to urban SMEs.

COMPETITIVE ADVANTAGES AND URBAN–RURAL LOCATION

The above findings thus appear to suggest that recent rural small business growth reflects the development of new specialised opportunities and markets for profitable production at the wider national economy level which small rural firms have been able successfully to target. The reasons for their success in this respect may well lie in the personal qualities, expertise and contacts of the previously urban entrepreneurs who have established these rural businesses. However, the survey also and explicitly asked SME entrepreneurs themselves to assess the sources of their firm's competitive success, in terms of the contribution of a number of possible factors, and of a scoring system where 0 indicated the factor was completely insignificant and 9 highly significant. The results are recorded in Table 3.7 in terms of mean scores.

This shows that the five leading factors reported by SMEs in all four locational groups as being most significant for their competitive success were personal attention to customer needs, the quality of the product or service, the firm's established reputation, speed of customer service, and specialisation, in terms of providing specialised products or expertise. The nature of these key competitive advantages, with their clear stress on quality, customisation and specialisation, further and strikingly substantiates the contemporary importance of 'flexible specialisation' attributes in explaining recent small business development in the UK. Considerations of cost and price are revealed as being at best of only secondary importance in small firm growth, as experienced and reported by their owner-

Table 3.7 Urban-rural differences in SME assessment of competitive advantages

| | Average score (0–9) | | | |
	Conurbations	Large towns	Small towns	Rural areas
Personal attention to client needs	7.45	7.60	7.43	7.75
Product quality	6.49	7.06	6.61	7.15
Established reputation	6.65	6.87	6.71	6.97
Speed of service	6.32	6.69	6.49	6.97
Specialised expertise or product	6.34	6.42	6.27	6.73
Price	5.16	5.39	5.46	5.62
Range of expertise or products	5.09	5.48	5.25	5.47
Flair and creativity	4.77	4.57	4.40	4.81
Product design	4.10	4.48	4.41	4.72
Marketing skills	4.35	4.20	4.22	4.33
Cost advantages	4.08	4.33	4.21	4.79
Total SMEs	788	313	677	177

Source: Cambridge University Small Business Research Centre Survey, 1992

managers (for the whole sample, cost advantages are in fact ranked lowest of all 11 factors).

Table 3.7 also shows, however, that there is a considerable urban-rural difference in SME ratings, with rural firms recording the highest mean scores for all five leading attributes, and conurbation firms the lowest for three. Rural SMEs also record the highest ratings for most of the remaining factors, including product design and cost advantages. Altogether, rural firms occupy the lead position for 9 of the 11 factors, contrasting with conurbation firms which are in bottom position for seven. These differences are, moreover, equally true for both manufacturing and service firms, and cannot therefore be explained by sectoral composition. They seem to indicate that rural businesses are appreciably more sensitive than urban firms to the contemporary importance and relevance of service, quality, customisation and specialisation in achieving business success, a difference which could of course be linked to their better employment growth record noted earlier. The reasons for the difference are not easy to judge, but might possibly reflect more dynamic, professional and customer-conscious rural owner–managers. The latter ties in with the suggestion at the beginning of this section concerning the possible importance of personal qualities and expertise associated with in-migrant rural entrepreneurs.

INNOVATIVE ACTIVITY AND TECHNOLOGY

The above discussion leads naturally to consideration of urban-rural differences in levels of innovation and technological intensity in the Cambridge SBRC sample of small and medium-sized firms. If rural enterprises and their owner–managers are indeed more dynamic and sensitive to rapidly changing market demands than their urban counterparts, they ought to record significantly higher rates of production innovation and technological change. This is indeed exactly what the survey reveals (Table 3.8). For no less than four of the five different types of innovation listed, rural SMEs exhibit a higher proportion of innovating firms than any of the other locational groups, with conurbation firms recording the lowest proportion for three of these innovation types. Over half (51 per cent) of rural firms had introduced a major innovation in products or services in the last five years, compared with only 42 per cent of conurbation firms, while 41 per cent of rural firms had introduced major new production processes compared with only 28 per cent of conurbation SMEs. And in both these cases, the urban-rural contrast applies independently to both manufacturing and service enterprises, indicating that it is location, not sector, which is of paramount influence in its association

Table 3.8 Urban-rural variations in frequency of introduction of major innovations by SMEs

| | Firms successfully introducing major innovations during last five years (% of total) | | | |
	Conurbations	Large towns	Small towns	Rural areas
Products or services	41.5	45.7	44.0	51.1
Production processes	28.4	33.0	28.9	41.0
Work practices, organisation	29.5	33.0	28.2	28.1
Supply, storage, distribution	11.2	10.8	11.3	13.5
Administration, office systems	40.2	40.6	41.3	42.1
Total SMEs	797	315	688	178

Source: Cambridge University Small Business Research Centre Survey, 1991

Table 3.9 Urban-rural contrasts in technological intensity and research and development activity

	Conurbations	Large towns	Small towns	Rural areas
Importance of in-house technological expertise in firm's commercial success?				
% responding 'very important'	50.7	52.7	55.4	60.1
Use of external sources of technical information in developing new products or processes?				
% responding 'yes'	53.2	57.8	61.6	62.4
Frequency with which firms carry out research and development into:				
new products	42.9	45.1	47.4	48.9
new processes	31.2	31.7	34.4	39.9
new services	36.6	31.4	33.6	30.3
R & D employees as % total	2.4	3.7	3.5	6.0

Source: Cambridge University Small Business Research Centre Survey, 1991

with innovative activity. This finding is, moreover, further replicated by the quite separate Department of Environment study of accessible rural firms noted earlier (Keeble *et al.*, 1992). Table 3.8 also reveals an urban-rural difference in innovation rates in adoption of new supply, storage and distribution systems, and new administrative and office systems. Only in the adoption of new work practices and labour organisation do conurbation firms out-perform rural firms.

Greater rural SME innovativeness is, moreover, reinforced by higher rural levels of technological intensity and systematic research and development (R & D) activity. Table 3.9 shows that more rural businesses rate in-house technological expertise as 'very important' for their competitive success than do any other group, with a striking urban-rural gradient of percentage values from a conurbation minimum to a rural maximum. A clear urban-rural gradient also characterises the proportion of firms carrying out systematic R & D into both new products and new processes, as well as the percentage of those employing external sources of technical information in developing new products or processes. Rural firms thus record the highest percentages of all three of these technological intensity indicators, with differences in nearly all cases applying separately and independently to both manufacturing and service enterprises. The only exception to greater technological intensity is R & D into new services, where conurbation firms – almost certainly concentrated in

London – record the highest values. Finally, rural firms employ on average more than twice the share of R & D workers found amongst conurbation firms (6.0 per cent compared with 2.4 per cent). Interestingly, in this one case the difference is entirely due to greater R & D intensity amongst professional and business service firms (11.8 per cent compared with 2.6 per cent), with no urban-rural difference for manufacturing enterprises. Overall, however, the survey reveals clearly that rural and small town firms are significantly more frequently technologically based and research-intensive than their urban counterparts. And this is generally true independently and equally for both manufacturing and service SMEs, indicating that these striking urban-rural differences are not simply – or largely – due to sectoral composition.

The above findings on technological orientation are of course exactly in line with that of the urban-rural shift of high-technology industry evident from aggregate data, as outlined earlier in this chapter. The explanation suggested there, of the particular importance of attractive rural residential environments as a major influence on the migration of both 'boffin' entrepreneurs and essential research and technical staff, is certainly entirely consistent with the evidence on SME characteristics provided by the SBRC and Department of Environment (DoE) surveys. It is also strongly supported by the direct evidence of the importance of migration and residential attractiveness provided by the founders of technologically advanced and innovative accessible rural businesses in the latter study (Keeble *et al.*, 1992, 14–15). This environmental influence is of course reinforced by greater rural and small town production space availability and room for expansion for innovative and growing technology based enterprises. But whatever its cause, the greater technological sophistication, dynamism and innovativeness of rural and small town firms revealed by the SBRC survey must play an important if not determining role in explaining the general urban-rural shift of economic activity and employment in the UK charted earlier.

THE CONSTRAINTS ON URBAN AND RURAL BUSINESS GROWTH

The final set of results from the Cambridge SBRC survey concern the important issue of constraints on enterprise growth and efficiency in these different urban and rural business environments. The possibly greater incidence of constraints in congested and higher-cost urban areas might, for example, help explain urban economic and small firm decline, as argued by both 'constrained location' and 'production cost' theories of the urban-rural manufacturing shift. The role of urban agglomeration diseconomies has certainly recently been suggested as a possible cause of above-average rates of firm deaths and below-average rates of small business growth in Britain's major urban centres during the 1980s (Keeble *et al.*, 1993). Alternatively, the greater dynamism and better employment growth of rural businesses might possibly cause them to experience greater constraints than their urban counterparts, as growth brings them up against ceilings on further expansion in the form, for example, of difficulties in labour recruitment because of small rural labour markets.

A starting point in this regard is the reported growth objectives over the next three years of the different groups of SMEs, as recorded in Table 3.10. This shows that rural and small town firms differ from urban enterprises in containing the highest proportion of businesses seeking to grow at a moderate rate (68 per cent, compared with 61 per cent for conurbation firms), and the lowest wanting to stay the same size. In contrast, conurbation SMEs record the highest proportions both for 'no-growth' and rapid growth, hinting at a more bi-modal distribution, with different groups of urban firms wanting both substantial expansion and no expansion. The rural pattern of growth objectives would seem likely to provide a more stable basis for local economic growth than the conurbation one.

With this background, Table 3.11 reports the relative incidence of constraints on growth ('factors significantly limiting your firm's ability to meet its business objectives in the last three years'), measured in terms of mean scores (0 = completely unimportant, 9 = highly important) for each of the four urban-rural groups. In general, the table shows that spatial variations in the levels of constraints are relatively small, and show little systematic pattern. This is evident, for example, in the premises constraint, which perhaps surprisingly rates very low and with similar scores in all four samples. However,

Table 3.10 Urban-rural contrasts in SME growth objectives

Growth objective	Conurbations %	Large towns %	Small towns %	Rural areas %
Grow smaller	2.2	3.2	1.3	2.3
Stay same size	12.9	11.2	9.3	9.1
Grow moderately	61.2	63.3	68.0	67.6
Grow rapidly	23.7	22.4	21.4	21.0

Source: Cambridge University Small Business Research Centre Survey, 1991

Table 3.11 Factors significantly limiting firms' ability to achieve business objectives

	Conurbations	Large towns	Average score Small towns	Rural areas
Finance availability and cost	4.64	5.27	5.18	5.19
Overdraft finance	4.69	5.29	4.99	5.22
Demand growth	4.81	4.42	4.56	4.80
Increasing competition	4.37	4.18	4.32	4.12
Marketing and sales skills	4.14	4.03	4.08	4.12
Management skills	3.91	3.65	3.78	3.95
Skilled labour	3.39	3.45	3.42	3.60
Acquisition of technology	2.31	2.31	2.22	2.47
Difficulties in implementing new technology	2.22	2.09	2.11	2.08
Premises or site availability	2.07	2.08	2.16	2.04
Access to overseas markets	2.01	1.73	1.88	1.69

Note: 0 = completely unimportant, to 9 = highly important.
Source: Cambridge University Small Business Research Centre Survey, 1992

three differences are noteworthy. First, rural firms record the lowest constraint levels for 'increasing competition' and 'access to overseas markets', the latter despite recording the highest level of exports as a percentage of 1990 turnover of all four groups (10.5 per cent compared with 10.4 per cent for conurbation firms, 9.1 per cent for those in large towns, and 10.1 per cent for those in small towns). These findings almost certainly reflect the greater degree of rural SME targetting of specialised, customised, and perhaps technologically intensive market niches identified earlier, this specialisation shielding them from increasing competition, both nationally and internationally.

Secondly, conurbation firms stand out as recording by far the lowest incidence of financial constraints, in terms of 'the availability and cost of finance for expansion'. This pattern, while evident for both manufacturing and service firms separately, is particularly marked for services. Small and medium-sized conurbation firms – and probably particularly those in London, close to the financial and capital markets – would thus appear to be advantaged in obtaining capital for growth relative to their counterparts elsewhere. This provides interesting confirmatory evidence of a pattern of differential capital availability spatially within Britain which has frequently been hypothesised by academic observers, as with Martin's work (1992) on the London orientation of venture capital provision.

Thirdly, rural firms do record the highest level of constraints in relation to the availability and difficulty of recruitment of skilled labour, with conurbation firms recording the lowest level for this factor. This last finding is particularly noteworthy, in that both this Cambridge SBRC survey and that of the Department of the Environment study (Keeble *et al.*, 1992, 28–9) highlight a clear and significant difference in skilled labour availability as between rural and urban firms. Thus a specific question in the present survey reveals that more rural firms experience difficulties in recruiting suitable employees in particular jobs or skills (42.1 per cent) than is the case with any of the other groups (36.1 per cent, conurbations: 40.6 per cent, large towns: 39.8 per cent, small towns), and that this labour recruitment problem is focused on skilled workers. Perhaps as a result, rural firms do report higher levels of provision of formal training to their workers (66.9 per cent, compared with only 60.1 per cent for conurbation firms). This pattern of greater labour recruitment difficulties, especially of skilled labour, is almost certainly to be explained by the fact that rural firms operate within much smaller labour markets than do their counterparts in urban areas, especially the conurbations, while their more rapid employment growth results in a greater relative need for additional workers. These workers are also more likely to be skilled because of the greater technological intensity of rural enterprise. This skilled labour constraint on rural businesses is the more significant, of course, because of their above-average innovativeness, technological intensity, and export performance and hence wider national economic importance. The issue of labour and skill shortages in rural Britain is thus an important one for Training and Enterprise Councils (TECs) concerned with rural areas, as well as for district and county councils in relation to their housing and planning policies.

A final issue investigated by the Cambridge survey but not included explicitly in the list of possible constraints presented to firms (Table 3.11) is that of access to external business advice. The use of such advice by both large and small firms has been increasing steadily in recent years, as a response to increasingly complex, turbulent and dynamic market and technological environments. Thus the SBRC survey found not only that 86 per cent of firms had used external advisors during the previous three years, but that 59 per cent of these reported increased use, compared with only 10 per cent reporting decreased use (Cambridge University SBRC, 1992, 32). In turn, this increased demand has generated a remarkable growth in numbers of small business service firms (Keeble *et al.*, 1993), many of which are included in the SBRC survey itself. In the present context, however, the interesting further finding is that rural firms report the lowest frequency of use of external business advice of all four groups in no less than five of the seven areas of use specified in the questionnaire. The biggest differences come in the use of external advice on taxation and financial management (only 57.9 per cent of rural firms compared with 62.1 per cent of conurbation firms), on the introduction of new technology (19.1 per cent compared with 26.2 per cent for conurbation firms), and on computer services (43.3 per cent compared with 52.7 per cent for large town firms). To the extent that external business advice is valuable in improving efficiency and competitiveness – and the Cambridge survey does find a clear link between use of such advice and small firm growth (Cambridge University SBRC, 1992, 32) – the lower rate of use evident for rural firms is perhaps of policy concern. Its cause is of course likely to be found in the greater relative distance of rural enterprises from urban-based business services, and hence greater difficulty of access to such advice, notwithstanding the efforts of such public sector rural advisory agencies as the Rural Development Commission (formerly CoSIRA). The present findings do thus provide support for continuing public sector initiatives targeted specifically at rural enterprise, to provide small rural businesses with more equal access to specialised expertise in such key areas as financial management and planning, and the use of computers and other new technologies.

CONCLUSIONS

The Cambridge SBRC survey, with its authoritative and nationwide coverage of Britain's population of small and medium-sized enterprises in manufacturing and business services, thus yields a series of findings which throw new light on the urban-rural shift of business activity and employment. It shows that while manufacturing firms have spearheaded this shift, it is also clearly evident in professional and business services. And rural and small town businesses are not only younger and newer, but have also achieved appreciably faster employment growth during the 1980s than their conurbation counterparts. The origins of rural and urban SMEs also differ somewhat in that the former are characterised by higher proportions of spin-offs from existing firms, management buyouts, and acquisitions. Their founders are also more likely to report that the firm formation decision was influenced by threatened or actual unemployment. This interesting set of findings are argued here as perhaps likely to reflect the reluctance for environmental reasons of managers and professionals already living in residentially attractive rural areas to move away from these areas when faced with unemployment or problems affecting their existing local employer. Their urban counterparts are in contrast more likely to be able to find alternative employment, rather than establish their own businesses.

The survey also provides considerable support for the thesis, recently argued by Keeble *et al.* (1992), that rural and small town SME development is closely related to the growth in the wider economy of new specialised market niches which small firms can supply as efficiently if not more efficiently than large firms. These niches in turn reflect rising consumer incomes and increasing technological and business complexity (Keeble, 1990). Rural SMEs thus report fewer serious competitors and more frequent orientation to consumer markets – but equal orientation to manufacturing customers – than urban firms. They also rate more highly as factors in their business success such attributes as personal attention to customer needs, product quality, speed of customer service and provision of specialised products, suggesting perhaps greater awareness on the part of their owner–managers of the importance of specialised and customised market opportunities in contemporary competitive success, as well as professional commitment and expertise in supplying them.

These findings are almost certainly closely linked to perhaps the single most important set of results of this analysis, namely those which clearly identify rural SMEs as the most innovative, technologically intensive and research focused of all four groups of firms. As with the accessible rural firms surveyed in the Keeble *et al.* study (1992), the rural enterprises included in the Cambridge SBRC survey are appreciably more innovative in terms of developing new products and adopting new production processes, new supply, storage and distribution systems, and new administrative and office systems, than are firms in the other locational categories and especially the conurbations. And this greater general level of innovativeness is accompanied by higher levels of technological expertise and systematic research and development activity, indicating that rural areas are characterised by a higher proportion of technologically focused and research intensive small businesses than urban areas. This of course exactly fits the wider evidence of a marked urban-rural shift of high-technology industry in Britain during the 1980s noted earlier, as well as suggesting that technological change has also played a significant role in enabling and underpinning rural small business growth. A probable explanation for this greater rural SME innovativeness and technological intensity focuses on the importance of quality of life and residential attractiveness considerations for professionally qualified workers, entrepreneurs and high-technology firm founders, as well as greater space availability and room for expansion for innovative and growing businesses.

The final set of conclusions arising from the Cambridge SBRC survey concerns the nature and intensity of constraints on business efficiency and growth in urban and rural locations. Perhaps surprisingly, the reported incidence of constraints, including premises constraints, is low and does not vary much spatially. Rural SMEs are, however, less likely to report 'increasing competition' and 'access to overseas markets' as significant constraints, despite relatively high export levels, probably reflecting their orientation to specialised and protected market niches. Conurbation firms report the lowest level of financial constraints, suggesting as is often argued that proximity to conurbation-based – and especially London-based – sources of capital is an advantage to this group of firms. Labour shortages, and especially shortages of skilled labour, are greatest among rural businesses, probably because of their employment growth and the small size of rural labour markets. This is an area in which continuing policy intervention, for example by Training and Enterprise Councils, is arguably justified. Finally, rural firms also make less use of specialised external business advice and expertise, perhaps because of relative distance from urban based sources of such advice. Again, this finding provides justification for continuing public sector provision of business advisory services specifically targeted at rural enterprises by such agencies as the Rural Development Commission.

4 The growth and survival of mature manufacturing SMEs in the 1980s: an urban-rural comparison

David Smallbone, David North and Roger Leigh

1 INTRODUCTION

This chapter aims to contribute to our understanding of the potential for small business development in contrasting geographical environments by focusing on the development during the 1980s of a sample of manufacturing SMEs in remote rural locations, and comparing them with the development of a similar group of SMEs located in London. The rural and urban firms will be compared in terms of their capacity for growth as well as the adjustments they have made over the decade with respect to products and markets, production processes, labour processes, location, ownership and organisational change. In our previous analysis we have focused on the adjustments made by firms in London with different performance characteristics (Leigh *et al.*, 1991; Smallbone *et al.*, 1992) highlighting the difference in the nature and extent of the adjustments necessary for survival on the one hand and high growth performance on the other. This analysis will be used to provide a basis for the comparison with change in the remote rural firms in this chapter. The key question that is addressed therefore, is whether mature SMEs in remote rural locations differed significantly in their development during the 1980s from the London firms; if so, we want to explore those aspects of their development where the differences were most apparent.

The empirical evidence on which this chapter is based is drawn from a study of mature manufacturing SMEs in eight manufacturing sectors. In 1979, the base year for the study, all these firms were independently owned and employed less than 100 employees. The core of the project consists of a panel of firms in London which were the subject of a previous research project in the early 1980s. These firms were interviewed in 1979 and 1981 and the owners and/or senior managers of surviving firms were recontacted in 1990 and interviewed to discuss the changes which had occurred in their businesses over the 1980s. In this way we were able to build up a picture of the conduct and development of these businesses between 1979–90. In fact 58 per cent of the 293 firms in the original study (which met the criteria for inclusion in the present study) actually survived until 1990 and of these 126 were interviewed in 1990. In addition to the London firms we also compiled two further panels of firms drawn from outer metropolitan locations (in Hertfordshire and Essex) and from northern rural counties in order to compare the development of firms in contrasting geographical environments. This chapter is based on a comparison between the London (126 firms) and the northern rural panels (80 firms).

The panel of rural firms was compiled especially for this project with the aim of maintaining the same sectoral mix as that for London, in order to control for sectoral influences on adjustment processes affecting firms over the period. In selecting the rural panel, the other criteria for eligibility which were used in London were also applied (i.e. a firm had to be independently owned and employing less than 100 employees in 1979); in addition, rural firms had to be located in a settlement of below 10,000 population to justify inclusion. Using lists supplied by the Rural Development Commission (RDC) together with local authority business directories we identified a sample of firms to be interviewed which met the criteria, drawn mainly from northern rural counties. In the event it proved impossible to produce a rural sample which was divided between the eight sectors in the same proportions as the London sample because there were insufficient qualifying firms in certain sectors. Whilst it was possible to obtain sufficient numbers of firms in the craft sectors from the more northern rural counties (Cumbria, North Lancashire, and North Yorkshire), it proved necessary to extend the boundary of the study area southwards (into Derbyshire and Lincolnshire) in order to find mature SMEs in the electronics and instruments sectors.

It should be emphasised that all of the firms included in this study are 'mature' in the sense that they were at least ten years old at the time they were interviewed in 1990, and most were a good deal older. As a number of writers have argued recently, if the contribution of the smaller business to the economy is to be maximised, one of the most important issues is how to encourage established SMEs to maintain and improve their competitiveness (e.g. Hughes, 1991). By analysing the development of a group of mature SMEs with a range of performance characteristics over a ten-year period, this chapter aims to contribute to this particular debate.

It is important to emphasise that the urban-rural comparison in this chapter is between conurbation-based firms in London on the one hand and firms located in remote rural regions on the other. Another recent study has emphasised the differences in both the characteristics of, and the opportunities and constraints facing, 'remote rural' and 'accessible rural' firms in comparison with urban firms (Keeble *et al.*, 1992). This would seem to be an appropriate distinction since the degree of rurality is likely to vary with distance from the main centres of economic activity. The northern rural counties, from which the sample of rural SMEs in this chapter were drawn, are part of the 'remote rural' category. In the same way the London based firms cannot necessarily be taken as typical of urban based SMEs throughout the UK. Thus the comparison we make in this chapter is between a group of London-based firms with a similar group drawn from remote rural areas. The extent of the contrast between these two types of location increases the expectation that we will find differences in the nature and extent of adjustments which firms have had to make in order to survive and grow.

Following this introduction, the second section of the chapter compares the remote rural and London firms in terms of characteristics such as their activities, their age and their size. In the third section we will compare the two panels in terms of how they performed during the 1980s, mainly in terms of turnover growth and employment change. In the fourth and main part of the paper we will compare the nature and extent of adjustments made by rural firms over the decade with those made by London firms. Since our analysis of the London firms has already demonstrated that the nature and extent of adjustment is related to growth performance (Leigh *et al.*, 1991; Smallbone *et al.*, 1992), the framework we shall use for this analysis is one which attempts to relate the extent and nature of adjustment (in terms of products, markets, production methods, etc.) to a firm's performance over the decade. We will be interested to see whether the remote rural firms have had to be more active than their urban counterparts in making the various types of adjustment necessary for survival and growth. Finally, in the concluding section, we will summarise the main similarities and differences, highlighting some of the policy implications and paying particular attention to the potential for, and problems of, developing SMEs in the remote rural regions.

2 COMPARING THE CHARACTERISTICS OF RURAL AND URBAN FIRMS

Although the rural SMEs were drawn from the same sectors as those in London and all were 'established' firms in the sense that they were in existence in 1979, it may be possible to identify some other distinctive characteristics (e.g. age, size) which may help to explain any observed differences in the nature and extent of adjustments made over the decade. Indeed it might be suggested that one aspect of successful adjustment to the opportunities and constraints offered by remote rural environments could be the precise nature of a firms' activities, as well as the way in which they are produced and delivered. In this way active adjustment by a firm can help to turn a constraint into an enabling factor which means that a successful business in a rural environment may have different characteristics to a firm engaged in an apparently similar activity in a more central urban location.

Sectoral structure

As shown in Table 4.1, the composition of the rural panel is weighted more towards the craft based sectors than the London panel. Whilst we encountered little difficulty in finding a sufficient number of qualifying firms in sectors like furniture and printing in northern rural counties, we were unable to find any pharmaceutical firms which met our criteria, and had greater difficulty in obtaining a sufficient number of electronics and instruments firms than in London. Given the steps taken to find firms in these sectors, we can say that one of

Table 4.1 Sectoral structure of London and rural panels

Sector	London		Rural		Total	
	No.	%	No.	%	No.	%
Printing	26	22	23	29	49	24
Instruments	10	8	4	5	14	7
Pharmaceuticals	6	5	0	0	6	3
Clothing	12	9	10	12	22	15
Industrial plant	20	16	15	19	35	17
Toys	4	3	2	2	6	3
Electronics	22	17	7	9	29	14
Furniture	26	20	19	24	45	22
Total	126	100	80	100	206	100

the characteristics of remote rural industry is a relative absence of established SMEs in these more scientific and medium–high technology sectors. Thus part of the distinctiveness of mature manufacturing firms in remote rural areas is a higher proportion of craft-based firms and a lower proportion of firms in the science and technology based sectors than is the case in London.

When we compare the firms in the London and rural panels at the subsectoral level, some other important differences are apparent which reflect the different market opportunities in the different operating environments. In several sectors, the rural firms were drawn from a narrower range of subsectors than were the London firms. Thus for example in the printing sector, the rural firms were all engaged in general commercial printing, whereas the London panel included firms which supplied specialist markets (e.g. the corporate/City market) as well as firms specialising in particular types of printing service (e.g. typesetting). Similarly in the furniture sector, nearly all the rural firms were concerned with the production of wooden furniture of some sort, whereas the London panel also included firms which specialised in upholstery, cabinet making, and shop and office fitting. In these sectors firms in rural areas appeared more isolated and more self-sufficient than their London counterparts rather than being part of an industrial agglomeration with the network of interdependencies between firms which that implies. In the clothing sector, the composition of the rural panel was in fact more diverse at the sub-sectoral level than in the London case. Whereas the majority of London firms were concentrated in the womens outerwear and light outerwear sub-sectors, the rural firms were spread across several sub-sectors (including lingerie and infants' wear) and also included firms which were applying their garment-making skills to other related activities (e.g. the making of tents). A focus on a specific market niche appeared to be a particular feature of these remote rural clothing firms. Thus when comparison is made at the more detailed sub-sectoral level, it is possible to detect some differences between the rural and London firms within a given sector.

Age structure

Whilst our rural firms are all 'mature' in the sense that they were established prior to 1979, analysis of the age structure (Table 4.2) does indicate that the rural SMEs tended to be younger than their London counterparts. Nearly half the rural firms (48 per cent) were founded in the 1970s compared with a quarter (27 per cent) of the London firms and three quarters since 1959 compared with just over a half (54 per cent) in London. To a considerable extent the difference in the age structure of firms reflects the contrast between London's history as an industrial centre especially in clothing, electronics, printing and furniture, and areas in which industrialisation has often been much more recent. However, despite the fact that the firms in the rural panel do tend to be younger than those in the London panel, it should be noted that a quarter of the rural firms were founded before 1960 and thus we do have a sufficient number of older established rural SMEs to make it possible to compare their development with that of the London firms.

Table 4.2 Age structure of London and rural panels

Year of formation	London		Rural		Total	
	No.	%	No.	%	No.	%
Pre 1950	36	29	17	21	53	26
1950–9	21	17	3	4	24	12
1960–9	34	27	22	28	56	27
1970–9	33	27	38	48	71	35
Total	124*	100	80	100	204*	100

Note: * indicates 2 missing data items

It is interesting to note that from our evidence only a minority of entrepreneurs move to rural areas in order to set up their business. The founders of three quarters of the firms in the panel lived and worked in the area previously, suggesting that the main source of new rural businesses is to be found in the local rural economy and not from outside. In this respect the finding confirms previous research which has shown that the majority of new business founders set up their businesses in the locality in which they are living (Mason, 1991). At the same time, the fact that 24 per cent of the founders of these established SMEs had moved into the area in order to set up their business is arguably significant, and similar to the 20 per cent reported in the recent survey by PA Consultants Ltd. Interestingly, this latter study also showed that the majority of new firm founders in remote rural regions were not born locally, suggesting a link between recent inmigration to these rural areas and the rates of new firm formation there (Keeble *et al.*, 1992).

Size structure

As might be expected given the youthfulness of the rural firms, they also tended to be smaller than the firms in the London panel. At the start of the period (1979), just over half (54 per cent) of the rural firms employed fewer than ten employees compared with just over a quarter (28 per cent) in London, and over three quarters (79 per cent) employed less than 20 employees compared with under a half (44 per cent) of the London firms. Not surprisingly, this difference in the size distribution was still there in 1990 (see Table 4.3) although there was some convergence as a result of the different employment performance of the two panels (see section 3 below). Thus by 1990 just under half (48 per cent) of the rural firms still employed fewer than ten employees compared with a quarter of the London firms. Whilst the proportion in each of the other three employment size groups is correspondingly lower in the rural areas, it is the 20–49 size group where the difference is the greatest (26 per cent in the rural compared with 39 per cent in London). Our evidence would seem to indicate therefore that part of the character of established SMEs in remote rural areas is a tendency for them to be smaller than their counterparts in London.

Table 4.3 Size structure of London and rural firms

1990 Employment	London		Rural		Total	
	No.	%	No.	%	No.	%
1–9	31	25	38	48	69	33
10–19	24	19	11	14	35	17
20–49	49	39	21	26	70	34
50+	22	17	10	12	32	16
Total	126	100	80	100	206	100

The difference in the size structure of the two panels is also reflected in the relative importance of the different types of legal form. Whereas in London at the start of the decade, 93 per cent of firms were incorporated businesses, in the rural panel only half the firms were incorporated in 1979 and only a handful changed their legal status over the decade. Thus the smaller average size of these established rural firms was associated with a lower propensity to be limited liability companies.

3 COMPARING THE GROWTH PERFORMANCE AND EMPLOYMENT CHANGE IN RURAL AND URBAN FIRMS IN THE 1980s

In this section we compare different aspects of the performance of the mature SMEs in the rural and London panel. It might be considered, a priori, that rural firms will tend to be more conservative in their attitude to growth than urban firms. One factor might be the more easy-going life style that might be associated with businessmen choosing to live and work in a rural area. The predominance of craft-based businesses in the rural panel may be another reason for expecting the growth rates of the firms to lag behind those of the London firms; there might be a greater expectation for such firms to be managed for stability not growth, or for their owners to have other objectives than increasing the size of the firm. Alternatively, it could be argued that the younger age of the rural businesses might be indicative of a greater dynamism and commitment to the pursuit of growth. Besides comparing the sales growth performance of the firms, we will also compare their profitability and their employment performance over the period.

Growth performance during the 1980s: attitudes and achievements

Rather surprisingly there is no difference between the two panels in the extent to which firms were growth orientated. When we asked the owners and managers of rural firms about the aims for their business during the 1980s and specifically about the extent to which they had been growth orientated, 40 per cent reported a clear growth objective (compared with 41 per cent in London) and only 25 per cent said they had not had a growth objective (compared with 32 per cent in London). Thus whilst it is important to recognise that a significant minority of firms in both panels were not aiming for growth over the decade, there is no basis for expecting any difference between the two panels in the actual performance because of differences in management attitudes to growth.

When we come to measure the actual performance of the firms over the 1979–90 period, each firm was assigned to one of five performance groups, based on the change that occurred in real sales turnover over the period, with additional criteria used to identify the 'high growth' and 'strong growth' firms. The groups are defined as follows:

Group 1: *High growth firms*, i.e. firms that more than doubled their turnover in real terms over the decade, that reached a size by the end of the decade likely to ensure continuing viability (£0.5 m turnover), and that were consistently profitable in the late 1980s.

Group 2: *Strong growth firms*, i.e. firms that at least doubled their turnover in real terms over the decade, but failed to reach a large enough size or to maintain the consistent profitability needed to be in the high growth category. Their 'success' was arguably less secure than that of the high growth firms in that they remained small or lacked consistent profitability but on the criterion of sales growth they were clearly successful.

Group 3: *Moderate growth firms*, i.e. firms which increased their turnover in real terms by a factor of between 1.5 and 2 over the decade.

Group 4: *Stable firms*, i.e. firms that stayed at about the same size in terms of the real value of their output, having increased their real turnover by a factor of between 1.0 and 1.5. These are survivors rather than growers.

Group 5: *Declining firms*, i.e. firms which actually declined in terms of their real turnover over the decade, these being the weakest firms in the panel.

The main conclusion to be drawn from an examination of the distribution of the firms in the two panels between the five performance groups (Table 4.4) is that the performance of the rural firms compares very favourably with that of their London counterparts. Whilst it is true that only 19 per cent of the rural firms achieved high growth compared with 25 per cent of the London firms, this is mainly because of their smaller size and the failure of a substantial number of them to attain a turnover of £0.5 m by 1990. For this reason, and not because of poor profitability, these smaller rural firms have been classified in the 'strong growth' group; in fact 15 of the 16 rural firms in this latter group were excluded from the high growth group because they were too small to justify inclusion by 1990. If we combine the high growth and strong growth groups together, we can see that 39 per cent of rural firms at least doubled their real turnover over the decade compared with 35 per cent in the case of London. Similarly, at the opposite end of the performance hierarchy, although there were fewer declining firms in the rural areas than in London, there was a similar proportion of 'stable' and 'declining' firms in the rural panel (43 per cent) to that in London (46 per cent).

We can conclude therefore that the sales growth performance of

Table 4.4 Growth performance in the 1980s

Performance group	London		Rural		Total	
	No.	%	No.	%	No.	%
High growth	31	25	15	19	46	22
Strong growth	12	10	16	20	28	14
Moderate growth	25	20	15	19	40	19
Stable firms	25	20	18	23	43	21
Declining firms	33	26	16	20	49	24
Total	126	100	80	100	206	100

the remote rural firms over the decade is similar to that of the London firms; there is certainly no indication from this evidence that remote rural areas have a greater share of 'satisficers' than urban areas nor that growth is harder to achieve in a rural environment than an urban one. The only aspect where the comparison does highlight a possible weakness in the rural businesses is that a significant proportion of them still had to achieve the critical size necessary to give them the resilience to withstand external shocks of various kinds. Clearly one of the challenges for business support organisations in rural areas (such as the Rural Development Commission) is to try to ensure that as many of these smaller, fast growing firms as possible achieve the minimum size necessary in order to become secure high growth firms.

The favourable growth performance of the rural firms over the period is further emphasised by the fact that the sectors which had a high proportion of high growth firms in the London panel (notably pharmaceuticals and instruments) were either not represented or under-represented in the rural panel. Comparing the performance of firms in those sectors where we have a reasonable number of firms in both panels (a minimum of ten), shows remarkable similarity in the distribution between the performance groups. If we compare the proportion of firms within these sectors which managed to achieve at least 'moderate growth' over the decade we find that in printing the figure is 65 per cent in both panels; in clothing 42 per cent London, 40 per cent rural; in furniture 54 per cent London, 47 per cent rural; and in industrial plant 40 per cent London and 53 per cent rural. The conclusion must be that there are similar opportunities for obtaining growth in these sectors in both urban and rural areas although the nature of these opportunities and the adjustments firms need to make to take advantage of them may be different.

In view of the predominance of young firms in the rural panel, it is interesting to compare the youngest firms in the two panels to see whether the young rural firms have grown more or less rapidly than their London counterparts. If we compare the performance of the firms which were founded in the 1970s, it shows that a very similar proportion of firms achieved high growth or strong growth perform-ance in the 1980s (rural 52 per cent; London 51 per cent). However, fewer of the rural firms reached the £0.5 m turnover threshold to justify 'high growth' status so that, if anything, the growth perform-ance of the youngest rural firms is slightly less impressive than that of their equivalents in London. Closer analysis of the performance of the rural firms in relation to the age of the firm shows that the best growth performance was achieved by firms which were established in the 1960s. It would appear therefore that the bias towards younger firms in the rural panel does not account for the favourable growth performance of the rural firms during the 1980s.

Profitability of rural and London firms

Some comparison of the relative profitability of rural firms and London firms is possible for the late 1980s period, although because of the difficulties of measuring profits in small firms it is impossible to describe the level of profitability with accuracy. Our measure of profitability was pre-tax profits as a percentage of turnover and for some of the firms which were limited companies we were able to check profits figures given by managers against the published accounts. Since 1986, however, many of these firms have only been required to submit modified accounts which do not normally include any profits data. For firms which were not incorporated there were no published accounts and whilst we sought to obtain a comparable pre-tax profits figure, the reliability of such data is inevitably imperfect. For these reasons, we have chosen to classify our data into a set of ranked nominal categories and a comparison of the profitability of rural and London firms for the 1987–9 period is presented in Table 4.5.

Table 4.5 shows that rural firms reported a consistently higher level of profitability during the late 1980s period than the London firms: 69 per cent of rural firms reported pre-tax profits of 5 per cent or more in 1987 compared with 21 per cent of London firms, 68 per cent in 1988 compared with 20 per cent of London firms, and 70 per cent in 1989 compared with 22 per cent of their London counterparts. The difference between the panels is less pronounced if we combine the two 'profits' categories although again it is the rural panel in which there is a higher proportion of firms reporting profits being made: in

Table 4.5 Pre-tax profits for London and rural firms

Pre-tax profit/loss as a % of turnover	1987 % of firms London	Rural	1988 % of firms London	Rural	1989 % of firms London	Rural
Profit of 5% or more	21	69	20	68	22	70
Profit of less than 5%	54	18	58	20	57	14
Breakeven	4	7	5	5	7	6
Loss of less than 5%	16	4	13	7	14	8
Loss of 5% or more	5	1	3	0	3	3
No. of respondents	113	72	115	76	106	79

Notes: (1) The percentages refer to the proportion of firms in each panel.
(2) Since there are 126 firms in the London panel and 80 in the rural panel, there are a number of firms in both cases for which we do not have any profits data.

1987, 87 per cent of rural firms reported profits compared with 75 per cent of London firms, in 1988, 88 per cent of rural firms were 'profitable' compared with 78 per cent of London firms, and in 1989 the proportions were 84 per cent and 79 per cent respectively. It does appear therefore that a higher proportion of rural firms were making profits compared with their London counterparts and the difference increases if we focus on firms reporting pre-tax profits of 5 per cent or more.

Employment change in rural and London firms

Whilst the distribution of the rural panel between the various growth performance categories was broadly similar to that of the London panel, there was a much clearer difference between the two panels when we look at their employment performance over the decade.

As Table 4.6 shows, the rural firms were more active in terms of job generation than firms in London. The rural firms created half as many jobs again by the end of the decade as they provided in 1979, whereas the net increase in the London firms was only 6.7 per cent. Thus the mean increase in the number of jobs per firm in the rural panel was seven compared with just two in the case of the London firms. The fact that the median values were lower than the means in each case indicates that a relatively small proportion of firms accounted for a high proportion of the increase in employment (for

Table 4.6 Employment change 1979–90

	London panel	*Rural panel*
Total employment 1979	3611	1067
Total employment 1990	3852	1606
Net absolute change 1979–90	+241	+539
% Change 1979–90	+6.7%	+51%
Absolute change per firm		
Mean	+1.9	+7.0
Median	0	+2.0
Average employment 1979		
Mean	28.7	13.9
Median	21.0	7.0
Average employment 1990		
Mean	30.6	20.9
Median	22.0	10.0
Number of firms	126	77*

Note: * indicates 3 firms where 1979 employment data was unavailable.

a more detailed analysis of employment change in the two panels, see North *et al.*, 1993).

Another way of comparing the growth of rural and London firms over the decade is to use transition matrices (Tables 4.7 and 4.8) which enable us to identify the number of firms which have moved between employment size groups over the period. Tables 4.7 and 4.8 show that a similar proportion of the firms which employed fewer than ten employees in 1979 had grown sufficiently to be in a larger size group in 1990 (30 per cent rural; 31 per cent London) although as Table 4.9 shows, the average increase was higher in the case of the rural firms. In the case of firms in the 10–19 size band in 1979, the mean increase was again higher for rural firms but this reflects some extreme cases as the comparison with the median increase shows (see Table 4.9). Although a similar proportion in each panel had grown to employ more than 20 in 1990 (37 per cent rural; 33 per cent London), a higher proportion of rural firms had declined sufficiently in employment to be in the lowest size band in 1990 (42 per cent rural; 29 per cent London). The stronger employment growth performance of the rural panel is therefore only slightly attributable to the higher average growth of employment in the smallest firms.

Interestingly, it is the somewhat larger rural firms which have the strongest employment performance compared with their equivalents

Table 4.7 Employment growth of rural firms, 1979–90

Employment 1979	Employment 1990				
	1–9	*10–19*	*20–49*	*50+*	*Total*
1–9	30	6	5	2	43
10–19	8	4	6	1	19
20–49	–	–	9	4	13
50+	–	1	1	2	4
Total	38	11	21	9	79*

Note: * indicates one firm where 1979 employment data was unavailable and which we were unable to classify.

Table 4.8 Employment growth of London firms, 1979–90

Employment 1979	Employment 1990				
	1–9	*10–19*	*20–49*	*50+*	*Total*
1–9	24	5	6	–	35
10–19	6	8	7	–	21
20–49	1	9	28	9	47
50+	–	2	8	13	23
Total	31	24	49	22	126

Table 4.9 Employment change by size of firm

	1979 Employment			
	1–9	*10–19*	*20–49*	*50+*
London panel				
Mean change	+4.1	+3.5	+4.4	−7.9
Median change	+1.0	−2.0	0	−10.0
Standard deviation	7.5	10.6	22.3	37.0
Rural panel				
Mean change	+6.9	+7.4	+19.5	−34.8
Median change	+3.0	−2.0	+10.0	−8.5
Standard deviation	11.9	27.0	28.4	64.0

in London. Whereas 21 per cent of the London firms in the 20–49 employment size group had declined sufficiently to move into a lower size group by the end of the 1980s, none of the rural firms in this size group had declined sufficiently to be reclassified into a lower size group by the end of the decade. Moreover, 31 per cent of the rural firms in this size group had grown to employ more than 50 by 1990, compared with just 19 per cent in London. The average increase for the rural firms was substantially greater than that for London firms. It is also striking that the number of firms in the rural panel employing more than 50 workers had more than doubled during the decade, whereas the number in the London panel had remained static. It appears therefore that rural SMEs employing more than 20 employees in 1979 were a significant source of job growth in the 1980s.

As we found when we looked at the growth performance in relation to the age of the firm, the strong employment performance of the rural firms cannot be attributed to the fact that a higher proportion of them were young firms. In fact, when we compare the 1990 employment of those firms founded in the 1970s in the two panels it appears that the youngest rural firms have been less dynamic in terms of job generation as over half of them (53 per cent) still employed less than ten in 1990 compared with only a quarter of London firms, and three quarters employed less than 20 compared with less than a half (48 per cent) in London. As with sales growth performance, it was rural firms founded in the 1960s which proved to be the most dynamic in terms of employment creation.

When we consider employment change in relation to the five growth performance groups, it is clear that the bulk of the additional jobs are to be found in those firms which at least doubled their sales turnover in real terms over the decade. In the case of the London firms, we find that 86 per cent of all the additional jobs were created by the high growth (73 per cent of additional jobs) and strong growth firms (13 per cent). Similarly, in the rural panel 79 per cent of all the additional jobs were created by the high growth (67 per cent of additional jobs) or strong growth firms (12 per cent). From the point of view of the employment generation potential of mature SMEs in both urban and remote rural areas therefore, it would appear that firms have to at least double their size in output terms in order to be capable of generating a significant number of jobs.

Summarising, it would appear that in comparison with established manufacturing SMEs in London, our mature rural firms were generally smaller, younger and more likely to be in craft based sectors such as furniture or industrial plant than in one of the more scientific or medium-high technology sectors such as electronics or instruments. Whilst the rural firms have achieved turnover growth which is broadly comparable with that achieved by the London firms, their smaller average size means that fewer have been able to achieve the minimum size necessary to become secure, high growth businesses. At the same time however, as a group the rural firms appeared to have been more profitable than their London counterparts, during the late 1980s at least. They have also been the more dynamic in terms of employment growth, and it tended to be some of the more established and larger rural firms which made significant increases in employment rather than the younger and smaller ones.

4 COMPARING THE NATURE AND EXTENT OF ADJUSTMENTS MADE BY RURAL AND LONDON FIRMS

The frequency of adjustments

If adjustment is defined as changes introduced by firms to meet the competitive conditions of the market place, it is likely that most firms continuing to trade over a ten-year period will need to make some form of adjustment in order to survive. As our previous analysis demonstrates, the nature and extent of these adjustments will tend to vary with a firm's performance (Leigh *et al.*, 1991; Smallbone *et al.*, 1992). Nevertheless as Gibb and Scott have argued 'firms can be dynamic without this necessarily being reflected in conventional growth measures such as turnover or employment' (Gibb and Scott, 1985). Whilst some firms which may not have grown (or which have even declined) over the period may have had to be actively adjusting to changing circumstances simply to survive, it is the firms which have achieved high rates of growth which are likely to have been the most active adjusters. Factors specific to sectoral conditions can also be an influence.

In this section of the chapter we aim to compare the nature and extent of adjustments made by rural firms with those made by London firms at different levels of performance. In order to facilitate this comparison we have used an index of adjustment which resulted from our previous analysis of change in the panel of London firms (Smallbone *et al.*, 1992). This analysis resulted in the selection of 26 indicators of adjustment which we identified to cover each of the main adjustment dimensions included in the study. In selecting these 26 variables (listed in Appendix 1), we aim to capture the extent to which firms had been active in relation to changes in the following aspects of the business: products and markets, production processes, the use of labour, ownership, internal organisation and location. As Appendix 1 shows, under each of these headings specific forms of business behaviour were identified to represent the different types of adjustment being made by firms in the period. The extent to which a firm was involved in this portfolio of changes gives an aggregate index of a firm's adjustment activity and more selectively a profile of the type of adjustments made. It is the combination of these variables in the summary index which is used as the starting point for the comparison of adjustment by rural and urban firms in this chapter.

There is very little difference between rural and London firms in terms of the overall extent of their adjustment over the decade (chi-square = 1.5928 with df = 3). Very few firms in either panel had made none of the specified adjustments and the mean number of adjustments per firm was very similar in the two panels: 7.3 for London, 6.9 for the rural firms (see Table 4.11). Indeed as Table 4.10 shows, the frequency distribution of the total number of adjustments made by urban and rural firms is remarkably similar: the slightly lower mean adjustments per firm in the rural panel is reflected by the fact that 20 per cent of rural firms made three or fewer adjustments over the period compared with 13 per cent of London firms.

Table 4.10 Comparing the frequency of adjustment in rural and London firms

No. of adjustments	London firms		Rural firms		All firms	
	No.	%	No.	%	No.	%
0–3	17	13	16	20	33	16
4–7	54	43	31	39	85	41
8–11	39	31	24	30	63	31
12–15	13	10	8	10	21	10
16+	3	2	1	1	4	2
Total	126	100	80	100	206	100

Table 4.11 Mean number of adjustments per firm by performance group

Performance group	London firms	Rural firms	All firms
High growth firms	10.1	10.1	10.1
Strong growth firms	7.4	8.0	7.7
Moderate growth firms	7.4	6.9	7.2
Stable firms	6.6	4.4	5.6
Declining firms	5.1	5.8	5.3
Total	7.3	6.9	7.2

Table 4.11 shows that there is a tendency for the total number of adjustments made by firms over the decade in both panels to be related to their performance. Comparing firms at the extremes of the performance range, high growth firms were the most active making 10.1 adjustments on average over the period compared with only 5.3 adjustments per firm by declining firms. A more detailed comparison of the frequency of adjustment by firms in the five performance groups in each panel can be made from Figures 4.1 and 4.2.

As Figures 4.1 and 4.2 show, high growth firms in both panels typically made eight or more of the 26 adjustments over the period: the modal class was 8–11 adjustments and 74 per cent of London firms and 73 per cent of rural firms made eight or more in this performance group. For the strong growth firms (Group 2) the frequency of adjustment was lower than in the high growth firms (Group 1): 42 per cent of London firms made eight or more adjustments compared with 56 per cent of rural firms in this group. The moderate growth group (Group 3) showed more variation with some very low adjusting firms and a few very active adjusters. As our previous analysis of London firms has shown, this group contained a few firms where active adjustment was associated with improved performance over part of the period but whose growth performance over the decade as a whole was insufficient to meet our high growth or strong growth criteria.

It is in the stable performance group (Group 4) that the clearest contrast between London and rural firms is apparent in terms of the average adjustments per firm. Table 4.11 shows that rural firms in this group made only 4.4 adjustments per firm on average over the decade compared with 6.6 by their London counterparts. Comparing Figures 4.1 and 4.2 we can say that whereas 28 per cent of 'stable' performing firms in London made eight or more adjustments over the period, in the rural panel only 11 per cent did so. It would appear that rural firms needed to be less active than the London firms simply in order to achieve stable real turnover. The majority of declining firms (Group 5) in both panels made fewer than eight adjustments with many firms making less than three. However, there are some potentially interesting exceptions of firms which were more active adjusters in this group, particularly in London. As our previous analysis of London firms has shown, active adjustment by declining firms tended to be a combination of product and market adjustment and internal organisational adjustments, in most cases associated with turnaround efforts made after either acquisition or a management buyout.

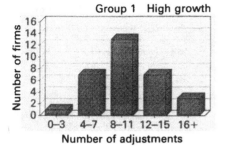

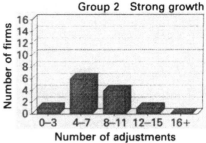

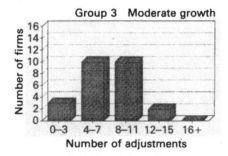

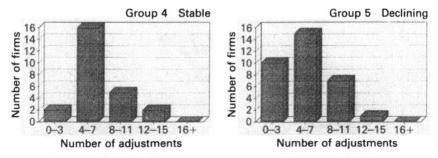

Figure 4.1 Frequency of adjustments by performance group: London firms

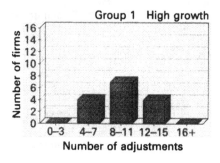

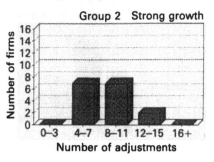

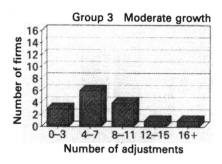

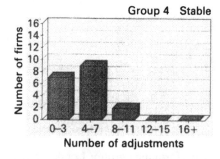

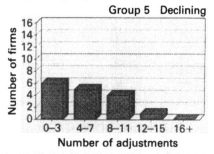

Figure 4.2   Frequency of adjustments by performance group: rural firms

Although there is a relationship between the frequency of adjustment and a firm's performance over the decade, there are also sectoral variations. Using the average number of adjustments per firm in each panel as the reference points, it was firms in the instruments, electronics and printing sectors which were 'above average adjusters' and those in toys, industrial plant and furniture 'below average adjusters'. In furniture for example, 81 per cent of London firms and 79 per cent of rural firms had made seven or fewer adjustments over the period and in general it was firms in the craft based sectors which tended to be the least active in this respect. Clothing is a potentially interesting sector since in London there was a contrast between the high growth clothing firms which had been very active adjusters on a number of dimensions (in moving from being 'cut make and trim' subcontractors to developing their own design and manufacturing role), and those clothing firms which were able to survive yet remain relatively inactive along most dimensions (Leigh *et al.*, 1991). It would appear that in the rural panel the polarisation between the active and inactive adjusting clothing firms was much less pronounced.

The level of overall adjustment described by the index is to some extent sensitive to firm size: labour process adjustments in particular (such as a change in numerical or functional flexibility) were not made by the smallest firms and some ownership and organisational changes (such as 'disposal of part of the business' or 'increased division of managerial responsibility') also tended to be more common in the larger firms. Not surprisingly therefore, the frequency of adjustment does tend to increase as firm size increases. Interestingly, however, rural firms were more active than London firms in each employment size group except the 10–19 category (1979 employment).

In view of the fact that the rural firms tended to be smaller and also biased towards the craft based sectors, it is not surprising that the rural firms show a slightly lower average propensity to adjust overall. When we control for size and sector, however, the rural firms begin to appear more active than their London counterparts and this applies throughout the performance range with the exception of the stable performance category (Group 4). This is mainly due to the composition of the stable category in the rural panel in which there is a predominance of relatively small firms in craft based sectors (such as furniture, printing and industrial plant) which meant that they were able to survive without being active adjusters.

So far we have compared urban and remote rural firms in terms of

Table 4.12 Number of adjustments per firm (by type of adjustment)

Type of adjustments	Max. no. possible	Mean no.		% firms making 1 or more	
		London	Rural	London	Rural
Product and market adjustments	6	3.2	3.6	92	96
Production process adjustments	3	0.7	0.5	46	41
Labour process adjustments	4	0.6	0.4	49	31
Ownership change	5	0.6	0.5	47	44
Organisational adjustments	5	1.5	1.4	71	61
Locational adjustments	3	0.7	0.5	58	48
Total adjustment	26	7.3	6.9	98	97

the overall frequency of adjustment over the decade. In order to understand the strategies and types of business behaviour associated with survival and growth in the two types of location, we shall now disaggregate the adjustment index into its main components and examine some of these in more detail. In this way the 26 variables incorporated in the summary index will be used as a starting point for the comparison and we shall highlight those variables where there appears to be a significant difference between the two panels (see Appendix 2).

Table 4.12 shows the mean number of adjustments per firm for each of the adjustment dimensions and also the proportion of firms in each panel which made at least one of the specified adjustments on each dimension. The table shows that rural firms appear to have been slightly more active than their London counterparts in making product and market adjustments but less active on each of the other adjustment dimensions. We shall focus on those dimensions in which there appear to be some interesting differences between London and remote rural firms. This means that we shall emphasise adjustments in terms of products and markets, and production processes whilst discussing changes in labour processes, location, organisation and ownership more briefly.

Product and market adjustments

Most firms (94 per cent) made at least one of the six product and market adjustments over the period. Very few firms were able to survive without making some form of adjustment of this type and some firms were very active indeed: 31 per cent of all firms made either five or six product or market adjustments and there was no difference between the panels in this respect (see Table 4.12). There was a relationship between the frequency of product and market adjustment and performance however, in that the mean number of product and market adjustments per firm was higher in the high growth and strong growth firms and lower in the firms with stable or declining performance over the period. Thus we can say that survival depends on firms making at least some changes in products and markets but to achieve growth over a ten-year period, firms need to be particularly active on this dimension.

As Table 4.12 demonstrates, product and market adjustment was the only dimension on which rural firms had a higher mean number of adjustments per firm than their London counterparts (rural: 3.6 per firm; London: 3.2 per firm) and only three rural firms had made none of the six product and market adjustments compared with ten firms in London. Rural firms appeared more active than their London counterparts in all performance groups except for the stable category in which there was a group of small craft based firms which had been able to survive with minimal product or market change. Because this is one of the major points of contrast in the behaviour of firms in the remote rural and London locations over the period, we will look in more detail at the types of changes made and the reasons why rural firms apparently have to manage their products and markets more actively to survive and prosper. For example, is it the case that small firms in remote rural areas faced with limited local market opportunities and relatively isolated from the major market areas, have had to be more proactive in managing their products and markets than their more centrally located London counterparts? A more detailed examination of the type of product and market adjustments made by firms in the two panels over the period should help to answer this question.

Market adjustments

The two variables included in the summary index to describe market adjustment are the identification and development of new markets and the creation of a broader customer base (see Table 4.13).

Table 4.13 Market adjustments by performance group

Type of adjustment	High growth	Strong growth	Moderate growth	Stable firms	Declining firms	All firms
New market opportunities						
London	81%	92%	60%	52%	21%	56%
Rural	100%	94%	80%	61%	63%	79%
Wider customer base						
London	71%	58%	68%	56%	30%	56%
Rural	100%	94%	87%	56%	50%	76%
Number of firms						
London	31	12	25	25	33	126
Rural	15	16	15	18	16	80

(i) It could be argued that one of the most important forms of adjustment for an evolving business is the ability to spot and take advantage of new market opportunities which could mean finding new products or services to offer existing customers, obtaining new customers for existing products or possibly diversification into other activities. This was one aspect of adjustment in which the rural firms had been more active over the decade than their London counterparts: 79 per cent of all rural firms had *identified and responded to new market opportunities* over the decade compared with only 56 per cent of firms in London (chi-square 9.84 with df = 1, significant at the 0.01 level: see Appendix 2). Although the tendency for rural firms to be more active in this respect is apparent in all performance groups, the difference between the panels is most pronounced in the declining group (Group 5); it would appear that these established rural SMEs have had to be more active to simply survive the decade, and not just to grow.

One particular aspect of the development of new markets by rural firms was the *extension of the geographic extent of market coverage* either by increasing the proportion of sales in national rather than just local or regional markets, or by increasing exports. In London, on the other hand, firms generally kept the same geographic market orientation over the period. Contrary to our initial expectations, in London, not even high growth performance was linked to market evolution in the sense of moving from local to regional to national markets, or by increasing export sales. In general the scale and diversity of the market in Greater London meant that there was good scope for growth without a need for firms to change their regional market orientation; this was particularly the case in sectors such as furniture and printing. In the case of the rural firms however, there was more evidence of the development of new markets meaning an extension of the geographic extent of the market, although this was by no means a dominant process.

We classified the geographical market orientation of each firm in 1979 and 1990 on the basis of where the majority of their sales revenue was generated (international market orientation = more than 50 per cent of total sales revenue from exports; national market orientation = more than 50 per cent of sales outside the local/regional market; local/regional market orientation = more than 50 per cent of sales in local or regional markets). Comparing the geographic market orientation of rural firms at the start and end of the decade we find that 16 per cent had extended their geographic market coverage over the decade, in most cases by re-orientating themselves away from a regional market focus. (Other firms had increased the proportion of their sales outside their local area but still remained below the 50 per cent threshold.) In London on the other hand, only 5 per cent of firms were re-classified in this way. Not surprisingly the majority of the firms which had extended their geographic markets tended to be firms which had performed well over the period, and this applied to both rural and London firms.

Interestingly, however, there was a difference between the panels in the sectoral mix of the firms which had extended their geographic markets in this way. In London, the majority of the firms involved were in either electronics or instruments, these being sectors in which many firms need to sell outside the region because of the highly specialised nature of the market segment they were aiming to serve. In the case of the rural panel on the other hand, all seven sectors were represented. It would appear that for rural firms, the more limited local market opportunities made it necessary for growth firms to be more active in developing markets further afield in sectors which in London would have given reasonable opportunities for growth within the regional market. For example, in the case of the clothing sector (where rural firms tended to be more national market orientated throughout the period), 70 per cent of firms were making more than 50 per cent of their sales outside the region by 1990, compared with only 25 per cent of clothing firms in London. It was therefore more common to find rural firms in the craft based sectors which had increased their geographical market scope, whereas in London the size and diversity of the regional market made this strategy less important for the majority of firms.

In general, those rural firms which had been active in shifting from a regional to a national market focus did tend to be the more successful firms: for example 11 of the 13 were in performance groups 1–3. They were typically focused on a particular market niche so that geographic market extension was almost a requirement of growth. At the same time a strategy of geographic market extension can create other demands on the company and its management. Additional costs may result directly from the extension of sales and marketing over a wider geographic area and there may also be indirect costs which arise from the increasing problems of management control.

This would seem to be a particular challenge for those engaged in offering policy support such as the Rural Development Commission. The priority currently being given to support for market research and marketing needs to be set in the context of the development of all aspects of the business if it is to lead to sustained business growth in the longer term. This needs to include both a financial plan and an organisational structure which is capable of supporting what may become a more dispersed complex business. It should also be recognised that rural firms will have to grow by market extension at an earlier age and from a smaller initial size base than similar urban firms which who can depend on a larger local market i.e. a stage in the business when the firm has less experienced managerial resources.

As mentioned earlier, another way in which firms can extend their geographic market areas is through exporting. If we combine those firms which have changed their geographic market orientation domestically and those which have increased exports as a proportion of turnover, 29 per cent of rural firms can be said to have increased the extent of their geographic markets over the decade compared with a total of 16 per cent of London firms. In the case of increased exports, however, it was mainly a question of rural firms moving into export markets for the first time. The proportion of rural firms which were exporting at all increased from 14 per cent in 1979 to 26 per cent in 1990 whereas in London the proportion changed from 41 per cent to 49 per cent respectively. Exporting was also more important to London firms: 17 per cent exported more than 25 per cent of turnover in 1990 compared with just 8 per cent in the rural panel. It should be noted however, that with a smaller proportion of firms in the instruments, electronics and pharmaceuticals sectors (14 per cent compared with 30 per cent in London), the rural panel was less well endowed with firms in those sectors which in London had tended to show a higher propensity to be involved in export markets. Indeed when we combine those rural firms which have increased their geographic market areas nationally with those which have increased the proportion of exports, we find that clothing and furniture firms are again particularly well represented, pointing up the differences between the types of firm in these sectors in remote rural areas and in London.

(ii) Another measure of market adjustment included in the summary index was *a change in the breadth of the customer base:* firms which were able to point to a widening of their customer base over the period were considered to be active adjusters in this respect. As shown in Appendix 2, this was another aspect where rural firms had been significantly more active adjusters over the period (chi-square of 8.18 with df = 1 which is significant at the 0.01 level). Table 4.13 shows that in both panels there was a relationship between a firm's performance and its ability to broaden its customer base although the proportion of rural firms making this adjustment was equal to, or greater than, that of London firms in all five performance groups. It would appear that in general a broadening of the customer base was more commonly associated with growth and more necessary for survival in the case of remote rural firms than was the case in London. This possibly reflects the finding of another recent study that key customers of rural firms tend to be smaller than those of urban firms, resulting in less scope for the expansion of output (SBRC University of Cambridge, 1992).

Although the rural firms had been more active in increasing the total number of customers, their *market dependence* (in terms of dependence on a limited number of major customers) was similar to that of the London firms: 41 per cent of rural firms and 44 per cent of those in London were dependent on three customers for more than 40 per cent of sales in 1990. However, whereas in London the high growth firms showed the lowest level of dependency (i.e. only 29 per cent of them), in the rural case the proportion of high growth firms which were dependent on their top three customers for at least 40 per cent of sales was slightly above that for all firms in the panel. This suggests that their high growth status may be less secure than that of their London counterparts with their broader customer base, possibly resulting from a combination of their smaller average size and the more limited local market opportunities.

These remote rural firms were also less dependent on *subcontracting* than their London counterparts. Only 14 per cent of rural firms gained more than a third of their turnover from subcontract work compared with 30 per cent in London. This suggests that their remote rural location may place these firms at a disadvantage in competing for subcontract work, and it follows that their growth is likely to depend more upon their ability to develop and market their own proprietary products than in the case of similar firms based in large urban areas. Once again this emphasises the difference between the opportunities offered within a large industrial complex such as London and those in a more isolated remote rural environment with implications for the nature of strategies for successful adjustment.

This comparison between the market adjustments made by remote rural firms with their London counterparts does reveal certain differences in the nature of the opportunities and difficulties facing firms in the two types of location but also a key similarity. In both panels it was the more successful firms over the decade (in terms of growth performance) which had the greatest propensity to identify and develop new markets, and to broaden their customer base. At the same time certain differences can be identified. For remote rural firms, the limited size of their local markets coupled with the distance from the main centres of population and economic activity, often meant that management needed to be more active in seeking out new market opportunities than was the case in London. This applied to firms which just survived the decade as well as those which performed well.

London based firms faced rather different problems. They may have had the advantage of a substantially larger local/regional market than the remote rural firms but they typically also faced rather more competition and a generally more hostile market environment. When managers were asked to describe the characteristics of the demand conditions facing their firms during the 1980s in terms of market trends, its cyclical or seasonal variation and the strength of competition, the pattern of responses suggested that in general remote rural firms had faced less hostile market conditions than their London counterparts. Whilst there were sectoral variations, the picture which emerged overall was one in which remote rural firms faced market trends which were more buoyant and showed less periodicity than those facing London firms and, for some rural firms at least, a lower level of competition.

Part of the explanation for this reported difference in market conditions may be a result of a lower level of competition in what are often relatively small local markets in these northern rural areas. However, a further contributory factor almost certainly reflects the fact that in some sectors at least, the rural firms are more sharply niche focused than the London based firms. This emphasises that we cannot view the firm and its environment as totally independent of one another. To an extent, the development of a successful firm (whether this is defined in terms of growth or simply survival) represents an adaptation to a particular set of external conditions.

Product adjustment

The types of product adjustment included in the summary index are a change in the product range, the number and type of steps taken during the decade to try to make products more competitive, and the introduction of innovative products (see Table 4.14).

(i) One of the clearest forms of product adjustment is where a firm has made some *change in its range of products over the period.* In our summary index a firm is considered to have been an active adjuster if it developed either a broader or different range of products, or if the firm had actively narrowed its range as part of a refocusing of its activities.

Although as Table 4.14 shows, the rural firms appear to have been more active in this respect overall, the difference between the panels was not a significant one (see Appendix 2). The difference becomes

Table 4.14 Product adjustments by performance group

Type of adjustment	High growth	Strong growth	Moderate growth	Stable firms	Declining firms	All firms
Change in product range						
London	84%	83%	60%	64%	42%	64%
Rural	93%	94%	80%	50%	50%	73%
Number of competitive steps						
London	61%	17%	44%	40%	27%	40%
Rural	47%	56%	33%	28%	25%	38%
Type of competitive steps						
London	77%	50%	72%	76%	48%	66%
Rural	73%	81%	67%	50%	56%	65%
Innovative products						
London	45%	33%	36%	36%	18%	33%
Rural	33%	31%	33%	6%	31%	26%
Number of firms						
London	31	12	25	25	33	126
Rural	15	16	15	18	16	80

significant however if a 'narrowing of the product range' is excluded since a larger number of London firms had adopted this strategy, particularly but not exclusively at the weaker end of the performance range. The more hostile competitive environment in London meant that a number of firms in the stable and declining categories were forced to refocus their businesses, either in response to declining demand or because their own lack of competitiveness had led to a loss of customers. Becoming more focused on a particular market niche was a common strategy associated with survival (but not growth) in craft based sectors in London, such as furniture and clothing in particular. In remote rural firms on the other hand, active management of the product portfolio was almost always associated with a broadening of the product range.

Table 4.14 also shows that a firm's propensity to actively manage its product portfolio varied with the firm's growth performance over the period, particularly where this involved some broadening of the product range. This relationship applies in both panels although the more active nature of the rural firms overall is reflected by a higher proportion of active adjusters in all performance categories except the stable group (Group 4). An active broadening of the product range appeared to be one of the attributes associated with both survival and growth for firms in remote rural areas.

(ii) Managers were also asked how they attempted to make their products competitive against those of other firms and were invited to specify up to three *steps taken to improve the competitiveness of their products/service over the decade*. For the purpose of the summary index, active adjustment was defined where managers could point to and substantiate three specific steps. Table 4.14 shows that there was little difference between London and rural firms in respect of the number of competitive steps taken overall, and there was a similar contrast between firms at the extremes of the performance range in the two panels. Active management of the product portfolio which included taking tangible steps to make their products more competitive, differentiated the best from the worst performing firms in both panels.

(iii) Our summary index also includes a measure of the *type of competitive steps taken by firms*. Since cost focused steps are present in all groups, active adjustment is defined here as the introduction of steps which are customer or market focused (such as increased resources to sales and marketing, improved service to customers, new product development or the development or adaptation of existing products). As Table 4.14 shows, there was little difference between rural and urban firms in the overall proportion of firms in which such customer focused competitive steps could be identified. What the table also shows is that declining firms in London and the stable and declining firms in the rural areas showed considerably less customer awareness in the steps taken than growing firms. The only competitive step to be mentioned with any consistency by declining firms was 'measures taken to reduce costs' which is linked to their tendency to place more emphasis on price and less on product differentiation in their competitive tactics than did firms in the other performance groups.

(iv) Another way in which firms could be active in managing their product portfolio is in possessing or developing products or services which are innovative in some way. *Product innovation* is also included in our summary index of adjustment, and Table 4.14 shows that 26 per cent of rural firms and 33 per cent of London firms had products which their managers considered to be innovative. The importance of product innovation to a firm's competitiveness varies considerably between industrial sectors however, being relatively important in the more scientifically based sectors such as electronics, instruments and pharmaceuticals and less important in the more craft based sectors such as furniture, clothing and printing. Since the rural panel is less well endowed with those sectors in which product innovation tends to be a more important part of a firm's competitive tactics, one conclusion might be that having access to sources of product innovation (or the ability of owners to manage innovation) is less important as a prerequisite of growth than say the ability to successfully broaden the geographical market coverage, or the breadth of the customer base.

Production process adjustment

Although 73 per cent of the London firms and 78 per cent of rural firms had made some change to their production methods over the decade, in the majority of cases this involved fairly minor modifications to existing processes rather than a more substantial adjustment. In the summary index the aim was to focus on the more substantial changes in production processes which were defined as a move to a new technological base, the introduction of new technology or the externalisation of a substantial part of production. Less than half of firms in either panel made one of the three specified production process adjustments over the period (see Table 4.12) and although rural firms were even less active in this respect than the London firms, the overall difference between the panels was not significant. However, closer examination does reveal that the most active adjusting firms in terms of production process changes were in London: six firms in London had made all three of the production process changes over the period compared with none in the rural panel.

As Table 4.15 demonstrates there was a tendency in both panels for the firms which had been more active in making changes in production processes to be the firms showing the better growth performance over the decade although the difference between the high growth and the declining firms is more pronounced in the case of the London firms. This is mainly a result of the fact that there is a lower level of production process adjustment by rural firms overall,

Table 4.15 Mean number of production process adjustments by performance group

Performance group	London firms	Rural firms	All firms
High growth firms	1.0	0.7	0.9
Strong growth firms	0.8	0.5	0.6
Moderate growth firms	0.6	0.5	0.6
Stable firms	0.6	0.4	0.5
Declining firms	0.4	0.5	0.4
All firms	0.7	0.5	0.6

Note: Maximum number of adjustments per firm = 3.

Table 4.16 Production process adjustments by performance group

Type of adjustment	High growth	Strong growth	Moderate growth	Stable firms	Declining firms	All firms
Move to new technical base						
London	35%	25%	24%	24%	3%	21%
Rural	40%	25%	13%	11%	19%	21%
Introduction of new technology						
London	39%	33%	12%	24%	6%	21%
Rural	33%	25%	33%	33%	25%	30%
Change in % subcontractors						
London	29%	25%	28%	12%	27%	25%
Rural	–	–	–	–	6%	1%
Number of firms						
London	31	12	25	25	33	126
Rural	15	16	15	18	16	80

and also that there is relatively little difference between the performance groups in the propensity of rural firms to have introduced new
technology.

Table 4.16 shows the propensity of rural and London firms to make
any of the three particular types of production process adjustment
included in the summary index, each of which is discussed briefly
below:

(i) Only a fifth of firms in both the rural and London panels had
moved to a new technological base involving a shift to new production
processes or new ways of organising production. It is clear, therefore,
that fundamental changes in production methods during the ten-year
period were relatively uncommon. The majority of firms in both
panels ended the decade with essentially the same production
methods as they had in 1979. Not surprisingly perhaps, it was the
high growth firms which were more likely to have made fundamental
changes in production methods. In London the main differences were
at the extremes between the high growth firms and the declining
firms. Only one of the declining London firms had moved to a new
technological base, though 42 per cent of them had carried out minor
changes to production such as the reorganisation of production layout
or investing in power tools. In fact, the proportion of firms making
minor production changes of this sort showed relatively little variation between the performance groups. In the rural panel also it was
the high growth firms which showed the highest propensity to have
shifted to a new technological base, although in this case the
difference was with all other survivors rather than mainly between
the high growth and declining firms.

(ii) The second measure of production process adjustment used in
the summary index is the *introduction of some new or advanced
technology* over the decade. The way in which new technology was
defined varied between sectors but to be included in the index a firm
needed to have introduced new technology into all or a substantial
part of the production process. Although rural firms appear to have
been more active in introducing advanced technology than firms in
London, this was mainly concentrated in the printing sector which
accounted for two thirds of the rural firms introducing advanced
technology. In the majority of cases this involved change at the pre-
print stage and typically a shift to computerised typesetting. In other
cases the change was more gradual as advanced technology was
introduced as and when individual machines were replaced. A more
detailed comparison shows that rural printing firms in the lower
performance groups (Groups 3–5) have been more active than their

London counterparts. This appears to be mainly a result of a time lag in the introduction of new technology in the rural printing firms compared with those in London, together with some difference in the characteristics of the firms themselves. Whereas in London most of the surviving printing companies had replaced hot metal by computer typesetting in the 1970s, in the rural panel this change had commonly been made during the 1980s. There was also a difference in that whereas in London, some of the printing firms specialised in part of the production process, in the rural panel it was more common for firms to offer a full printing service including typesetting, printing and finishing. This meant that more of the rural firms were involved in the pre-print processes where the impact of technological change has been particularly dramatic.

(iii) Another way in which firms can make adjustments to their production processes over the period is by changing the extent to which they *externalise part of their production to other firms*. An increase in subcontracting could be a way of maintaining (or increasing) a firm's competitiveness by reducing costs in markets where price competition is severe. Increased externalisation of production can also be attractive to firms as a way of moving out (either in whole or in part) of what their managers see as troublesome manufacturing with its high fixed costs in plant and machinery, high labour costs and in some cases skill shortages. A reduction in subcontracting on the other hand could be associated with an attempt to improve quality in circumstances where firms did not want to compromise product quality by sourcing from unreliable subcontractors.

Although the proportion of firms in the two panels which sometimes used subcontractors was fairly similar (78 per cent London; 69 per cent rural), there was a distinct difference in the regular use of subcontractors which was lower in the rural case (30 per cent compared with 48 per cent in London). The greater importance of subcontracting to London firms is further supported by the fact that only one rural firm subcontracted out more than 25 per cent of the value of its production in 1990, compared with a fifth of the London firms which were subcontracting out at the end of the period. This reinforces the view that in London small firms are more bound into networks of interdependent (and specialised) businesses, compared with a higher degree of self-sufficiency in similar remote rural firms.

The most common reason given by firms in both panels for subcontracting out was that some work required specialist equipment or skills which they did not possess in-house (72 per cent of London firms and 73 per cent of rural firms which subcontracted out). Whilst this can be rationalised in terms of being more cost effective than firms investing in the specialist capability themselves, in most cases this was not part of an explicit cost-reduction strategy. In fact one of the differences which can be noted between the two panels is the higher proportion of London firms which explained their subcontracting out in terms of cost reduction (26 per cent London; 15 per cent rural).

Focusing specifically on the firms in which there had been a change in the use of subcontracting over the period, two criteria were used to identify the active adjusters: an identifiable change in the proportion of work subcontracted out, and subcontracting having been an important part of production organisation (defined as 25 per cent of turnover value) for at least part of the period. Table 4.16 shows that firms which had made such a change in the proportion of production subcontracted out were largely confined to the London panel; only one of the rural firms had changed its production organisation in this way over the decade. However when the 'importance' criterion is relaxed, the proportion of firms in the two panels which changed the proportion of work subcontracted out over the decade is broadly similar. In London 40 per cent of firms which subcontracted out at some point during the decade reported an increase compared with 35 per cent of rural firms; 17 per cent of London firms reported a decrease compared with 16 per cent in the rural areas.

There is some evidence to suggest that in the case of London firms, subcontracting has been used during the 1980s to reorganise production and achieve cost reduction, whereas this has not been the case in the rural panel. We can infer that London firms are better able to do this because of the richer network of specialist supporting and supply firms which exists in London. This suggests that London offers a locational advantage for small firms seeking to regain competitiveness by this strategy. In London, 40 per cent of firms which increased their subcontracting over the period did so as part of a cost-reduction strategy compared with only 11 per cent of those experiencing an increase in subcontracting in the rural panel. It is also noticeable in the case of the London firms which used subcontracting for this purpose, that the value of production subcontracted out was higher than in those firms which externalised production for other reasons; nearly half of the 26 London firms which externalised to reduce costs put out more than a quarter of their production.

The use of subcontracting for cost reduction was a particular feature of several electronics firms in London and this was often associated with a strategy to restore profitability and competitiveness. Various cost advantages were identified, including the transfer of the costs associated with the purchase of materials and components on to the subcontractor, the avoidance of investment in specialist machinery, and a reduction in the cost and hassle of employing workers. The only functions to remain internal in these firms were the design, assembly and testing of the products; the production of the various components being subcontracted out to other firms. In comparison, none of the electronics firms in the rural panel had externalised their production to achieve cost reduction during the 1980s. Most of them did subcontract a small part of their production, but this consisted mainly of specialist processes which they could not provide internally. However, it is interesting to note that at the time of the interview the two largest rural electronics firms were considering subcontracting out an increasing proportion of their production. Their managers saw this as a way of coping with increasing demand whilst avoiding the additional costs associated with investing in more factory space and expanding the workforce. There are some tentative signs therefore that the externalisation of production may be becoming a more important feature of the organisation of production in rural as well as London electronics firms; but apparently remote rural firms need to be larger before they can manage such a strategy, i.e. manage a network of necessarily dispersed supply and service subcontractors.

Investment in plant and machinery

The summary index emphasises major adjustment rather than incremental change but another way of measuring changes in production is to compare the rates of capital investment in London and rural firms. Table 4.17 shows that on average rural firms were investing more than London firms in the late 1980s with a median of £500 per employee per annum compared with £380 for London firms. The table also shows that the annual level of capital investment per employee by rural firms was higher in most sectors. The only sectors in which London firms were higher investors were printing and electronics although if the mean rather than the median is used, the level of investment in rural firms exceeds that in London in these sectors also. Thus on average, rural firms appear to have been investing more in capital equipment than their London counterparts in the late 1980s.

Table 4.17 Median annual capital investment in £ per employee in the late 1980s (by sector)

Sector	London firms		Rural firms	
Printing	£1850	(25)	£1670	(23)
Instruments	£250	(10)	£445	(4)
Pharmaceuticals	£980	(6)	–	
Clothing	£110	(12)	£195	(10)
Industrial plant	£230	(18)	£770	(15)
Toys and games	£40	(4)	£105	(2)
Electronics	£400	(20)	£360	(7)
Furniture	£250	(24)	£333	(18)
All firms	£380	(119)	£500	(79)

Note: The figures in brackets show the number of firms for which we have data on this variable.

When the annual level of capital investment per employee is compared between the performance groups we find that in both panels there is some tendency for the level of investment to be positively associated with performance (see Table 4.18). At the same time a comparison of the mean and median investment levels shows that there is a considerable variation within most performance groups and a tendency for a relatively small number of firms to be very high investors. Because of this tendency towards skewness, the median gives a more reliable measure in this instance.

However, it is interesting to note that whereas in the rural firms there is a consistent tendency for investment to decrease with performance, in London the picture is less straightforward. Whilst the median annual investment per employee for firms in Group 1–3 (£667) is markedly above that of stable (£255) and declining firms (£140), the high growth firms in London cannot be uniformly characterised as high investors. Their median investment of £580 per employee is below that of London firms in the strong and moderate growth categories and substantially below that of their high growth rural counterparts. Closer analysis shows that this is not so much a result of differences in sectoral composition so much as the kind of growth strategies which the high growth firms in London have adopted. For example, all three high growth clothing firms in London have moved out of manufacturing and in other sectors such as electronics increased externalisation by high growth firms reduced the necessity for in-house investment in production capacity. In other sectors such as printing, some of the high growth firms diversified into activities which were related but which did not involve increased investment in productive capacity.

Table 4.18 Average annual capital investment £ per employee in the late 1980s by performance group

Performance group	London firms			Rural firms		
	Median	Mean		Median	Mean	
High growth firms	£580	£1352	(30)	£1340	£2135	(15)
Strong growth firms	£1485	£1895	(12)	£1040	£1462	(15)
Moderate growth firms	£670	£1025	(23)	£500	£1719	(15)
Stable firms	£255	£920	(22)	£415	£780	(18)
Declining firms	£140	£556	(32)	£235	£437	(16)
All firms	£380	£1050	(119)	£500	£1276	(79)

Whilst on the basis of the evidence presented here we cannot say that remote rural firms are technically more backward than their counterparts in London, it would appear that they have been rather slower to have introduced new production technologies. Nevertheless, during the late 1980s at least, the remote rural firms have been more actively investing in capital equipment than their London counterparts. This is partly explained in terms of the catching up process described and partly by their stronger commitment to manufacturing as a group than the London firms, where there was both a higher level of externalisation and some diversification from core manufacturing activities which was largely absent from the rural panel.

Labour process adjustments

Four indicators of *labour process adjustment* are included in the summary index: a change in the ratio between manual/non-manual staff, evidence of numerical flexibility, functional flexibility and a substantial increase in labour productivity over the decade. Less than half the firms in the two panels (42 per cent) made one or more of the specified changes over the decade (see Table 4.12). It would appear that active labour process adjustment was not a central feature of the development of firms in either panel over the period although there are a small number of interesting exceptions (see North *et al.*, 1992 for a more detailed analysis of labour process changes in the London panel). A comparison between the panels shows the London firms to have been the more active, although the difference in average size of firms is undoubtedly one factor (very small firms tend to be excluded from indicators which measure proportional change in the type of labour employed for example). In terms of performance it would appear that in both panels improvements in productivity are particularly associated with the better performing companies but there did not appear to be any consistent relationship between any change in labour flexibility and performance. In the London panel in particular, stable and declining firms were as likely to have increased either numerical or functional flexibility as growth firms.

A more detailed comparison of the way in which labour is managed by SMEs in different locations shows very little difference between remote rural and London firms in terms of *numerical flexibility*. Not only was the extent to which firms used 'peripheral' sources of labour broadly comparable in the two panels but there was no evidence of a greater use being made of 'peripheral' labour over the period in order to achieve flexibility on any scale (North *et al.*, 1993).

However we were able to detect differences between London and remote rural firms in terms of *functional flexibility*. It would appear that remote rural firms used labour more flexibly than the London firms. We asked managers to assess the degree of workplace flexibility on a four-point scale from strongly demarcated to totally flexible and their responses were used alongside evidence from elsewhere in the interviews to code each firm. On this basis, 81 per cent of rural firms were considered to be either 'highly flexible with little demarcation' or 'totally flexible' in the use of labour compared with 59 per cent of London firms. Whilst this is partly a reflection of the smaller size of the remote rural firms, closer analysis shows that all sizes of firm in the rural panel tended to be more flexible in the use of labour than their London equivalents. This may indicate more flexible attitudes of workers in these remote rural regions and the absence of traditional approaches to job demarcations.

It is also interesting to note that the proportion of skilled workers in the workforce does tend to be smaller in the remote rural firms than in those in London, especially in the clothing and industrial plant sectors. Indeed this may be one factor contributing to the higher reported level of functional flexibility in the rural firms. The lower proportion of skilled workers in these remote rural firms is not so much the result of a deliberate strategy on the part of management however, as a reflection of the difficulties experienced by remote rural firms in recruiting skilled workers. Skills shortages were also a problem for the London firms, however. When we asked managers if their firm had faced any labour problems during the three years prior to the interview, 59 per cent of firms in each panel referred to skilled labour shortages. The problem is a national one of course, and a major investigation of the constraints on the growth of small firms in Britain concluded that the shortage of skilled labour was much more of a constraint than finance for example (Department of Trade and Industry, 1991).

What is interesting here is the difference in the way in which firms in these different geographical environments have responded to these skills shortages. In London the shortage of skilled workers and recruitment problems generally, had contributed to increased externalisation of production in some firms and to diversification in others. In the remote rural firms on the other hand, the response was more typically to try to increase the level of skill within the workforce (48 per cent of the firms in the rural panel) compared with London (30 per cent) and this strategy was particularly evident in the printing and furniture sectors. Remote rural firms in general, faced rather fewer opportunities for subcontracting out production tasks to other 'local' firms which meant they had to be more self-sufficient. There was also evidence that they experienced fewer problems with labour once it had been recruited compared with their London counterparts. If this was also combined with lower rates of pay and less competition in local labour markets, there was also a greater likelihood of the rural firms receiving a return from their attempt to increase the skill levels of their workers.

Locational adjustments

For a firm to be considered locationally active and thus included in our summary index of adjustment, it needed to have either relocated, opened additional facilities of some sort at another site or closed a site over the period. Surprisingly perhaps, more than half of all firms (54 per cent) had made some form of locational adjustment (see Table 4.19). Although London based firms appear to have been more active than the rural firms, this is almost entirely due to the fact that very few rural firms had closed facilities over the period. As shown in Appendix 2, there was a significant difference between the panels in the propensity of firms to have *closed facilities* over the decade (chi-square = 10.5 significant at the 0.01 level) which is mainly a result of the fact that there were fewer rural firms which were multiplant firms in 1979 (8 per cent compared with 23 per cent in London). This difference had narrowed by the end of the decade, however, (17 per cent rural; 22 per cent London), partly because of the closures made by some London firms and partly because

Table 4.19 Firms making locational adjustments by performance group

Type of adjustment	High growth No.	Strong growth No.	Moderate growth No.	Stable firms No.	Declining firms No.	All firms No.	%
Relocation							
Urban	9	7	14	4	8	42	33
Rural	7	12	3	2	5	29	36
Additional site							
Urban	10	1	2	5	2	20	16
Rural	5	3	1	1	–	10	13
Closure							
Urban	9	1	4	7	8	29	23
Rural	–	–	2	1	1	4	5
At least one adjustment							
Urban	19	9	18	11	16	73	58
Rural	11	14	4	4	5	38	48
All firms							
Urban	31	12	25	25	33	126	100
Rural	15	16	15	18	16	80	100

of the increase in the number of rural firms which opened additional sites.

By contrast, there was little difference between London firms and rural firms in their propensity to relocate or establish additional facilities over the decade. Fifteen per cent of all firms *opened additional facilities* (such as another production plant, sales office or retail outlet) over the decade and predictably this form of locational adjustment was associated with growth, particularly with high growth performance. The only difference between the panels appeared to be that whereas in the case of London, a third of new site openings involved production plants, in the case of the rural firms the majority of new site openings (66 per cent) involved additional production facilities. Although approximately two thirds of new facilities were opened in the same region in both panels, in the case of the rural firms those few cases which did involve establishing a site outside the region were either production plants or sales offices located in the SE region.

As Table 4.19 shows, *relocation* was the most common of the three types of locational adjustment included in the index. About a third of all firms relocated over the decade, with a predictable tendency for this to be more common in the case of growing firms (Groups

1–3) although there was a significant minority of declining firms (27 per cent overall) which had also moved. Overall there was an association between relocation and age of firm: 40 per cent of relocating firms in London had been founded in the 1970s and 66 per cent in the case of the rural panel. Put another way, half of the firms founded in the 1970s, relocated in the 1980s. It is the combination of age and growth characteristics that explains why the strong growth firms (Group 2) have the highest propensity to relocate in both panels. It is this performance category which contains a subset of relatively young firms whose growth over the decade meant that they outgrew their premises; relocation was an integral part of their development process.

When managers were asked why the firm had relocated, the most common reasons given were related to site characteristics and to property in particular. 'Space constraints' was the most common reason given for relocating by firms in both panels: 41 per cent of movers in London and 62 per cent in the rural panel and 'poor condition of building' was the second most commonly mentioned reason for moving, again in both cases (22 per cent of relocating London firms, 24 per cent in the rural panel). However, there were certain differences in the other reasons given which were mainly a result of a difference in the importance of the different types of property tenure between the two panels (65 per cent of rural firms owned the freehold of their main sites in 1979 compared with 45 per cent of London firms). In view of the higher proportion of rural firms owning freehold sites in 1979, and since in both panels firms in freehold property showed a lower propensity to relocate than firms in rented sites, this makes the rural firms appear relatively more active in terms of relocation. In both panels there was a tendency for the reasons given by managers for moving to vary between the performance groups. The overall picture is one where relocating firms which are expanding, move to acquire more space and better quality premises whereas declining firms move to cut costs, realise assets or because they are forced to.

Whilst in both panels, there was a tendency for the majority of relocating firms to move over a relatively short distance, in the case of the rural firms this was even more pronounced than in London. In London 48 per cent of relocating firms moved to another part of the same borough and a further 26 per cent to elsewhere in London. In the rural panel on the other hand, 90 per cent of relocations were 'local' in that they were either to another part of the same village or to a neighbouring village; only three relocating rural firms moved outside their 'local' area and the longest distance was approximately 30 miles.

These results provide supporting evidence for the importance of floorspace constraints and premises related factors as a stimulus to relocation in both urban and rural areas. One implication for policy is to emphasise that if the growth potential of SMEs is to be realised, it is important that an adequate supply of suitable premises for expanding firms to move into is available in all types of location. Rural firms appear to be particularly tied to their local areas. This presents a particular challenge for policy makers in these remote rural areas since there may be planning implications involved in responding to the need for larger local premises for growing firms in some localities. The contribution of local authority planning policies to the shortage of larger industrial premises in rural settlements was referred to in another recent study which also found a higher level of dissatisfaction with the small size of their premises among remote rural firms compared with their urban based counterparts (Keeble *et al.*, 1992).

As in the case of the other adjustment dimensions therefore, there are both similarities and differences in the nature and extent of locational adjustments made by these urban and rural firms over the decade. In both panels, relocation was particularly associated with young growing firms and the fact that half of the firms founded in the 1970s relocated in the 1980s has clear implications for policy in terms of the provision of an adequate supply of larger industrial premises in all areas. The main difference between the panels lies in the lower level of site closures by remote rural firms although as argued above, this would appear to be mainly as a result of a difference in the characteristics of the firms at the start of the period than because of a difference in either business strategy or the environment they faced.

Ownership change and organisational adjustments

Five types of *ownership change* were included in the summary index: acquisition of the firm, a management buyout, a change in the principal shareholders (which normally involved either a change in the balance between existing shareholders, family succession or new directors being brought into the business), disposal of part of the business and the acquisition of another firm. Although there was a higher average number of ownership adjustments per firm in London than in the rural areas, this was mainly because of a minority of

London firms which were affected by more than one change in ownership over the period.

In general it is the similarity in the nature and extent of the ownership changes affecting the two panels which is more striking than any differences. A similar proportion of firms in the two panels were affected by either acquisition or management buy-out (16 per cent rural; 13 per cent London) and a change in the principal shareholders (21 per cent of firms in both panels). There was also a similar tendency in both cases for the majority of cases of acquisitions and buy-outs to be concentrated in the lower performance groups (specifically Groups 3–5). Changes in principal shareholders on the other hand, affected firms in all performance groups. One difference between the two panels is in the declining category (Group 5) where acquisition or management buy-out was commonly followed by a period of active adjustment. The higher proportion of declining firms in London which were either acquired or subject to management buy-out (24 per cent compared with 16 per cent in the rural panel), helps to explain the larger number of active adjusting declining firms in London compared with the rural panel. For example, six of the eight declining firms (Group 5) in London which made eight or more of the 26 adjustments in total were firms where there had been a change of ownership.

Sale of part of the business was a form of ownership adjustment which only affected a small minority of firms in either panel (7 per cent London; 3 per cent rural). London firms were the more active acquirers, however: 24 London firms (19 per cent) made 28 acquisitions over the period compared with eight rural firms (10 per cent) which made a total of nine acquisitions. The higher level of acquisition activity by London firms is probably partly a result of the fact that they tend to be larger firms and partly that in London there are simply more opportunities for acquiring firms locally. Although the extent of acquisition activity was lower among the rural firms it showed a similar relationship to performance; in both panels it was the high growth and strong growth firms which accounted for approximately half the firms making at least one acquisition over the period. The acquisition experience of the high growth firms in London suggests that whilst a few were able to grow successfully using external means, others found that the success of such a strategy is by no means guaranteed.

The summary index also includes five indicators of internal *organisational adjustment*: a change to professional management; a change in the number of managers; evidence that more time had been created for carrying out management functions within the firm; a change in the division of management responsibility; and a change in leadership. Overall, as Table 4.12 shows, rural firms were slightly less active than urban firms in making one or more of these organisational adjustments although in general it is the similarities rather than the differences between the panels which are the most striking. Comparing urban and rural firms on each of the five organisational adjustment variables, however, reveals no statistically significant differences (see Appendix 2).

Surprisingly perhaps, there was little difference between the panels in the propensity of firms to have introduced professional managers over the decade (by professional managers we mean managers who have either some management qualification and/or management experience in another company). In fact at the time of the interview, a similar proportion of firms in the two panels were led by managers with a craft background: 48 per cent of rural firms compared with 43 per cent in London although rural firms had fewer managers from a financial or management background than their urban counterparts (20 per cent compared with 33 per cent in London).

Our analysis of London firms has shown that the organisational adjustment variable which most clearly differentiated the best from the worst performing firms was 'creating more time to manage': in London this was identified in just 5 per cent of stable and declining firms compared with 42 per cent of those in the high growth group. As other writers have emphasised, creating more time to cope with change is one of the key internal factors influencing the process of change in small firms (Gibb and Dyson, 1982). An important threshold for owners and managers of small manufacturing companies to make is the transition from being in effect a factory manager to managing the assets of the company so as to maximise the profit potential of the business. To pass over this barrier requires time to be created for management tasks beyond those associated with day-to-day operational matters. On this criterion, whilst the difference is not statistically significant, our remote rural firms compare favourably with those in London (28 per cent compared with 18 per cent in London) and the contrast between the extremes of the performance range is similar to that in London. However, since the proportion of firms in both panels which had made this type of adjustment was relatively low, in only a minority of firms could it be demonstrated that the development of the firm over a ten-year period had involved some evolution of the role of the leader which resulted in more time being devoted to the higher level management tasks.

Organisational development often lags behind other aspects of the firm's development although remote rural firms do not appear to be any worse than their London counterparts in this respect.

5 CONCLUSIONS

This comparison of the development of mature SMEs in two very different geographical environments shows both similarities and differences in the types of strategies and business behaviour associated with survival and growth over a ten-year period. In some instances the issues raised by this chapter are applicable to the development of mature manufacturing SMEs in general, whilst others refer to the problems and opportunities facing firms in specific types of environment. Of particular interest may be those conclusions which can be drawn about the potential for developing small firms in remote rural areas, the types of problems they face and the type of adjustment strategies which appear to be the most successful. In this final section, we will summarise the main conclusions paying particular attention to any implications for policy:

(1) In terms of assessing the capacity for the growth of SMEs in remote rural areas, our analysis has shown that the growth performance of the remote rural firms is broadly similar to that of the London firms over the decade: 39 per cent of the rural firms at least doubled their sales turnover in real terms compared with 35 per cent of those in London. The proportion of rural and London firms in which sales remained stable or declined over the period is also similar. This similarity in the actual performance of firms in the contrasting operating environments would seem to indicate that there are opportunities for growth in remote rural as well as urban locations. The one noticeable difference was that fewer of the growing rural firms managed to reach the minimum size required (i.e. £0.5 m turnover) in order to qualify for high growth status. Arguably there is a case for making these particular firms the target of business support policies in rural areas in order to enable them to achieve the size required to become more resilient to external shocks of various kinds.

(2) It did appear that the remote rural firms were particularly active in terms of employment generation during the 1980s, achieving a net employment increase of 51 per cent compared with only 7 per cent in the case of the London firms. Contrary to our initial expectations, the difference was not simply attributable to the higher proportion of young firms in the rural panel. It was also due to the

ability of some of the larger, more well established rural firms to expand their employment, and the lower proportion of rural firms which shed jobs over the decade compared with their London counterparts. It did appear that the remote rural firms were more labour intensive than those in London however, which was associated with lower productivity levels, less externalisation of production and possibly with cheaper labour. Interestingly, the tendency for rural SMEs to out-perform their urban counterparts in terms of employment generation is confirmed by two other recent studies which covered service sector as well as manufacturing firms (Keeble *et al.*, 1992; SBRC University of Cambridge, 1992).

It is worth emphasising that in both the rural and London panels, the bulk (i.e. more than 75 per cent) of the additional jobs were created by the firms which at least doubled their sales turnover over the decade. Employment generation by SMEs over a long period of time is clearly dependent upon their growth in output which suggests that the best way of increasing employment generation in SMEs in the longer term is to focus on policies aimed at mobilising their growth potential.

(3) Turning to the types of business behaviour and strategies associated with survival and growth over the decade, there are important similarities demonstrated by firms in the two panels which should be highlighted. In both panels, there was a clear relationship between the frequency of adjustments made and growth performance, with the high growth firms making the most adjustments and the declining firms the least. Whilst only a minority of firms had survived with minimal adjustment over the decade, it was the best performing firms which had been the most active adjusters of all, co-ordinating adjustments along a number of dimensions.

At the same time certain types of adjustment appeared to be particularly associated with different levels of performance. For example, the benefits of active adjustment in terms of identifying and developing new markets and active management of the product portfolio, are reflected by the fact that in both panels more than 80 per cent of high growth and strong growth firms were able to demonstrate they had been active in these respects. Referring to product and market adjustment more generally, very few firms in either panel had survived the decade without making some form of adjustment on this dimension and some of the best performing firms had been very active indeed. Better performing firms in both panels could usually point to more steps which had been taken to improve their competitiveness than the stable and declining firms. There were also qualitative differences in the type of steps taken by firms at different levels of performance: declining firms for example not only took fewer steps on average than growing firms, they also tended to focus on reducing costs (reflecting their emphasis on price rather than product/service differentiation in their competitive tactics), compared with the greater emphasis on customer focused tactics by the growing firms.

Active production management on the other hand, was generally less apparent and the majority of firms in both panels ended the decade with basically the same production methods as they started it with. The nature and extent of these changes in production varied between sectors however, since sectoral conditions affected the extent to which firms needed to invest to remain competitive. In both panels, improvements in productivity over the period were more commonly found in the growth companies but there did not appear to be any consistent relationship between a change in labour flexibility over the decade and a firm's performance. In terms of locational adjustment, in both panels it was the younger, better performing companies which showed the highest propensity to have relocated over the period which emphasises the need to maintain an adequate supply of premises of all sizes for expanding companies in both types of location. Organisational adjustment was not a major feature of the development of firms in either panel over the decade.

(4) Whilst there is an underlying similarity in both the nature and extent of adjustment with performance in the London and remote rural firms, there are also a number of differences in the types of adjustment made by firms in the two types of location.

For remote rural firms, the limited size of their local markets and the distance which typically separates them from major centres of population and economic activity means that they have to place a particularly high priority on market development. Thus the rural firms tended to be more active in making product and market adjustments than the London firms, particularly in terms of identifying and developing new market opportunities. This often involved extending the geographical market area for their products beyond the confines of the local or regional market. The growth of niche focused rural firms invariably necessitated extending the market geographically whereas this was not so important for similar London firms because of the large and diverse nature of the London market, especially in some of the craft sectors. From a policy perspective, it is important to recognise that the need to extend their markets geographically can create additional demands on rural businesses in terms of finance and management control which business support agencies need to help firms plan for. Rural firms also face fewer opportunities compared with London firms as a result of not being part of a large industrial complex. There are fewer opportunities for picking up subcontract work locally as well as for the subcontracting out of production.

At the same time, rural firms do have certain advantages compared with their London counterparts. Although London firms have the advantage of a large and diverse market on their doorstep, they also typically face more hostile market conditions than the remote rural firms. In addition, in the craft sectors at least, London based firms also appear to have faced more serious labour constraints. Firms in both types of location face the problem of skills shortages but for London firms the highly competitive local labour markets means that small firms are often uncompetitive in terms of the pay and working conditions which they offer.

Thus whilst there are underlying similarities in the types of strategy which appear successful in the different environments, managers need to take steps to minimise the constraints and maximise the opportunities presented by the particular external conditions which they face. For small firms in particular, this can mean an ability to adapt to local environmental conditions which may have implications not just for the way in which products are produced or sold but also for the precise nature of the firms' activities. In this way the relationship between the internal characteristics of the business and external conditions they face can be considered a dynamic one and this is reflected in some of the specific differences in the types of adjustment made by rural firms compared with their London counterparts.

(5) In terms of production, whilst there was little difference between the rural and London firms overall in terms of the extent of production process adjustments made during the 1980s, the rural firms did have higher investment levels towards the end of the period. The reasons for this include the fact that they appeared to be more committed to growth in manufacturing than some of the London firms (particularly some of the high growth firms) which were either diversifying into non-manufacturing activities or externalising production to other firms. In addition, some of the rural firms (especially in the printing sector) were investing in the new technologies which their London counterparts had already invested in. Another difference between the panels overall was that the rural firms tended to be less involved in subcontracting out production than

the London firms, most notably where subcontracting was being used as part of a cost reduction strategy. As a result rural firms needed to invest more in in-house production equipment, and this often required more factory space and also more labour.

(6) Whilst there was little difference in the frequency with which rural and London firms made locational adjustments over the decade, the growth of the rural firms was more likely to involve relocation than in the case of the London firms. To some extent, this is a reflection of the smaller size of the rural firms since they were more likely to outgrow their premises than the larger London firms. Most relocations within the rural areas were local and there was a stronger preference for obtaining freehold property than was the case in London. These findings demonstrate that a key element of any policy for rural industrial development must be the provision of a variety of industrial space in terms of size and tenure in order to meet the needs of firms at different stages of their development.

Finally, while local environments can present particular opportunities and constraints for the development of small and medium-sized companies, it is clear that the underlying principles influencing growth and survival are not locationally specific. Allowing for the fact that the rural panel tended to be biased more towards the craft sectors and towards younger firms than the London panel, there was surprising similarity in the extent and nature of the adjustments made over the decade which we have detailed above. Thus whilst the comparison has revealed some interesting differences in the problems, opportunities and types of business behaviour associated with firms in different types of location, these must not be over-emphasised.

APPENDIX 1: VARIABLES INCLUDED IN THE SUMMARY ADJUSTMENT INDEX

Variable	Definition
Product and market adjustment	
1. New market opportunities	Managers could point to new markets they had identified and exploited over the decade.
2. Number of competitive steps	Managers could identify up to three steps introduced over the decade to make their products more competitive. Active adjustment is defined as three competitive steps.

3. Type of competitive steps	Active adjustment is defined as the introduction of steps which are customer/market focused.
4. Change in product range	Active adjustment is defined as a broadening of the product range, a different range of products or an active narrowing of the range to increase market focus.
5. Wider customer base	This refers to an increase in the total number of customers.
6. Innovative products	This refers to the possession of a product or service which is innovative in some way.

Production process adjustment

7. Change in production methods	Active adjustment is defined as a substantial move to a new technological base.
8. Introduction of new technology	Active adjustment is defined as investment in new technology over the decade.
9. Change in % subcontracting out	An increase/decrease in the % of production subcontracted out (excluding cases where the % has remained below 25% of turnover).

Labour process adjustment

10. Change in manual/non-manual ratio	A change of more than 25% in the ratio (excluding the smallest firms).
11. Numerical flexibility	A significant increase/decrease in either p/t, homeworkers and/or temporary labour.
12. Functional flexibility	A significant increase in functional flexibility.
13. Increased productivity	A more than 100% increase in the sales/employment ratio and managers able to point to productivity improvements.

Ownership change

14. Firm acquired	Acquisition of business by another firm in 1980s.
15. Management buy-out	Existing management purchase at least a majority shareholding in company.

16. Change in principal shareholders	This normally involved a change in the balance between existing shareholders, family succession or new directors being brought into the business (excluding management buy-outs).
17. Disposal of part of business	Sale of part of the business.
18. Acquired other firms	Firm acquired at least one other company over the decade.

Organisational adjustment

19. Change to professional management	Change to managers who have either some management qualification and/or management experience in another company.
20. Increased time to manage	Manager could show that more time had been created for management tasks other than day to day operational matters.
21. Change in the number of managers	Increase/decrease in the number of managers.
22. Change in division of management	Some adjustment to the organisation which changed the division of management responsibility.
23. Change in leadership	Change in the leader of the management team.

Locational adjustment

24. Relocation	Relocation of main site.
25. Opening additional sites	Opening an additional facility of some kind.
26. Closed sites	Closure of a site.

Note: Since firms scored 1 or 0 on each variable the maximum possible score was 26 for each company.

APPENDIX 2: STATISTICALLY SIGNIFICANT DIFFERENCES BETWEEN URBAN AND RURAL FIRMS

Criteria	Chi-square	Significant difference at 0.01 level	Significant difference at 0.05 level
1. New market opportunities	9.84	Yes	
2. Number of competitive steps	0.08		
3. Type of competitive steps	0.00		
4. Change in product range	1.15		
5. Wider customer base	8.18	Yes	
6. Innovative products	0.85		
7. Change in production methods	0.00		
8. Introduction of new technology	1.50		
9. Change in % subcontract	18.60	Yes	
10. Change in manual/ non-manual ratio	0.10		
11. Numerical flexibility	5.47		Yes
12. Functional flexibility	1.20		
13. Increased productivity	0.48		
14. Firm acquired	0.03		
15. Management buy-out	0.00		
16. Change in principal shareholders	0.00		
17. Disposal of part of business	1.30		
18. Acquired other firms	2.40		
19. Change in type of manager	0.13		
20. Time for management	1.94		
21. Increase in number of managers	0.05		
22. Change in division of management responsibility	1.69		
23. Change in leadership	0.03		
24. Relocation	0.08		
25. Additional sites	0.22		
26. Closed sites	10.50	Yes	

Notes: df = 1 in each case.

5 Spatial variations in the role of equity investment in the financing of SMEs

Colin Mason and Richard Harrison

INTRODUCTION

Traditionally, locational analysts have regarded financial capital as being, in Weberian terms, a ubiquitous factor. Small businesses were therefore assumed to have equal access to finance regardless of location. Estall (1972) was one of the first commentators to dissent from this view, arguing that 'capital is not equally available at all locations, given identical risks and opportunities' (Estall, 1972: 196–7). He went on to suggest that the constraints that operate to impede its availability must, by extension, act also as a constraint upon regional economic development.

Spatial variations exist in both the cost and availability of finance (Estall, 1972; Estall and Buchanan, 1980). Admittedly, there is little evidence on spatial variations in the cost of capital and the information that does exist is contradictory. Keeble (1976) cites a newspaper report that commercial interest rates on loan finance for industrial development were lower in the South East of England than in peripheral regions. This evidence is contradicted by McKillop and Hutchinson (1990: 28) who claim that 'there are no inter-regional differences in interest rates charged to businesses. This is clearly the case for large businesses, given the strength of competition for this segment of the corporate finance market. Where SMEs are concerned, there again appears to be no direct evidence of inter-regional differences in the charging structure.' This view, in turn, is challenged by a recent survey by the Institute of Directors which found that just over half of those small businesses surveyed were being charged 1 to 2 per cent above base rates on their overdraft, with 39 per cent paying 3 to 4 per cent above base rate. In the North, 79 per cent of businesses paid 1 to 2 per cent over base rate compared with only 44 per cent of businesses in the south (*Financial Times*, 10 August 1992,

p. 7). However, it seems likely that this finding will have been influenced by the fact that the survey was undertaken at a time when the South East was leading the rest of the country into recession.

Interest rates are only one aspect of the cost of finance. An equally important factor is the collateral required for a loan. Collateral requirements are, of course, especially important to small businesses. Hutchinson and McKillop (1992) note that the higher the collateral required, at a given interest rate, the higher the cost of finance, on a risk adjusted basis, to the firm. They go on to suggest that because small business loans are normally made at the discretion of the local bank manager there can be a considerable variation in the attitude and standards applied in assessing such loans. This allows for the possibility that there may be spatial variations in the collateral requirements that banks place on small businesses. However, more detailed research in Northern Ireland suggests that these variations may be highly localised rather than systematic or regional in nature (McKillop and Barton, 1992).

There are a variety of factors which contribute to spatial variations in the availability of capital. First, there may be an absence of suppliers in particular areas. This is most marked in the case of venture capital where funds are highly concentrated in large urban centres (Martin, 1989; Mason and Harrison, 1991; Florida and Kenney, 1988; Green, 1989; Florida and Smith, 1990; McNaughton and Green, 1988; Perry, 1988a). Secondly, the willingness of the financial community to invest in particular kinds of project may vary between locations. On this point, a study by Deutermann (1966) noted the contrast between the attitude of financiers in Boston and Philadelphia to the financing of science-based industry. Thirdly, there may be spatial variations in the capability of financial institutions to support industry by means of advice, expert assistance and networking.

Access to finance is particularly problematic for small firms. Large firms can tap into national or international sources. However, small businesses are generally limited to local financial institutions. Estall (1972) notes that small business owners are more likely to be successful in raising finance from their local bank to whom they are known and visible, whereas non-local banks are likely to regard a small business owner who is not known to them and located in a distant location as being too great a risk. This is confirmed by Buss and Popovitch (1988) who note that 90 per cent of loans for business start-up in rural North Dakota were obtained locally; 91 per cent of those receiving bank loans indicated that either they or their families were well known in the community and over half believed that the lender's familiarity with them was a factor in the loan approval. Thus, 'insofar as much small enterprise depends on local sources of funds, the differing capabilities and attitudes of financial institutions in different locations will act to support growth in one area and impede it in another' (Estall, 1972: 196).

The particular focus of this study is on the financing of small businesses in rural areas. Small firms in rural areas may be expected to be disadvantaged in terms of access to finance in a number of respects. First, rural areas suffer from a lack of depth of supply because there are few players on the supply side (Economic Council of Newfoundland and Labrador (ECNL), 1988). For example, because of the location of most venture capital funds in major financial centres, typically in core regions, allied to their preference for investing in businesses located within easy travelling distance, good quality projects in remoter rural areas have less chance of being funded. Indeed, Malecki (1991: 337) comments that 'rural areas tend to be at a severe disadvantage in terms of venture capital'. Similarly, in some rural areas there may be only a single branch of a bank. In such circumstances there is limited competition amongst institutions to finance bankable businesses and businesses that are dissatisfied with that bank's services have limited financing alternatives. More particularly, there is evidence to suggest that in a diversified banking regime, such as that in the United States, small banks are especially significant to smaller firms (Guenther, 1991): small banks generally do not make large loans; large firms prefer to conduct business with larger banks both because their credit needs may be large and because they value the opportunity for one-stop shopping for a range of financial services; smaller firms prefer to deal with a bank to which their needs are important in relative terms; small banks (particularly in non-metropolitan areas) are often the most convenient or only bank available; and small business owners are likely to prefer to deal with senior bank officials, which is more likely in a smaller bank. Given this, changes in the competitive structure and increases in the level of concentration in the banking system are likely to be prejudicial to the interests of small firms, and to those in non-metropolitan areas in particular.

Secondly, bank managers in smaller communities may have less discretion in making loans. The consequence of their more limited decision-making power is that loan requests are more frequently referred up the managerial hierarchy. However, Perry (1988b) reports no evidence of differences between urban and rural areas in the proportion of loans that are referred up the management hierarchy. It has also been argued that the banking sector in rural areas suffers from the frequent turnover of account managers. As a result, managers will rely on head office lending criteria whereas personal knowledge of the customer would allow for a more flexible lending policy which can be more closely attuned to the local economic needs and realities (Jackson and Peirce, 1990). Perry (1988b) also suggests that bank managers in rural areas have lower levels of expertise than their urban counterparts.

Thirdly, changes in the regulatory environment are likely to have a differential spatial impact. In one recent study of small banks in the United States (where small is defined as a bank with assets under $100 m), changes in regulatory attitudes, interpretations and practices may inhibit lending to small firms (Guenther, 1991). Although some changes, as in increased premia for deposit insurance, will have a particularly detrimental effect on small firms located in metropolitan areas, a key conclusion is that in future

> for non-metropolitan smaller banks where depositors are more likely to face limited competitive alternatives there is likely to be a net flow out of the local bank or banks into other communities . . . [and] . . . some anecdotal evidence of such shifts out of smaller banks already exists. Such flows will have some net negative impact on the availability of funds in non-metropolitan areas, including funds for small firm financing
>
> (Guenther, 1991: 29).

Fourthly, O'Farrell (1990) suggests on the basis of research in Nova Scotia, Canada that banks appear to be more reluctant to lend to small firms in rural areas because if the firm fails the bank considers that it will be more difficult to sell the assets.

Fifthly, the concentration of financial institutions in core regions typically results in an outflow of savings from rural and peripheral regions for investment elsewhere. For example, there is frequent comment in the local and regional development literature in Canada that most personal savings accounts and registered savings plans are deposited at local branches and sub-branches of national banks and finance companies; these provide a conduit through which such potential sources of local capital flows out of local communities and peripheral provinces to the country's major financial centres and from there it is invested primarily in central Canada and overseas (Newfoundland Royal Commission, 1986; ECNL, 1988; Wickham *et al.*, 1989). Inter-regional capital flows have also been highlighted in the UK in the case of the Business Expansion Scheme, a scheme which provided tax incentives to encourage personal investments in unquoted small firms. The result was a net flow of investment funds to the South East from all other regions of the country (Mason *et al.*, 1988; Mason and Harrison, 1989).

Finally, there are also inadequacies on the demand side. As Sweeney (1987: 174) notes, 'the entrepreneur is highly local, dependent on the opportunities and networks of the locality . . . His contacts are personal, face-to-face and by phone. He lives within a half hour contact potential.' Because of the concentration of the business services sector in large urban areas (Leyshon and Thrift, 1989) small firm owner-managers in rural areas are likely to have poorer quality information about financing alternatives, may lack access to the specific skills that are required to prepare financial proposals, and may lack knowledge about the role of equity capital in business growth and, specifically, how venture capital funds operate. As a consequence, they may exhibit a greater unwillingness to share control with outside investors (Jackson and Peirce, 1990). These issues have not been addressed in the entrepreneurial networks literature. However, some evidence which supports this scenario is provided by a recently published wide-ranging study of small businesses in rural areas of England, jointly sponsored by the Department of the Environment (DoE) and the Rural Development Commission (RDC), which found that firms in remoter rural areas had a lower frequency of use of sources of external advice on financial planning and taxation than those in accessible rural areas and urban areas (Keeble *et al.*, 1992).

However, reaching any definitive conclusion on whether small firms in rural areas are disadvantaged in terms of access to finance is limited both by the paucity of studies which have examined the financing of small firms in rural areas and also by the fact that these studies contradict one another on a number of key points. In one of the few comprehensive studies of this issue, Shaffer and Pulver (1985) identify a number of contrasts between urban and rural areas in Wisconsin. First, a higher proportion of small firms in urban areas utilised 'borrowed' (or quasi-) equity (i.e. personal loans from friends, relatives, insurance policies, banks). Secondly, there were variations in the type of loan. Thirdly, there was little difference in the proportion of firms which experienced credit denial, a finding that is confirmed by Perry (1988b) in New Zealand. However, Shaffer and Pulver (1985) note that the reasons for credit denial differ between urban and rural areas. A higher proportion of rural firms were denied credit because of a lack of equity while a higher proportion of rural firms were denied credit because of a lack of collateral. Fourthly, Shaffer and Pulver (1985) concluded that a higher proportion of rural firms suffered from 'capital stress'. This conclusion is contradicted by Buss *et al.* (1991) who found little evidence of capital stress in their study of rural small firms in four US states. Most businesses did not encounter any reluctance by lenders in acquiring start-up finance and most obtained financing locally. Buss and Popovitch (1988) suggest that 'close links between local residents seeking to start a business and local lenders may be an important aspect of the lending environment in rural areas' (p. 25). Perry (1988b) also found no clear evidence that small firms in a rural region of New Zealand are disadvantaged in the search for debt finance: the typical firm had few problems, although this reflects their modest financial needs. However, the smaller number of growth-orientated firms – which tend to require more outside fundings more regularly – did experience a higher rate of rejection.

British evidence on this issue is even more limited but no less contradictory. The DoE/RDC-sponsored study of the performance of rural enterprise devoted just two paragraphs to the examination of financing issues, concluding that 'no significant differences actually exist in frequency or valuation of different sources between the . . . [matched] . . . samples of urban and rural firms' (Keeble *et al.*, 1992, p. 34). However, a large-scale national survey of small firms in Britian noted that conurbation-based firms recorded a lower level of constraints with respect to the availability of finance than rural firms (University of Cambridge, 1992).

This literature on the financing of small businesses in rural areas has a number of limitations in addition to its sparsity and the inconsistent nature of the findings. First, these studies have been based on surveys of surviving firms so are unable to identify any effect of constraints in the availability of finance upon discouraged entrepreneurship and business failure (Shaffer and Pulver, 1985). The one exception is the study by Buss and Popovitch (1988) which also examined the sources of finance used by discontinued businesses. They found that such businesses had been successful in obtaining loan finance. A second limitation is that most of the studies refer to North America. In view of the very different characteristics of rural areas to those in the UK, notably in terms of their remoteness to major urban areas, such studies are unlikely to provide a good guide to the UK situation. Thirdly, the focus of these studies has been on the availability and use of *loan* finance by firms in rural areas. In contrast, there is little equivalent information on external equity finance. However, a recent paper by Hustedde and Pulver (1992) concludes that 'proximity to urban settings is critical in the acquisition of equity capital' (p. 368): in their study of the search for equity capital by firms in Minnesota and Wisconsin businesses in rural areas were less successful in acquiring venture capital.

More generally, there are substantial reasons to believe that small firms face greater problems with agency costs and asymmetric information between suppliers of external capital and the owner-manager (Pettit and Singer, 1985), not least because small firms have more flexibility in altering their financial and operating structures, and outside suppliers of capital have greater difficulty in monitoring their behaviour. Consequently, there is considerable evidence that such firms will finance their needs in a hierarchical fashion, using internal equity first (owners' capital and retained earnings), followed by debt and finally external capital (Walker, 1989; Marsh, 1982). This 'pecking order' (Myers, 1984; Scherr *et al.*, 1990) in financing preferences reflects the effects of asymmetric information and agency problems on the returns required by providers of various sources of funds (Myers and Majluf, 1984) and hence on the costs of that finance to the firm. Given the greater concentration of the supply of equity finance, and the predominant metropolitan concentration of the supply of equity finance (with the possible partial exception of informal venture capital), one consequence of the pecking order hypothesis is that any difficulties experienced by rural small firms in obtaining access to external debt finance will be intensified in terms of access to equity finance.

It is therefore clear from this review that the financing of rural enterprises remains an under-researched issue and there is little consensus on whether SMEs in rural areas encounter greater difficulties in obtaining finance. Further research is therefore clearly warranted. This study examines attitudes to, and use of, external sources of *equity* finance, including venture capital, by SMEs in rural areas of England. This restricted focus enables the study to make a number of distinctive contributions to the literature on the financing of rural enterprises and on the geography of venture capital. First, as noted above, previous studies have generally ignored equity financing. Secondly, in contrast to most of the literature in the UK on the geography of venture capital which has adopted a supply-side perspective, the focus in this chapter is on the demand side. Firm based data is used to examine the use of, and attitudes towards, venture capital in different spatial environments. Thirdly, the spatial focus of this paper provides a refinement of the coarse level of spatial aggregation (typically standard region) adopted by existing geographical research on the venture capital industry, particularly in the UK, which has been necessitated by their use of highly aggregate data (Martin, 1989; Mason and Harrison, 1991). Fourthly, all sources of venture capital are examined, including both formal and informal sources and also investments by non-financial corporations (i.e. corporate venturing). This allows the relative significance of various providers of venture capital to be assessed and a preliminary examination of the extent to which the use of informal and corporate sources of venture capital are characterised by spatial variations. In the case of informal venture capital the existing literature (e.g. Freear and Wetzel, 1992; Gaston, 1989; Mason *et al.*, 1991) has either adopted a non-spatial focus or else has examined spatial issues in a very superficial fashion.

DEFINITIONS AND SURVEY METHODOLOGY

Spatial definitions

Although rural areas are recognised intuitively as being different from urban areas, the actual definition of a rural area remains an elusive concept. Administrative units are generally of little help. The local authority areas that were created following local government re-organisation in 1974 deliberately combined towns with their rural hinterlands, hence their boundaries bear little relationship to urban and rural areas (Phillips and Williams, 1984). This difficulty in defining rural areas – recognised by virtually all authors on the subject (Phillips and Williams, 1984) – arises from the fact that while there is no shortage of indicators to use in order to characterise rurality (e.g. land use, population density, distance from towns, degree of reliance on agriculture) there is often little correspondence between these different variables in terms of the areas which are identified. This, in turn, suggests that a composite definition of rural areas would be more appropriate. However, in studies which use sophisticated multivariate statistical techniques, such as those which subject Population Census data to some form of classification procedure such as cluster analysis or principal components analysis, rural areas do not emerge as a distinctive locality type. For example, in the Office of Population, Censuses and Surveys (OPCS) framework used by Champion and Townsend (1990) *remoter, mainly rural* areas emerged as one of four distinctive types of locality by virtue of their traditional rural productive activities, low population density and absence of larger urban centres. These areas are concentrated in Scotland, the northern Pennines, mid-Wales, the South West peninsula and much of the east coast of England. However, the more accessible rural areas and small towns do not emerge as a distinctive locality type; they are grouped in a large and varied category which is described as *prosperous sub-regions* on account of their population and employment growth and above-average representation of more wealthy households. Even when this grouping is subdivided into four sub-groups a distinctive 'rural' category still fails to emerge.

This paradox arises from the fact that 'urban' and 'rural' are not dichotomous variables. Rather, there is a transition from urban to rural (Cloke, 1977). This is illustrated by Bryant *et al.* (1982) who offer a schematic model comprising three types of rural area. In the *urban–rural fringe* rural land uses dominate the landscape but the infiltration of urban-orientated elements is clear. The *urban shadow* is an area where physical evidence of urban influences on the landscape is minimal, but where the urban presence is felt, for example, in terms of a scattering of residential housing estates and commuting patterns. This merges into the *rural hinterland* but even in this area there may be urban influences, for example, in the form of weekend cottages. This urban-rural continuum is illustrated empirically for England and Wales by Cloke (1977) and Cloke and Edwards (1986). They developed an index of rurality using multivariate statistical techniques which separates rural areas into four categories ranging from extreme rural, through intermediate rural and intermediate non-rural, to non-rural (urban).

It is important to note that rurality is not a static phenomenon. Areas change over time in their *level* of rurality. Thus, over time increasing urban influence will lessen the rurality of some areas, although change may also occur in the opposite direction. For example, Cloke and Edwards (1986) note that the South West extended its extreme rural area between 1971 and 1981. In addition, there are changes over time in *nature* of rurality. This necessitates changes in how rurality is measured in order to avoid anacronistic interpretations of what constitutes a rural area (Cloke and Edwards, 1986).

The definitional issues are side-stepped in this study by adopting the Rural Development Commission's (RDC) Rural Development Areas (RDA) as the definition of 'rural'. RDAs comprise 27 areas designated by the RDC since 1984 for special assistance towards job creation and socio-economic development on account of their high

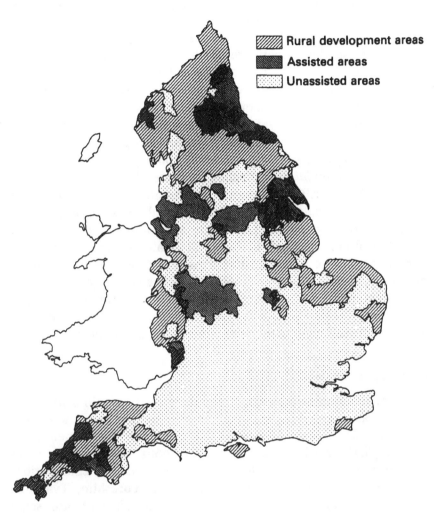

Figure 5.1 Location of study areas

levels of unemployment and economic decline. The RDC devotes the
greater part of its resources to these areas. RDAs are confined to
England. Rural areas in Scotland and Wales are the responsibility of
Highland Enterprise (formerly the Highlands and Islands Development Board) and the Development Board for Rural Wales respectively.

RDAs are mainly concentrated in the South West peninsula,
including most of Devon and Cornwall, along the Welsh border, in
the Pennine region of northern England and in the lowland areas
surrounding The Wash (Figure 5.1). As such, they closely correspond

to the *extreme rural areas* category identified by Cloke and Edwards (1986) and the areas identified by Champion and Townsend (1990) as comprising the *remoter rural districts*. Shaw (1979) suggests that the inhabitants of remoter rural areas suffer from two types of social problem. First, they experience *opportunity deprivation*. This takes various forms including a lack of jobs and a limited choice of jobs – especially well paying jobs – which arises from the narrow sectoral and occupational employment structure of such areas, and the decline of public and private services and housing, the latter arising from the sale of council houses, planning restrictions, in-migration and second home ownership. Secondly, poor public transport provision results in *mobility deprivation* for those who do not have access to a car. However, Champion and Townsend (1990) note that after decades of de-population many remoter rural areas are now characterised by recent population growth as a result of the reversal of net migration flows, although there is still localised de-population. In-migration to these types of rural areas is of three types: retirement migration; in-migration by economically active groups (including pre-retirement migration), some of which is related to new business formation (Keeble and Gould, 1985; Westhead, 1989; Keeble *et al.*, 1992); and, least significant of all, long-range commuting.

Sampling methodology

In order to examine whether there are spatial variations in equity financing amongst SMEs we have selected samples from three types of area: RDAs, assisted areas of England and unassisted areas (Figure 5.1). Assisted areas include both development areas and intermediate areas. These areas comprise the conurbations of Manchester, Liverpool, West and South Yorkshire, Tyneside, Cleveland, Humberside and the West Midlands and also some smaller industrial centres such as West Cumbria and Corby. Firms in the assisted areas are eligible to apply for a range of financial assistance to offset the costs of new investment projects. In addition, firms in assisted areas can benefit from infrastructure projects such as advanced factory development. The unassisted areas comprise virtually all of the area to the south of a line from Norwich to Exeter plus most of the East Midlands and Staffordshire as well as parts of North West England and West and North Yorkshire. There is an overlap between RDAs and assisted areas (see Figure 5.1). Firms in the sample which are located in these areas have been allocated to the 'rural' category.

Sample frame

In view of this study's focus on the use of external *equity* finance by SMEs it was clearly inappropriate to take a sample that was representative of the stock of small businesses in these study areas. Such a sample would be heavily weighted towards very small businesses, many of them sole traders and partnerships, the vast majority of whom would have been financed through a combination of internal sources and bank loans and overdrafts (Turok and Richardson, 1991). Such a sample would also be biased towards new and recent start-ups whereas it was thought more appropriate to select established firms that had completed a number of financing rounds in order to examine the use of external equity finance at various stages of firm development. These considerations dictated the use of a sampling frame which contained a listing of larger and more established SMEs. A further necessary attribute of the sampling frame was that it had a national coverage so that firms could be selected from each of the

Table 5.1 Survey response rates

	Assisted areas	Rural development areas	Unassisted areas	Total
Total number of questionnaires distributed	750	236	500	1486
Total number of usable returns	77	32	40	149
Crude* response rate (%)	10.3	13.6	8.0	10.0

Note: * This does not take account of unusable responses returned and questionnaires sent to firms no longer at the address on the mailing list and returned by the Post Office.

The distribution of respondents is as follows:

Firms in RDAs: North (Cumbria, North Yorkshire, West Yorkshire, Derbyshire, Lancashire, Northumberland) – 12 firms (37.5%); West Midlands (Shropshire, Hereford & Worcestershire) – 2 firms (6.2%); East Anglia (Norfolk, Suffolk) – 5 firms (15.6%); South West (Somerset, Devon, Cornwall) – 12 firms (37.5%); South East (East Sussex) – 1 firm (3.2%).

Firms in assisted areas: North East – 18 firms (23.4%); North West – 16 firms (20.8%); Yorkshire-Humberside – 11 firms (14.3%); West Midlands – 30 firms (39.0%); South West – 1 firm (1.3%); no location given – 1 firm (1.3%).

Firms in unassisted areas: Greater London and South East – 22 firms (55%); East Anglia – 3 firms (7.5%); South West – 4 firms (10.0%); East Midlands – 2 firms (5.2%); West Midlands – 4 firms (10.0%); North/North West/Yorkshire-Humberside – 5 firms (12.5%).

three types of area. The sampling frame that was used in this study which met these conditions was a mailing list provided by a direct marketing firm.

The data was collected by means of a postal questionnaire. This questionnaire sought information on the background characteristics of the firms (e.g. location, age, employment size, annual turnover), shareholders, source of external equity finance raised at various financial rounds and the amounts raised, and the sources of finance that the firm anticipated using to finance future growth. Firms which had raised venture capital from either formal or informal sources were asked series of supplementary questions.

Unfortunately, but inevitably in view of the geography of economic activity, the sampling frame contained relatively few firms that were located in RDAs. As a result, the RDA sample size was lower than intended. Questionnaires were sent to over 200 firms in the RDAs (representing all of the firms on the mailing list in RDAs) as well as to random samples of 750 firms in the assisted areas and 500 firms in the unassisted areas. Thus, just under 1500 questionnaires were dispatched in total. Usable responses were received from 149 firms, representing a *crude* response rate of 10.0 per cent, ranging from 8.0 per cent in unassisted areas to 13.6 per cent in rural areas (Table 5.1). A further 67 responses were received from firms that were not in scope (e.g. not independent), were in receivership/ liquidation, refused to complete the questionnaire or were returned 'gone away' by the Post Office. Although somewhat lower than the norm for postal surveys this response rate is nevertheless higher than that achieved in the postal survey undertaken for the DoE/RDC-sponsored study of rural enterprise (Keeble *et al.*, 1992).

Table 5.2 Age of firms

Date of formation	Assisted areas No.	%	Rural development areas No.	%	Unassisted areas No.	%	Total No.	%
pre-1918	20	26.0	3	9.7	6	15.4	29	19.7
1918–45	9	11.7	6	19.4	9	23.4	24	16.3
1946–59	12	15.6	1	3.2	7	17.9	20	13.6
1960–79	32	41.6	15	48.4	12	30.8	59	40.1
1980–91	4	5.2	6	19.4	5	12.8	15	10.2
No information	–		(1)		(1)		(2)	
Total	77		31		39		147	

FIRM CHARACTERISTICS

As the preceding section has made clear, our sample of SMEs is not representative of the stock of businesses in the UK. Rather, our survey methodology has sought to target larger and longer-established enterprises. The characteristics of the enterprises which responded to our survey reflects this. In comparison with the DoE/RDC survey of rural enterprises (Keeble *et al.*, 1992) which provides a useful benchmark, the respondents to this survey are longer established and larger.

Age

The vast majority of firms in the sample were established prior to 1980 and over one-third were started before 1945 (Table 5.2). However, there are contrasts in the age distribution of firms in each of the three areas. In the RDAs over two thirds of firms in the sample have been established since 1960 compared with fewer than half in the other areas. Moreover, nearly one in five of the firms in the RDA sample have started since 1980, compared with 13 per cent in unassisted areas and only 5 per cent in the assisted areas. This contrast, which is also found in the Cambridge study of small enterprises in the UK (University of Cambridge, 1992), is a reflection of the uneven geography of new firm formation rates in the UK

Table 5.3 Industrial structure of firms

Sector	Assisted areas No.	%	Rural development areas No.	%	Unassisted areas No.	%	Total No.	%
Primary sectors*	0	–	0	–	0	–	0	–
Manufacturing	39	51.3	18	56.3	14	35.0	71	48.0
Building/ construction	13	17.1	0	–	4	10.0	17	11.5
Retail/wholesale distribution	19	25.0	7	21.9	13	32.5	39	26.4
Transport	2	2.6	1	3.1	1	2.5	4	2.7
Producer services	3	3.9	2	6.2	3	7.5	8	5.4
Consumer services	0	–	0	–	0	–	0	–
Other services	0	–	4	12.5	5	12.5	9	6.1
No information	(1)		(–)		(–)		(1)	
Total	76		32		40		148	

Note: * Primary sectors comprise agriculture, forestry, fishing and mining during the 1980s (Keeble, 1990; Mason, 1992). Specifically, the greater youthfulness of the respondents in the RDAs is what would be anticipated given the much higher rate of new firm formation, especially in the manufacturing sector, in remoter rural areas during the 1980s (Keeble, 1990).

Industry sector

The sample is weighted towards the manufacturing sector which accounts for almost half of all the firms which responded to the survey (Table 5.3). However, within this sector there is an almost complete absence of high technology manufacturers. The retail and wholesale distribution sector is also well represented (26 per cent) but there are relatively few firms in other parts of the service sector. Comparing the industrial distribution of firms across the three areas indicates that manufacturing firms are of greatest significance in the RDA sample, where they account for 56 per cent of all respondents, and of least significance in the unassisted areas sample where they account for only 35 per cent of the total. These spatial variations in the industrial composition of firms are consistent with the much larger survey undertaken by the Small Business Research Centre at the University of Cambridge which also reported a bias towards manufacturing in rural areas (University of Cambridge, 1992). Within the sample, retail and wholesale distribution is of greatest significance in unassisted areas where it accounts for almost one third of firms and of least significance in rural areas. Firms in the construction industry (including plumbing and electrical contractors) are significant in the assisted areas where they comprise 17 per cent of the sample, but are absent from the rural sample. Conversely, the assisted areas sample has no firms in the other services sector.

The industrial composition of the sample is therefore clearly biased towards mature industrial sectors, especially in the assisted areas, and has a low representation of 'high tech' manufacturing firms and producer services firms – sectors where growth has been strongest and where demand for external capital would be anticipated to be high. The implication of this particular industrial composition is that it is likely to depress the revealed demand for external equity capital amongst the firms in the sample.

Employment and employment growth

The great majority of businesses in the sample are small. Over half have less than 50 employees, although only 13 per cent of firms have less than ten employees. At the other end of the size spectrum, 23 per cent of the respondents have over 100 employees (Table 5.4). Firms in the assisted areas are the largest in the sample, with over half employing 50 or more people, compared with just one third in both RDAs and the unassisted areas. The RDAs contain the smallest proportion of firms with 100 or more employees (16 per cent, compared with 22.5 per cent in the unassisted areas and 25 per cent in the assisted areas). Here again, this feature is confirmed by the much larger Cambridge survey (University of Cambridge, 1992).

Table 5.4 Total current employment of firms

Employment	Assisted areas No.	%	Rural development areas No.	%	Unassisted areas No.	%	Total No.	%
Less than 10	8	10.7	5	16.1	6	15.0	19	13.0
10–24	6	8.0	6	19.4	6	15.4	18	12.3
25–49	22	29.3	10	32.3	15	37.5	47	32.2
50–99	20	26.7	5	16.1	4	10.0	29	19.9
100+	19	25.3	5	16.1	9	22.5	33	22.6
No information	(2)		(1)		–		(3)	
Total	75		31		40		146	

As might be expected, there is a broad relationship between age of firm and employment size. In general, the longer established firms in the sample are likely to be larger: 27 per cent of the pre-1960 firms have more than 100 employees compared with only 16 per cent of post-1960 firms. A much smaller proportion pre-1960 firms have grown beyond 100 employees in RDAs than in either assisted areas or unassisted areas (10 per cent compared with 32 per cent and 27 per cent respectively). This may be a reflection of the constraints on business development and efficiency that firms in remote rural areas experience. In their DoE/RDC-sponsored study, Keeble *et al.* (1992) conclude that in comparison to firms in urban areas and accessible rural areas, firms in remote rural areas suffer from greater shortages of skilled and technical labour, management and professional staff, larger local premises and, for a small minority of firms, poorer telecommunications and goods transport facilities. However, these constraints do not appear to have affected the post-1960 cohort of start-ups in the RDA sample: the size distribution of post-1960 start-ups is similar in each of the three areas. This may reflect the fact that a high proportion of the new firm formation activity in remote rural areas during the past two decades has been undertaken by in-migrants who have moved to such areas specifically to establish their business (Keeble *et al.*, 1992). Because of their greater locational flexibility at start-up the firms that have been established by in-migrant entrepreneurs may be less affected by these locational constraints than the older cohorts.

In performance terms, the majority of firms in the sample have experienced recent growth in employment. The assisted areas contain the highest proportion of firms that increased their employment in the three years prior to the survey (59 per cent) while the unassisted areas contain the lowest proportion (47 per cent). Conversely, about one third of firms, ranging from 30 per cent in assisted areas to 39 per cent in rural areas, reduced their employment during the previous three years. The majority of firms in each of the areas anticipate future employment growth. The unassisted areas contained the smallest proportion of firms which anticipate adding to their employment in the next three years (67 per cent compared with 77 per cent in each of the other areas) while the RDAs contain the smallest proportion of firms anticipating a decline in employment (10 per cent compared with 14 per cent in the unassisted areas and 17 per cent in the assisted areas). Overall, therefore, the unassisted areas contain a smaller proportion of firms that have experienced recent employment growth and anticipate future job gains than the rural and assisted areas. To the extent that growth is a primary stimulus to the realisation of a demand for external finance, this implies that there will be a lower demand for, and use of, external finance than in RDAs and assisted areas.

Table 5.5 Turnover of firms

Turnover	Assisted areas No.	%	Rural development areas No.	%	Unassisted areas No.	%	Total No.	%
Under £0.25 m	5	6.5	5	15.6	4	10.0	14	9.4
£0.25 m–£0.99 m	13	16.9	7	21.9	9	22.5	29	19.5
£1 m–£2.49 m	19	24.7	8	25.0	10	25.0	37	24.8
£2.5 m–£4.99 m	14	18.2	5	15.6	9	22.5	28	18.8
£5.0 m–£9.99 m	14	18.2	4	12.5	4	10.0	22	14.8
£10 m and over	12	15.6	3	9.4	4	10.0	19	12.8
Total	77		32		40		149	

Turnover and turnover growth

In terms of their annual turnover, the firms in the sample are relatively small, a feature that is consistent with their employment characteristics. Over half have annual sales of less than £2.5 m while at the other extreme just 13 per cent have annual sales which exceed £10 m (Table 5.5). However, the proportion of firms in the assisted areas sample with a turnover in excess of £5 m is significantly greater than in either RDAs or unassisted areas (34 per cent, 22 per cent, 20 per cent respectively), a feature which is also consistent with larger employment size of firms in the assisted areas sample.

Table 5.6 Change in turnover during the previous three years

Change in turnover	Assisted areas No.	%	Rural development areas No.	%	Unassisted areas No.	%	Total No.	%
Increased by: 0– 9%	5	6.5	2	6.2	4	10.3	11	7.4
10–24%	22	28.8	9	28.1	12	30.8	43	29.1
25–49%	12	15.6	8	25.0	4	10.3	24	16.2
50–99%	3	3.9	3	9.4	3	7.7	9	6.1
100%+	4	5.2	3	9.4	2	5.1	9	6.1
Not specified	2	2.6	0	–	3	7.7	5	3.4
Static	14	18.2	5	15.6	5	12.8	24	16.2
Decreased by: 0–14%	6	7.8	0	–	2	5.1	8	5.4
15–30%	6	7.8	2	6.2	3	7.7	11	7.4
Not specified	3	3.9	0	–	1	2.6	4	2.7
Total	77		32		39		148	

Over two thirds of firms in the sample have experienced an increase in sales during the three years preceding the survey. In most cases this increase was less than 50 per cent. RDAs contained the highest proportion of firms reporting increased turnover (78 per cent) and the lowest proportion of firms reporting a declining turnover (6 per cent). The assisted areas had the lowest proportion of expanding firms (62 per cent) and the highest proportion of firms with a declining turnover (19 per cent) (Table 5.6). To the extent that growth rates are associated with size and age characteristics of firms, these spatial contrasts are likely to be associated, at least in part, with differences between the RDA and assisted areas samples in terms of the age and size distribution of firms. In particular, as Table 5.2 indicates, the sample of RDA firms is significantly younger than the assisted areas sample.

Firms in the sample are optimistic about future prospects for sales growth, with very few expecting sales to decrease or remain static. There are just two spatial contrasts of note. First, the proportion of firms in the RDA and unassisted areas samples which anticipate turnover growth in excess of 50 per cent during the next three years is twice that of the assisted areas (16 per cent, 15 per cent and 7 per cent respectively). Secondly, the assisted areas sample had the highest proportion of firms unwilling to estimate the likely percentage change in future turnover trends (14 per cent compared with 7.5 per cent of firms in unassisted areas and no firms in RDAs), perhaps indicating the greater uncertainty in economic conditions in these areas.

EXTERNAL EQUITY FINANCING

Use and sources of external equity finance

Despite the nature of the sample, which is weighted towards larger, longer established and incorporated businesses, only 10 firms – 7 per cent of firms in the study – have raised external equity finance since 1980 in a total of 13 financing rounds, little different from the proportion that is typically found in more representative surveys of small businesses (e.g. Small Business Research Trust, 1991). This study therefore provides yet further confirmation of the limited use of external equity finance even amongst larger and longer-established SMEs in Britain and clearly supports the widely held view that owner-managers of such companies regard equity finance as financing of the last resort (Walker, 1989; Scherr, Sugrue and Ward, 1990; Burns et al., 1992).

The amounts of finance raised per round ranges from £48,000 to £3.62 m, with a median of £240,000. Firms have raised external equity finance from a range of sources. However, the most significant sources are venture capital funds (five rounds) and private investors (three rounds). The majority of investments have involved management buy-outs and later stage investments (Table 5.7).

Any meaningful comparison of the characteristics of firms which have raised external equity finance with those businesses that have not is limited by the small number of firms in the former category. However, it can be noted firms which have raised external equity finance are predominantly post-1960 start-ups (eight of the ten firms) and in the manufacturing sector (seven firms). In terms of size, most have 25 or more employees (eight firms), although annual turnover

Table 5.7 Use of external equity finance

	Assisted areas No.	Rural development areas No.	Unassisted areas No.	Total No.
Firms raising external equity finance	5 (6.5%)	2 (6.2%)	3 (7.5%)	10 (6.7%)
Number of financing rounds	7	2	4	13
Source of finance		Number of rounds		
Private investors	1	–	2	3
Venture capital funds	4	1	–	5
BES funds and prospectus issues	–	–	1	1
Other financial institutions	1	–	1	2
Non-financial companies	1	–	–	1
Stock market	–	1	–	1
Stage of investment		Number of rounds		
Seed/start-up	1	–	–	1
Early stage	–	1	1	2
Later stage	2	–	1	3
Management buy-out	3	1	1	5
Management buy-in	–	–	–	–
Rescue	–	–	–	–
Other	1	–	–	1
No information	(–)	(–)	(1)	(1)

ranges from less than £250,000 to over £10 m. Not surprisingly, firms which have raised external equity finance since 1980 are growth-orientated, with eight firms reporting increased turnover during the three years prior to the survey (the two exceptions are management buy-outs) and all anticipate future turnover growth. The proportion of firms that have raised external equity finance is similar in each of the three areas: 7.5 per cent in unassisted areas, 6.5 per cent in assisted areas and 6.2 per cent in RDAs. Firms in the assisted areas account for four of the five rounds of venture capital investments, a feature which is linked to the fact that the assisted areas also contain three of the five management buy-outs in the sample.

Reasons for not raising external equity finance

There are a number of possible reasons why only a small minority of firms have sought outside sources of equity finance. First, some firms do not require to raise significant amounts of external finance because self-generated cash flow meets their continuing capital requirements. This may be associated with sector. Financing requirements vary by sector, and the lack of 'high tech' manufacturing firms in the sample may well have limited the number of ventures with significant capital requirements. Secondly, and more significantly, there is a wide range of evidence which suggests that most SMEs are reluctant to raise external equity finance because of the perception that the involvement of a third party in the financing of the business will result in a loss of control and unwelcome interference in management decisions. It has, in turn, been suggested that underlying such equity aversion is the failure of owner-managers to appreciate the different characteristics of loan and equity finance and their appropriate uses (NEDC, 1986). Such firms will gear their operations to minimise their need for external finance, limiting their external financing to bank overdrafts and, perhaps, loans. Thirdly, it is likely that some firms do not know how to go about seeking external funding and use their own resources by default. Finally, some firms will be unsuccessful in their search for external equity finance and so will be forced to rely upon internally generated sources.

Firms in this study have made limited use of external equity finance for two main reasons (Table 5.8). First, over two thirds of owner-managers stated that they had no need for equity finance because their financing requirements had been met through the use of retained earnings, often in conjunction with the use of bank loans or overdrafts or, less often, loans from finance houses. Indeed, a number of firms stated that they had substantial capital reserves. This supports more detailed evidence from a study by Leigh *et al.* (1991) that the majority of higher growth mature manufacturing companies have been able to expand through borrowing or self-financing, thereby balancing the need for funds to expand with the desire to retain ownership and control. An alternative possibility is that owner-managers have deliberately chosen to limit the growth of their businesses so that their ability to finance future developments without recourse to equity financing is not exceeded. It is not possible on the basis of the information available from the survey to assess adequately the importance of this factor. However, the fact that only a handful of owner-managers specifically stated that they had

Table 5.8 Reasons for not raising equity capital[1]

| | No. of firms | | | |
	Assisted areas	Rural development areas	Unassisted areas	Total
No need[2]	51 (76.1%)	15 (62.2%)	12 (48.0%)	78 (69.6%)
Examples of specific responses[3]				
other finance used: e.g. retained earnings; bank loan, overdraft	37	7	7	51
adequate capital reserves	3	2	1	6
finance not required	3	1	4	8
Did not seek[2]:	25 (37.3%)	5 (22.7%)	10 (40.0%)	40 (35.7%)
Examples of specific responses[3]				
loss of ownership/ control	14	2	5	21
high costs	2	1	1	4
other	3	2	4	9
Other reasons	3	1	1	5
Unsuccessful	0	1	2	3
Not applicable[4]	5	4	8	17
No response	5	7	8	20

Notes: 1. Firms could give multiple responses.
2. Firms giving no response (including 'not applicable' category) excluded from the calculation.
3. Not every firm provided a specific comment, hence numbers do not necessarily add up to total number giving 'no need'/'did not seek' response.
4. This includes firms which have raised external equity finance.

deliberately limited their growth in order to avoid the need for external finance suggests that it may be of only limited relevance.

Secondly, just over one third of firms stated that they did not seek equity finance, the overwhelming reason being their desire to retain ownership and control. In contrast, few firms cited the high costs of raising equity capital as a reason for not considering equity finance. However, this may simply reflect the fact that few firms had actually explored the market for equity finance. Only a handful of firms cited other reasons for not seeking external finance.

The remaining reasons why firms might not use equity finance proved to be insignificant. Only a small number of firms indicated by their responses that they did not understand equity financing. Even fewer – just three firms – stated that they had been unsuccessful in raising external equity finance.

These figures, and particularly the final statistic, therefore clearly suggest that, in the terminology used by the recent study by Aston Business School (1991) of financial constraints on small firm growth, *supply-side market failure* – where firms have been unsuccessful raising finance from potential suppliers – is a minor factor in accounting for the limited role of external equity capital in the financing of SMEs in the UK. Moreover, by no means every case where a firm is rejected by a supplier of finance signifies supply-side market failure. Supply-side market failure only includes situations where suppliers of finance have turned down proposals for reasons not connected with the viability of the project itself. Proposals that are rejected because of their poor quality, poor presentation or where funding quotas are exhausted are not signs of supply-side market failure. Of much greater significance is *demand-side market failure* where firms have not sought equity finance in appropriate circumstances either through lack of knowledge, poor or inexperienced management or simply inertia. This, in turn, raises the possibility of the existence of a *latent* demand for external equity finance amongst firms which currently rely upon internally generated finance and overdraft facilities and loans which could be articulated, for example, through information and advice.

However, it is important to insert a caveat here. This conclusion, based as it is on the findings of a sample that is biased towards larger, fairly long-established SMEs in mature industrial sectors, does not preclude the possibility that firms with particular characteristics, or combinations of characteristics (e.g. start-ups, 'high tech' firms, firms in peripheral regions) will encounter supply-side market failure.

Disaggregating the reasons why firms have not raised external equity finance by area highlights two significant spatial differences (Table 5.8). First, the proportion of firms citing that they had no need for equity finance because alternative sources of finance or capital reserves were available is highest in the assisted areas and lowest in the unassisted areas. The high proportion of firms reporting that they had no need for equity finance in the assisted areas may be, in part, a reflection of fact that these firms are the largest and longest established in the sample and so may have reached a growth plateau. The evidence presented by Leigh *et al.* (1991) on the ability of many mature manufacturing firms to finance their growth by a combination of borrowing and self-financing, discussed earlier, may also be relevant. Conversely, the survey found no evidence to suggest that firms have used regional development grants as an alternative to equity finance. Neither is there any evidence that firms in RDAs have used grants and loans from the RDC as a substitute for equity. Thus, what is termed the 'crowding out' hypothesis (Mason and Harrison, 1991) is not supported, albeit on the basis of a small sample.

Secondly, the proportion of firms stating that they deliberately did not seek external equity finance is much lower in RDAs than in the assisted areas and unassisted areas. This suggests that there is least explicit equity aversion amongst the sample of RDA firms. A number of factors might help to explain this feature. First, it is likely to be associated with the industrial structure of the sample of firms in the RDAs, which is weighted towards manufacturing and producer services (see Table 5.3), sectors where the demand for, and use of, equity is greatest. Secondly, as discussed earlier (see Table 5.6), the RDA sample contained both the highest proportion of growing firms, as measured by turnover, and also the highest proportion of firms with a growth in turnover in excess of 50 per cent during the three years prior to the survey. Thirdly, it may also be associated with the high proportion of post-1960 start-ups in the RDA sample (see Table 5.2). Many of the firms in the other areas, particularly in the assisted areas, are long-established family businesses. Responses to the survey indicate that such businesses have had a particularly strong desire to retain ownership and control and, as a result, are opposed to selling some equity to raise finance.

Future financing sources

The majority of firms in the sample plan to use retained earnings, in some cases in conjunction with bank finance, to finance future developments. Use of retained earnings was cited by just under three quarters of firms as highly likely, while just under one third of firms stated that loan finance was highly likely. In contrast, just four firms, 4.7 per cent of firms which responded to the question (and just 2.7 per cent of the total sample), stated that raising additional equity finance was highly likely, and a further 12 firms (14.1 per cent of firms responding to the question; 8.1 per cent of the total sample) stated that it was a probable source of future finance. This compares

Table 5.9 Likely sources of future finance

	No. of firms				
	Highly likely	Probable	Unlikely	Don't know	No response
Assisted areas (n = 77)					
retained earnings	57	10	1	4	(5)
loan finance	14	27	13	2	(21)
equity capital	1	6	35	7	(28)
Unassisted areas (n = 40)					
retained earnings	20	10	2	0	(8)
loan finance	14	11	2	0	(13)
equity capital	1	4	13	1	(21)
Rural development areas (n = 32)					
retained earnings	20	4	3 .	2	(3)
loan finance	4	13	4	1	(10)
equity capital	2	2	8	5	(15)

Table 5.10 Likely sources of future equity finance

	No. firms reporting 'highly likely' or 'probable'			
	Assisted areas (n = 7)	Rural development areas (n = 4)	Unassisted areas (n = 5)	Total (n = 16)
Other financial institutions	4	3	1	8
Sale of firm to another company	4	2	1	7
Founders/management	2	1	3	6
Private individuals	0	2	3	5
Venture capital funds	0	3	1	4
Non-financial companies	0	2	2	4
Stock market	0	1	2	3
Other	0	0	1	1

Note: Multiple responses possible.

with 66 per cent of respondents who stated that raising equity was highly unlikely (Table 5.9).

There was little consensus amongst those firms which stated that the use of equity finance in the future was highly likely or probable regarding the source of such finance (Table 5.10). The most frequently cited source of future finance was 'other financial institutions' (eight firms). The second most frequently cited source of future equity finance was sale of the company. The importance of this source confirms the observation of the Advisory Committee on Science and Technology (ACOST, 1990) that a significant number of companies overcome financial barriers to growth by becoming a subsidiary of a larger company. The report goes on to note that although this strategy has certain benefits there are also drawbacks, including possible managerial and organisational difficulties and the stifling of creativity. Of course, sale of the company may reflect a desire to 'cash out' rather than to raise additional finance. It is not possible from the survey responses to accurately assess the relative importance of each motive, although it can be inferred from the comments of some companies that the 'cash out' option was dominant in a number of cases. It is also possible that the three firms which cited the stock market as a likely source of equity finance may also have been seeking to cash out. Buckland and Davies (1989) found that a significant proportion of the owner-managers of firms which joined the Unlisted Securities Market (USM) were seeking to cash out at least some of their equity stake rather than raise additional finance. A flotation on the stock market is inappropriate for all but a tiny minority of SMEs. Owner-managers who are seeking to sell their businesses have few exit routes other than sale to another company (Birley and Westhead, 1989).

Six firms expected to look to the management team for further equity finance. Fewer than one-third of firms cited private investors (five firms), venture capital funds (four firms) and non-financial companies (three firms) as likely sources of equity finance. As these sources are conventionally used to extend the equity base of a business in order to undertake growth this may imply that only a small proportion of firms have growth ambitions. However, an alternative interpretation is that the small proportion of firms citing formal and informal sources of venture capital as likely sources of finance in the future reflects a lack of awareness and understanding amongst small firm owners and their professional advisers of the existence and role of these types of equity capital.

There are three contrasts of note between the three areas in terms of the sources of finance that firms anticipate using in the future. First, the proportion of firms citing loan finance as 'highly likely' is much higher in the unassisted areas than in RDAs and assisted areas. (This contrast remains, although less strongly, when firms citing loan finance as 'probable' are also included.) Secondly, and related to this, a lower proportion of firms in the unassisted areas stated that the use of retained earnings was highly likely (Table 5.9). Together, these features mirror the previous discussion which noted that the proportion of firms which cited no need for external equity finance was highest in the assisted areas. It cannot be established with any degree of certainty whether there are any spatial variations in the anticipated use of equity finance on account of the small number of firms citing equity finance as a likely source of finance, allied to the large number of firms which did respond to the question. However, bearing these caveats in mind, the proportion of firms in the sample citing equity finance as highly likely or probable is higher in the RDA and unassisted areas than in the assisted areas. The RDA sample also contains the lowest proportion of firms that are unlikely to raise equity finance in the future. This reinforces our earlier conclusion that equity aversion is lowest amongst the sample of RDA firms. Thirdly, firms in the assisted areas sample (comprising the largest *number* of firms citing equity finance as a likely source of future finance) consider the narrowest range of sources of equity finance. Just three potential sources are cited: sale of the company, other financial institutions and founders/management (Table 5.10). Thus, all of the firms that cite informal and formal sources of venture capital as well as the stock market and non-financial companies as likely sources of equity finance in the future are located in the RDAs and unassisted areas. The RDA sample contains three of the four firms which are likely to seek venture capital while three of the five firms considering private sources of venture capital are located in the unassisted areas.

Share ownership

There is remarkably little information on the structure of share ownership in unquoted SMEs. Indeed, the recent Cambridge study is one of the few studies to provide any information on this topic (University of Cambridge, 1992). In view of the limited recourse of firms in the study to external suppliers of equity finance it might be expected that share ownership in the vast majority of cases has been fairly stable over time and is concentrated in the hands of the chief executive and directors. However, neither expectation is confirmed. About one-quarter of firms were unable to give the share ownership structure at start-up/incorporation, although in view of the fact that many were established fifty years or more ago, it is not surprising that some firms did not have this information available. Of those firms which did provide the appropriate information (most of which were started in the post-war period) almost one-half reported a change in their distribution of share ownership. In view of the differences in the ages of firms in the three areas, it is not surprising to note that change in the share structure was least frequent amongst RDA firms (23 per cent) which are the most youthful of the three sub-samples.

Just over half of these changes involved a dilution in the ownership stake of the lead entrepreneur(s), predominantly in favour of the management team (some of whom are likely to be family members) and relatives of the entrepreneur and management team. Not surprisingly, in view of the limited use of external equity finance, few changes in share ownership have involved outside investors. Almost as common have been changes in share ownership which have involved an increase in the proportion of shares owned by the lead entrepreneur, although no such cases occurred in RDAs. This change has come about in two main ways. First, it is associated with the inter-generational transfer of shares within family-owned businesses. Secondly, it reflects the accumulation of shares by the lead entrepreneur from their founding partners. McMullen, Long and Tapp (1984) note that while this may be associated with their voluntary or involuntary departure from the firm this is not always the case.

Share ownership is therefore relatively dispersed within the SMEs in the sample. The lead entrepreneur owns 100 per cent of the equity in only 21 per cent of firms and the median shareholding of the lead entrepreneur is only 52 per cent. The management team are shareholders in over half of firms and relatives of the lead entrepreneur and management team are shareholders in 40 per cent of cases. In each case their shareholding is typically around 30 per cent. However, fewer than 10 per cent of firms have extended shareholding to their other employees, confirming the observation of Smith (1986) that employee share-ownership schemes are rare in small privately owned companies. Moreover, employee shareholding in these firms is generally very small (median of 5 per cent). Finally, 13 per cent of firms have outside investors, and on average they have a 25 per cent stake in these businesses.

It is in terms of ownership structure that the most significant spatial variations can be observed. Specifically, share ownership in the RDA sample of firms is much more concentrated in the hands of the lead entrepreneur(s) than in either the assisted areas sample or the unassisted areas sample. In RDAs the lead entrepreneur owns all of the equity in 44 per cent of firms, whereas the equivalent proportions in the assisted areas and the unassisted areas are 19 per cent and 9 per cent respectively. The median share ownership of the lead entrepreneur is also higher, at 59 per cent in RDAs, 57.5 per cent in assisted areas and just 50 per cent in unassisted areas. It also follows that fewer firms in RDAs have shareholders amongst the other categories. These differences are particularly marked for relatives of the management team, other employees and outside investors. The sharpest contrasts are between firms in the RDAs and firms in the unassisted areas.

CONCLUSION

Successful growth requires a company to solve the conundrum of balancing the retention of ownership and control with the need for cash. Relying simply on funds generated by the business is attractive but limiting, whilst the attraction of outside investors can be both liberating and painful (Employment Department, 1990). This study has provided confirmation that the majority of firms, including larger and longer established ones, have rejected the latter option. Few firms have raised equity finance from external sources. Most have been able to finance their development by means of retained earnings and, in many cases, bank loans and overdraft facilities. A significant proportion of firms have also deliberately avoided the need to raise external equity finance because they feared loss of ownership and control. Most firms expect to continue with this pattern of funding into the future. However, the survey was undertaken around the time that signs were emerging of a 'credit crunch' and a few firms did comment that their bank had tightened up their relationship. Indeed, there was one case in which a firm was forced to raise equity finance to replace a loan that had been withdrawn by the bank. Thus, there must be some concern about the ability of SMEs to continue to finance their development in such a traditional way. It is unclear whether other firms in this situation will be able to raise equity finance.

The small number of firms in the sample that have raised external equity finance limits the conclusions that can be reached concerning spatial variations in the financing of firms. Nevertheless, even with this limitation two conclusions regarding the financing of rural enterprises can be reached on the basis of the evidence presented in this study. First, there is no evidence to suggest that firms in remote rural areas are disadvantaged in terms of access to equity finance. Use of equity finance by firms in RDAs does not differ significantly from that in either assisted areas or unassisted areas. Moreover, the reasons why firms in RDAs chose not to seek equity finance are similar to those offered by firms in other spatial environments. The sample of RDA firms did not report a higher rejection rate by suppliers of equity finance.

Secondly, equity aversion amongst firms in the RDA sample is lower than in the other areas. Two particular findings point to this conclusion. The RDA sample of firms contained both the smallest proportion that specifically did not seek external equity finance and also the lowest proportion of firms that stated that they were unlikely to raise equity finance in the future. The RDA sample also contained three of the four firms that were likely to seek venture capital in the future. This lower equity aversion suggests that there may be a higher latent demand for equity finance by SMEs in remote rural areas. The characteristics of the RDA sample, notably youthfulness, more rapid turnover growth, and bias towards manufacturing and producer services, are likely to be associated with the greater need for external equity finance. In addition, our earlier review of the literature on spatial variations in the financing of SMEs implies that rural firms, because of their location, experience more significant problems in accessing sources of debt finance. This is likely to be intensified in conditions of a deepening credit squeeze facing the SME sector in general. However, the fact that this lower equity aversion is not reflected in higher than average use of external equity finance strongly indicates that rural SMEs may be experiencing supply-side market failure in the external equity capital market.

The likelihood that firms in remote rural areas have a high latent demand for external equity capital is reinforced by the fact that the lead entrepreneur in such firms is more likely to own all of the equity and there is less dispersal of shares amongst the management team, relatives of the management team, other employees and outside investors. The implication is that owner-managers of RDA firms have the greatest potential to sell shares in order to raise finance without losing overall ownership and control.

Thus, we have a number of findings which consistently point to the existence of a latent demand for equity capital in remote rural areas. Two policy recommendations follow from this conclusion. First, the RDC should adopt a pro-active role in promoting the use of both formal and informal venture capital to its clients in RDAs. Since there appears to be little fundamental equity aversion many firms may find venture capital to be an acceptable and suitable form of finance if made aware of this financing option. The RDA's business counsellors will play a key role in converting the latent demand for venture capital into actual demand by increasing awareness of the venture capital option. Accordingly, they should receive appropriate training to enable them to educate their clients in understanding what venture capital is and how to identify and approach both formal and informal suppliers of venture capital.

Secondly, and in parallel, the RDA should develop strategies to increase the supply of venture capital in remote rural areas. There has been an increase in the number of regionally based venture capital funds, particularly in the midlands and northern regions of England, in recent years (Mason and Harrison, 1991). The establishment of new funds with an explicit rural investment focus is therefore likely to be inappropriate in most circumstances, although in remote rural areas which lack regional sources of venture capital the RDA should seek to stimulate the creation of funds by identifying suitable fund managers and assisting in the raising of finance. However, the RDA's main efforts should be concentrated on working closely with existing regional funds. Florida and Kenney (1988) emphasise that venture capitalists place a heavy reliance upon information linkages with entrepreneurs, consultants, business executives, other financiers and a wide range of other actors who operate as networks to locate deals and mobilize the necessary resources for business formation and development. Because of the intensive nature of this information flow, these venture capital networks tend to be personalised, informal and localised. Such information sharing is based upon mutual trust which is earned through long-term interpersonal contacts. RDA counsellors must therefore seek to become part of these venture capital networks by establishing themselves as a trustworthy source of good quality deal flow.

Although regionally based venture capital funds have a lower average investment size than London-based funds few are willing to make investments of less than £100,000 (Mason and Harrison, 1991). Thus, a parallel supply-side strategy must be for the RDA to plug this equity gap by encouraging informal venture capital activity which is widely recognised as the major (and most appropriate) source of finance for businesses, especially start-ups and recently established firms, seeking small amounts of equity finance (typically up to £50,000) (Walker, 1989; Mason et al., 1991). The RDA should therefore be aware of, and even consider sponsoring, not-for-profit organisations which provide a business introduction service for 'business angels' and firms seeking equity finance. Examples of such organisations include enterprise agencies that belong to the LINC network and some Training and Enterprise Councils (TECs). In areas which lack such organisations, the RDA should seek to promote their establishment, although recognising that such organisations will need to operate on a sub-regional or regional scale. RDA offices should also be aware of any private sector organisations (e.g. accountancy firms) which seek to link up both companies that are seeking equity finance and also companies seeking a buyer (including those in receivership) with private investors so that they can refer appropriate firms to such organisations. As in the case of venture capital funds, private sector 'match-making' organisations rely on a network of sources to build up their client base of businesses and investors (Harrison and Mason, 1993). Here again, RDA staff should aim to become a trusted part of the network of these organisations. Finally, RDA offices should also aim to become part of the referral network of active 'business angels' in their area, and especially those who are 'lead' investors, or 'archangels', who have their own network of associates to whom they suggest investments (and who, in many cases, will place considerable reliance on the recommendation of the lead investor) and who play the key role in putting deals together.

6 In search of spatial differences: evidence from a study of small service sector enterprises

Robert Blackburn and James Curran

INTRODUCTION

The search for spatial differences and the assessment of their significance for the understanding of contemporary economic activities in Britain has become widely debated since the late 1980s (Savage *et al.*, 1987; Massey and Allen, 1988; Cooke, 1990). In the study of small-scale enterprise there has been a similar increase in interest in spatial considerations (Keeble, 1990; Pyke *et al.*, 1990; Mason, 1991). Only recently, however, has there been any detailed empirical consideration of the links between locality and small scale enterprise to inform the wider debate (Curran and Blackburn, 1991; Keeble *et al.*, 1991).

Even less attention has been given to the small business in rural areas and to the comparisons which might be drawn between small businesses in rural areas and their counterparts in urban areas. A good deal has been written on the small farm (Champion and Watkins, 1991) but those areas commonly labelled 'rural' in Britain now contain large numbers of businesses, many of them small, whose activities have increasingly little or nothing to do with agriculture.

Any discussion of the differences between small businesses in rural and urban areas presupposes some notion of how the terms 'rural' and 'urban' ought to be conceptualised. In turn, problematic conceptualisations of this kind beg questions on the significance of 'locality' as a unit of analysis in economic activities (Curran and Blackburn, 1992a). The long debate on the urban-rural contrast and the content to be attributed to the two key terms has been well summarised elsewhere (e.g. Newby, 1979; Keeble, 1980; Lee and Newby, 1983: ch. 4, *passim*). In this chapter, a rural economy is conceived formally as a locality designated officially by the Rural Development Commission (RDC) as a Rural Development Area (RDA). In 1984 the RDC set up an RDA covering the northern half of Suffolk, to which, for this research, is added the North East part of Suffolk which lies outside the RDA itself, parts of Norfolk just over the Suffolk border and parts of Mid-Suffolk immediately to the south of the RDA.

As was being pointed out even in the late 1970s, there is no such thing as a typical rural economy: 'in reality rural England still presents the much celebrated "patchwork quilt" of people, places, activities and environments which almost defies summary and certainly renders any simplistic generalisation impossible' (Newby, 1979: 261). Nevertheless, in a rural economy the production of food together with its associated processing, manufacturing and services activities, is a significant element in terms of employment and output. For instance, in the Mid-Suffolk District in 1989, the proportion of the work force in agriculture, forestry and fishing was estimated at 10.7 per cent (Regional Trends, 1991). In the North East Suffolk RDA itself, in some areas up to 30 per cent of the work force were employed in agriculture and related activities (Rural Development Commission, 1988). However, other kinds of economic activities, not related to agriculture, are increasingly important, and even dominant, in terms of employment and output. As in other designated rural areas, the prosperity of the area can no longer be measured in terms of the prosperity of agriculture alone even if it often continues to have a significant impact.

Historically, rural areas have suffered from depopulation, poor economic and social infrastructures and declining employment chiefly as a result of over-dependence on a shrinking agricultural employment base, low population density and the failure of alternative forms of economic activity to emerge sufficiently (Champion and Watkins, 1991). However, there is evidence of a reversal in this decline in rural areas, at least since 1980, in what has been termed 'counter-urbanisation'. This comprises an urban-rural manufacturing shift (Keeble, 1980; Fothergill and Gudgin, 1982; Townsend, 1991), a substantial increase in middle-class residents especially through net-inward migration, the expansion in car ownership, the improvements in housing and developments in communications which have all 'considerably reduced the isolation of rural areas' (Champion and Watkins, 1991: 14).

The notion of 'urban' used in the chapter is, in a sense, residual since the other four localities in which the small businesses in the study were located are areas where agriculture and agricultural activities are entirely absent or, at the most, as in the case of

Guildford, barely represented. The UK has one of the smallest agricultural sectors in employment and output terms of any advanced industrial society. By 1985, for example, it was estimated to be responsible for less than two per cent of gross domestic product (GDP) (Curwen, 1990: 29). In the most recent *Labour Force Survey* of 1991, agriculture, forestry, fishing and mineral extraction were recorded as employing 552,000 or just over two per cent of those in employment (Department of Employment, 1992: table 15). However, because of the residual status of the urban in the present analysis, covering the great majority of economic areas, there will be very substantial variations in levels of economic activities and these are likely to be much greater than the differences between the North East Suffolk and the urban areas. This will be especially the case because the areas representing the urban category were selected to provide maximum contrast to each other (see below).

It should be stressed that in the analysis below there is no intention of assuming an urban-rural contrast of the kind fashionable in earlier conceptualisations such as the 'rural-urban continuum' (Lee and Newby, 1983: 58–62). Instead, we present findings on the ways in which particular forms of economic activities which are common across the economy whatever the area geographically, function in particular kinds of localities. These by no means comprise a complete picture of economic activities in these localities and therefore cannot be taken to offer a full economic characterisation of the localities as a whole or of areas labelled 'rural' and 'urban'.

Recent developments in rural areas such as North East Suffolk have an enterprise dimension in terms of changes in the population of small businesses (Gould and Keeble, 1984). Precise data is not available but VAT figures provide broad indicators of starts and stops in different localities.[1] Although the patterns are not wholly uniform, VAT county based analyses show that rural counties match, and in many cases exceed, the net percentage growth in predominantly urban counties for 1980–90 (Daly, 1991). Of course, this may partly reflect a low base figure for 1980 in rural areas but, taken with counter-urbanisation, the results suggest that non-agriculturally related small-scale enterprise has become more significant in these areas.

SMALL BUSINESSES, SERVICES AND THE ECONOMY

The main aim of this chapter is to investigate spatial differences at the level of the firm in the rural and urban areas studied, in terms of small, service sector businesses. The service sector has attracted little attention until recently particularly in the study of small-scale enterprise (Burrows and Curran, 1989). Equally, in the wider analysis of regional economies, the emphasis has been on the 'export based' manufacturing sector rather than services as a means to generate income and employment (Armstrong and Taylor, 1983). However, it is becoming widely acknowledged that the service sector has become the heartland of the UK economy and many services themselves can be exported. In 1951, 36 per cent of Britain's GDP derived from manufacturing but by 1986 this had fallen below 25 per cent. In contrast, in 1986 two thirds of GDP came from services which also provided over two thirds of all jobs (Ball *et al.*, 1989). The need to focus attention on service sector smaller businesses is further buttressed by the finding that 63.5 per cent of businesses registered for value added tax (VAT) are in the service sector. This underestimates the total proportion of small firms in this sector because businesses in services are smaller than those in manufacturing and therefore are less likely to be registered.[2]

Small businesses in services and manufacturing have a differential regional presence (Mason, 1991). There are several reasons why differences between urban and rural service businesses might be expected but, broadly, these can be summed up in terms of the idea that 'specific places provide a specific incubator function for specific new activities' (Giaoutzi *et al.*, 1988: 3). While there are strong indications of a rural bias in new firm formation rates in manufacturing (Townsend, 1991: table 6.3), services provide a more complicated picture (Keeble, 1990). The dominance of the South East region in the two fastest growth sectors, 'finance' and 'other services', suggests that any urban-rural shift is unlikely to be uniform. That is, while rural areas such as North East Suffolk and even more so the East Anglia Region, may have benefited from gains in manufacturing, they may have not done as well in services.

Whatever the trends revealed at a regional level, they provide little information of the actual experiences of businesses in urban and rural areas. For instance, services small firms and especially those providing consumer services, depend on local income levels which in turn will influence their size and growth rates. Incomes in rural areas have been shown to be consistently below the national average (Townsend, 1979; Mclaughlin 1986). But the processes of counter-urbanisation will have offset at least some of the massive decline in agricultural jobs in rural areas such as North East Suffolk. The substantial increase in middle-class residents, both commuters and the retired, may well have begun to reverse the historical differences in income and expenditure. However, little is known about current trading patterns and business size in these areas and how these have changed over time.

At the same time, urban areas themselves are undergoing changes. The movement of population and business from inner urban to suburban areas and other intra-urban changes (Savage, 1989) also have important implications for small businesses. This is particularly the case for small businesses in services because it is in the mainly urban regions such as the South East, that services businesses have been expanding rapidly (Keeble *et al.*, 1991). In short, the comparison of the situations of service sector small businesses in rural and urban areas may well throw light on a number of more basic sets of changes occurring in the UK in the 1990s.

METHODOLOGICAL CONSIDERATIONS AND BACKGROUND TO THE STUDY

The findings presented are drawn from projects in a large scale research programme on the small, service sector business. In the *Lead Project* owner-managers of 350 small, service sector businesses were interviewed. The businesses were selected from seven areas of services: computer services; garages and vehicle repairers; employment secretarial and training agencies; plant and equipment hire; advertising, marketing and design agencies; video hire, health, beauty and leisure clubs; and free houses, wine bars and restaurants. The main reasons for this particular selection of economic activities were twofold. First, to cover a broad spectrum of services to ensure a range which would include producer services (e.g. advertising, marketing and design), consumer services (e.g. video hire and leisure businesses) plus others with a mixed customer/client base (e.g. garages and vehicle repairers). Secondly, it was also felt necessary to ensure that both older business types were represented such as small garages and vehicle repairers, as well as newer services enterprise which have emerged strongly since 1980 such as those in computer services and the leisure sector.[3]

Previous aggregate studies suggest that if spatial differences in the experiences of businesses are to be isolated, then business type must be controlled (Mason, 1991). In this way, particular locality effects may be isolated from any differential industry-mix effect. The research design described above takes this point into account by drawing approximately 70 firms from each locality covering the seven sectors but also ensured a diverse range of localities to allow spatial comparisons. Using an index of local prosperity devised by Champion and Green (1988), five localities were selected: Guildford, Doncaster, Islington, Nottingham and North East Suffolk.[4] As we have argued elsewhere (Curran and Blackburn, 1992a) there are problems in using formally defined areas of the kind in Champion and Green's index since they are unlikely to coincide with patterns of substantial relations (Sayer, 1984) between firms, interest groups and other social formations. Nevertheless, it is argued that the areas as defined here have some utility in the analysis of differences between them and have sufficiently contrasting socio-economic and political characteristics to allow such a spatial comparison.

The chapter also draws on data from three other projects. First, re-interviews with 81 of the owner-managers of the original 350 firms in the *Lead Project* collected information on *employment relations, labour recruitment and management strategies*. The interviews took place in North East Suffolk, Doncaster and Guildford. A further project concerned *owner-manager relations with the wider environment* involved re-interviewing 45 owner-managers, in all five localities, on how they coped with 'critical incidents' in the business. 'Critical incidents' here refer to one-off events with the potential to disrupt the routines of the business such as the loss or gain of a major customer, the loss of gain a new partner or director in the business or a major investment in new equipment or premises. The aim was to explore how such incidents were managed and to what extent sources external to the firm ranging from professional advisers to family and friends, were used to manage the incidents. Finally, all the surviving businesses were interviewed in a *telephone survey* in February 1992. As pointed out elsewhere (Mason, 1989: 335–6) the tendency to take data from single interviews of owners is questionable in many respects and data with a longitudinal element has considerable value. The re-interviewing of owner-managers in these subsequent surveys overcomes such problems and adds considerable validity to the results.

The localities

North East Suffolk, the rural area selected, is more difficult to define than the urban areas and it is worth reiterating a number of methodological points. As noted earlier, the core of the North East Suffolk area from which firms were recruited is an RDA. The actual area covered included Lowestoft which is not a rural town in many

respects since tourism and fishing are important sources of employment. However, it would be difficult to select almost any area of
Britain which might be described as 'rural' without including a
sizeable town of some kind. These towns often act as focal points for
the surrounding economy and, arguably, form part of a wider economy with substantial agricultural and agriculturally related activities
as well as more urban varieties of economic activities.

For the purposes of this study, North East Suffolk is considered
a rural locality, within which there are some large villages and
towns. These include Lowestoft (population 59,875), Great Yarmouth
(55,875), Beccles (10,815) and Woodbridge (9772) (Office of Population Censuses and Surveys, 1984) from which 30 businesses were
selected. The remaining 41 businesses were situated in areas of low
population density which were not joined to any of the urban areas
and are called 'more rural areas' in the chapter. As expected, there
were some sector differences between these two sub-groups. Whilst
there was a dearth of computer services and video shops in the more
rural areas, there was a higher proportion of free houses. However,
these sector differences were not statistically significant and it is
argued that a predominantly rural area with urban centres provides
a more realistic study environment than a sample of firms drawn from
different rural areas. Any other differences are noted in the further
analyses presented below.

The East Anglia region of which North East Suffolk is a part, was
a boom area for much of the 1980s (*Financial Times*, 1991) although
North East Suffolk itself remains relatively poor on a range of
indicators. In the RDA between 1981 and 1986, employment in
agriculture declined by 1.9 per cent per annum, to 2,119, and by 1987
employment in agriculture was 15.3 per cent (Rural Development
Commission, 1988; 1992). The type of farming is mainly large scale
– much of it based on cereals production – and capital intensive. As
in East Anglia as a whole, it experienced net inward migration in the
1980s, mostly of people who commuted to work outside the area and
people retiring. The area is also poorly served by major roads and
public transport and many of the RDA's 110 parishes lack basic
facilities: 60 have no post office, 63 have no shop, 86 have no school
and 95 have no doctors surgery (Rural Development Commission,
1988). The bulk of development within Suffolk county has been in
the South dominated by Ipswich and the A45 'corridor' through Bury
St Edmunds, Badbergh, Ipswich and the Suffolk Coastal local
District (Suffolk County Council, 1988; *Financial Times*, 1991),
outside the area covered in the three projects. One estimate is that

eight out of ten of the new jobs generated in Suffolk in the 1980s were located in towns along the A45 (Utting, 1991).[5]

The other four localities, the urban group – Guildford, Nottingham, Doncaster and Islington – are more easily described. Guildford is in a prosperous area in the South East region and was selected for its high rating on the index of prosperity. The economy is dominated by newer white collar and high tech industry and the population contains a high proportion of people with above average incomes, many of whom commute to London (Guildford Borough Council, 1989). The local authority's Economic Development Unit estimates that at the onset of the current recession, the labour market problems of local employers remained severe not only due to skill shortages but also because of high housing costs (Guildford Borough Council, 1989). Unemployment remains low at 6 per cent, and well below the national average (*Employment Gazette*, 1992). Guildford still has connections with agriculture in the area though the proportion of the labour force in the agriculture, forestry and fishing category is low at 1.5 per cent (Regional Trends, 1991).

Nottingham had a relatively high representation of manufacturing at the start of the research programme though a shift to services was also occurring reproducing national trends. It remains a centre for clothes manufacturing and still has several nationally known manufacturing companies such as TI Raleigh. The area suffered from high unemployment in the first half of the 1980s – reaching 20 per cent in the city itself in 1985 – and then declined as the economy recovered in the mid-1980s (Nottingham City Council, 1989). At 10.3 per cent unemployment is currently a little above the national average (Employment Gazette, 1992). But indications of growth in the late 1980s remain, as the experiences of many of the firms in the sample demonstrate.

Doncaster was chosen to represent a locality whose economy had suffered from a massive decline in older style industries, most notably coal mining and railway equipment manufacturing, but had not managed to replace these with more modern high technology and services industries. Long-term unemployment (those out of work for over a year) was 29 per cent in January 1991 (Regional Trends, 1991) and currently the overall level of unemployment is 13.2 per cent (Employment Gazette, 1992). Some employment has come through the establishment of branches of national firms in manufacturing which take advantage of local, skilled labour at relatively low wages.

Islington, the inner city economy in the research programme, is a very mixed economy. The southern end of the Borough is adjacent to the City of London and many of the businesses locate there because of close proximity to the City at cheaper rents than in the City itself. Elsewhere in the area there are pockets of poverty and very different economic conditions for smaller businesses. The Borough also contains several ethnic minority populations, most notably Greek Cypriots and Asians. Many of those who own businesses in the area live outside the area. Overall, Islington offers a good example of a cosmopolitan, inner city economy with widely varying levels of economic activity though, as the data from the present research programme showed, in comparison with the other four localities, its small businesses in services were among the most prosperous (Curran, Blackburn and Woods, 1991a: table 6).

INITIAL EXPECTATIONS AND COMPARISONS

To date, the bulk of research on urban and rural differences within a small business setting has tended to focus on aggregate variables such as new firm formation rates at regional levels (e.g. Fothergill and Gudgin, 1982; Allen and Massey, 1988; Mason, 1991). In this chapter the focus is on small service firms in urban and rural areas to assess in what ways they differ. It should be stressed again that, as the earlier discussion implied, there is no typical urban or rural area and, indeed, the terms 'urban' and 'rural' are problematic. Generalisations from the data must therefore be treated with caution.

The initial inter-locality comparisons revealed few spatial differences on a substantial range of key variables but strong sectoral differences (Curran, Blackburn and Woods, 1991a). The analysis in this chapter, however, brings a sharper focus to the analysis of the data. A strong urban-rural contrast might not have been expected on a number of grounds. For instance, there is the now familiar thesis of the trend towards the globalisation of production, distribution and exchange which might well dissolve urban-rural economic and employment differences. This is supported, for example, by data on manufacturing which suggests that rural areas have gained relative to urban areas. Manufacturing employment in rural areas now constitutes 21.8 per cent of the workforce in comparison to 24.0 per cent for Great Britain as a whole (Townsend, 1991: table 6.3) leading to the conclusion that 'what has quietly happened is a convergence of employment structures between urban and rural areas' (Townsend, 1991: 90).

Rural areas also seem to have coped better with the two recessions of the 1980s mainly as a result of holding on to manufacturing jobs better than urban areas. Between 1981 and 1987, factory employment fell by only 6.5 per cent in rural counties, and by 2.8 per cent in remote, mainly rural, areas in contrast to a national rate of 15.7 per cent (Townsend, 1991: 90). One possible explanation for this is that rural areas have experienced a very high proportionate growth in female and part-time forms of employment (Champion and Watkins, 1991). In other words they have not been held back by the labour and technological rigidities of a manufacturing heritage of the kind many urban areas have experienced.

The influx of migrants to rural areas, mainly from urban areas, may add further to these processes producing increased cultural and life style homogenisation between areas as well as providing income and expenditure boosting local rural economies. This might well tend to reinforce the development of indigenous consumer services which, at the same time, contribute to the erosion of many of the cultural values associated with rural living or, at least, interweave with local cultures to put the more specific, rural culture under strain (Savage, 1989).

Business size

An analysis of business size shows that North East Suffolk's small businesses are clearly much smaller than those in the urban areas as a whole with over double the proportion of businesses with turnovers of less than £50,000 (Table 6.1). Conversely, the proportion of businesses with turnovers over £250,000 in North East Suffolk is only a little over half of the proportion in Islington and significantly below that of the urban areas overall. The most obvious reason for this difference is the markets faced by small businesses in North East Suffolk. Those businesses relying on local markets are in an area of low population density with lower overall levels of earnings than in more prosperous areas such as the South East (New Earnings Survey, 1991) while those trading over more extensive areas such as those in advertising, marketing and design suffer from the disadvantages of being away from centres of the industry which is concentrated in London and South East. More generally, it is sometimes argued that a higher level of minimum efficient scale is necessary in urban areas to cover the assumed higher costs of production[6] though in some cases they may have the advantages of economies of agglomeration not available to businesses in rural areas (Allen and Massey, 1988: 62).[7]

A possible element in the explanation for the small size of

Table 6.1 Turnover of businesses in 1990

	All urban*	Islington**	North East Suffolk
Up to £50,000	11.5	12.1	23.9
£50,000 but under £100,000	20.6	16.7	19.4
£100,000 but under £250,000	22.9	18.2	28.4
£250,000 but under £500,000	21.0	22.7	11.9
Over £500,000	24.0	30.3	16.4
Total	262	66	67

Notes: * Chi-squared significance 0.036 for all Urban-North East Suffolk differences.
** Chi-squared significance 0.057 for Islington–North East Suffolk differences.
Six respondents were unable to answer the question because their businesses were too new. Information is not available for a further 15 firms.

businesses in North East Suffolk is that they are younger. There were, however, very few differences in the average age of firms between the different areas (Curran, Blackburn and Woods, 1991a: table 2). It is considered significant that the variation within the urban category in the table is also substantial. For instance, while only 28.8 per cent of Islington's firms had turnovers below £100,000, in Nottingham and Doncaster it was just over 41 per cent of the firms, a proportion approaching very close to the equivalent level in North East Suffolk (43.3 per cent). In other words, while North East Suffolk is relatively poor when compared with prosperous localities such as Islington and Guildford, the differential provides no basis for an overall urban-rural contrast measured in turnover levels. This suggests that size of business is more related to local prosperity than 'rurality'.

Premises and urban-rural differences

The complexities of comparisons between urban and rural businesses in the previous section particularly in relation to assessing prosperity levels, are shown again in the kind of premises occupied by the businesses. The premises from which the business operates are often a major asset of a small business. Freehold ownership often indicates a business which has achieved stability since a high proportion of businesses start initially from rented or leased premises. In addition, purchasing the freehold of the premises is attractive to owner-managers as an asset against which bank loans can be secured. (Important for a small, service business which often has relatively few physical assets acceptable to a bank or other source of outside

finance as security, compared with a manufacturing business.) Should
the business cease trading for any reason, the freehold of the
premises represents a realisable asset.

A major feature of previous discussions of urban-rural differences
has been the view that there may be a dearth of suitable premises in
rural areas whilst industrial conurbations' older industrial premises
may provide a seed-bed for young urban firms (Lloyd and Mason,
1984: 217). It might be that this divergence has become more acute
in regions such as East Anglia which have had rapid growth recently.
The Rural Development Commission in collaboration with English
Estates, have attempted to alleviate these problems in a variety of
ways but the provision of premises for businesses in areas undergoing economic change as agriculture declines and other forms of
enterprise are encouraged, is bound to be a continuing problem.[8]

Table 6.2 Occupational status of business premises

	*All urban**	*Islington***	*North East Suffolk*
Freehold	35.4	25.0	54.9
Lease or rented	61.7	70.6	42.3
Other	2.9	4.4	2.8
Total	277	68	71

Notes: * Chi-squared significance 0.010 for all urban-North East Suffolk differences.
    ** Chi-squared significance 0.001 for Islington North East Suffolk differences.

The findings from the research offer strong and somewhat
unexpected differences with regard to business premises (Table 6.2).
The majority of owners of businesses in North East Suffolk owned
their premises while in the other localities leasing or renting was by
far the most common tenancy form. The difference was especially
marked between North East Suffolk and Islington, and within North
East Suffolk itself there was a bias towards firms having a freehold
in the more rural areas. Given the advantages of businesses owning
their premises noted earlier, these findings suggest that, other things
being equal, businesses in North East Suffolk may be in a better
position to secure finance or use the freehold as a realisable asset for
other purposes, than the majority of businesses in the urban areas.
Additionally, the findings go against any rudimentary notion that
smaller businesses located in a rural area are less substantial than
their urban counterparts: a business may be small measured conventionally in terms of turnover or employment but this may not be the
whole story.

Respondents were asked whether lack of suitable premises was a hindrance to the expansion of the business. Since the recession was well in place by the time these interviews were conducted (February, 1992), it is possible that expansion was not an immediate concern for a high proportion of the businesses but availability of suitable premises was seen as a problem by less than 15 per cent of the businesses. Moreover, there was little difference between any of the localities. North East Suffolk's owners were slightly less likely to say they felt it was a problem but the difference was very small. Of course, if the economy was expanding and confidence was higher, more owners might be contemplating expansion and differences between the localities might then be greater. For instance, London has a glut of office premises at the moment as a result of the recession and over-supply. This may disappear in the future but at the moment there is no urban-rural difference on the availability of suitable premises for expansion.

OWNER-MANAGER MOTIVATIONS AND LOCALITY

The study of small business owner motivations has received an enormous amount of attention from researchers with a high level of consistency between the various studies (Curran, 1986: 17–28; Stanworth and Gray, 1991: 151–65). For instance, there is widespread agreement on the importance of independence and autonomy as motivations and the relative lack of importance of money making. There is, however, a problem in reducing what are often complex, and as the owner-managers in the study made clear, sometimes difficult to vocalise or only half-formed ideas on motivations in respondents' minds, into straightforward categories.[9]

Little or no attention has been given to locality differences in the motivational make up of small business owners still less to differences between those in rural and urban areas. It might be hypothesised, for example, that owner-managers in rural localities would be less entrepreneurially minded in terms of the adherence to some of the key values alleged to be associated with entrepreneurship in some analyses of the notion such as money making and profit maximisation (Chell *et al.*, 1991: ch. 2 *passim*).

Table 6.3 suggests that what distinguishes the North East Suffolk owner-managers is the lower proportion, under 6 per cent, who mentioned money-making as a main motivation for starting their own business in comparison with just over 14 per cent in the urban areas. This contrast was even stronger when North East Suffolk is compared

Table 6.3 Main motivations for starting in business

	All urban %	Islington %	North East Suffolk %
Autonomy and related reasons*	36.6	28.8	35.2
Money making	14.1	20.3	5.6
Total	265	69	71

Note: * Includes 'independence', 'wanting to be own boss', 'the challenge', 'felt I could do it better', 'could not work for somebody else' and similar reasons. Reasons which could not be classified clearly into either of the two categories have been excluded.

with Islington, where just over one in five mention money as the prime motivation for start-up, that is, almost four times as high as in North East Suffolk.

This would seem to support the notion that attitudes to small business ownership in a rural area show a lower commitment to material rewards. This might echo in some way a local culture stressing community, people-centredness and a less economistic outlook overall, that is, the kind of local cultural values often attributed to rural living and rural lifestyle choices. It also suggests that motivational influences related to small business ownership in rural areas cover a wider range than in urban areas since well over half of the reasons offered could not easily be placed into conventional categories employed by small business researchers. Again, this might suggest that the local culture gave more force to values and reasons less clearly linked to the individualism and materialism often seen as swamping other, alternative values in urban industrial settings. However, a disaggregation of the urban data suggests an alternative and rather more mundane interpretation is possible. Doncaster, the least prosperous of the urban economies, shows a striking similarity to North East Suffolk in terms of the motivations for starting a small business. Indeed, owner-managers in Doncaster show a *lower* commitment to money and a greater commitment to autonomy and other values than owner-managers in any of the other four localities, including North East Suffolk.[10] Fewer than 4 per cent of the Doncaster owner-managers reported that money was their main motivation for starting their business.

What the above might suggest as an interpretation is that a commitment to money-making might be related to local levels of prosperity. North East Suffolk and Doncaster had the smallest businesses measured by turnover and employment (Curran *et al.*,

1991a: tables 6 and 10 and below). North East Suffolk also has a lower population density than any of the other localities, an important market indicator for many small services businesses. Evidence from North East Suffolk and Doncaster therefore might suggest that lower levels of local prosperity leads to less of an emphasis on money-making as a motivation. In other words, it might well reflect a realistic assessment of the businesses' potential rather than any differences between rural and urban cultures.

Geographical mobility and small business ownership

As noted earlier, a significant feature of population movement in Britain has been net in-migration to rural areas and particularly into East Anglia. For example, the population in Suffolk grew from over 550,000 to over 590,000 between 1976 and 1985 and the population of the RDA itself grew from 54,617 in 1981 to 55,650 in 1986 (or 1.9 per cent a year) (Rural Development Commission, 1988: 3). Has this influx of newcomers produced an upsurge of entrepreneurial activity? It might be supposed that given the kinds of small businesses in the present sample, that is, services businesses predominately engaged in activities which have little to do with agricultural or agriculturally related activities, they are more likely to have been started or purchased by people with no local ties.

As Table 6.4 shows, in aggregate, there were few differences between the localities on the proportion of owners who have always lived locally. This probably reflects the fact that many of the in-migrants to North East Suffolk are commuters or have moved into the area to retire rather than to enter paid employment (Rural Development Commission, 1988: 2). But it also implies that the locality's long-term population have been entrepreneurial enough, compared with their counterparts in the urban areas, to take advantage of small business opportunities in newer areas of services such as computer services as well as to establish themselves in older forms such as small garages and vehicle repairers. In other words, the notion that rural areas are attracting incomers who wish to take advantage of cheaper premises and the alleged superior quality of life to start a small business, is not supported by this data despite the type of business and recorded high rate of in-migration favourable to the hypothesis. Indeed, when data for the urban areas are disaggregated, it is clear that the differences between the urban areas are greater than the difference between the urban areas as a whole and North East Suffolk. For example, in Islington 62.7 per cent of

Table 6.4 Proportion of business owners who have always lived in current locality

	All urban %	Islington %	North East Suffolk %
	44.7	37.3	42.3
Total	276	67	71

Note: The table is based on respondents' answers to a question asking them whether they had always lived 'locally' rather than any specified geographical distance. However, when this was widened out to cover the county, there was still no urban-North East Suffolk difference.

owner-managers were not born in the locality: in Doncaster only 42 per cent were not born in the locality.

What the above data suggests is that, if anything, it is the more prosperous, urban localities such as Guildford and Islington which appeared to attract in-comers who become business owners. North East Suffolk's overall high rate of inward mobility does not appear to increase the share of in-migrants in service sector business ownership or, from another perspective, does not reduce opportunities for those who are native to the locality to enter business ownership.[11]

Similar alternative explanations might be offered in relation to respondents' aspirations for growth. Asked 'Would you like your business to grow into a bigger business over, say, the next five years?' 45 per cent of North East Suffolk's respondents said 'No' in contrast to 30.3 per cent in Islington[12] and 25.6 per cent in all urban areas.[13] One interpretation here might be that lower levels of growth-mindedness in North East Suffolk reflected a lack of entrepreneurial spirit compared with the urban areas. Alternatively, these differences might simply reflect realistic assessments of the economic potential of the businesses in the areas in which they are located. Again, also, the differences within the urban group of localities are worth highlighting. In Doncaster, the least economically prosperous of the urban areas, the proportion of owner-managers wanting business growth over the next five years was 16.9 per cent, well below the average for the urban areas overall and the level in Islington.

TRENDS IN BUSINESS PROSPERITY IN URBAN AND RURAL LOCALITIES

One of the strengths of the research programme from which the data presented in this chapter is drawn, was its longitudinal aspect. The original *Lead Project* interviews were conducted in 1990 and owners of the surviving businesses in February 1992 were re-interviewed.[14] The major aim of these interviews, was to assess how many of the businesses were still surviving the severe recession which had only just begun to bite when most of the *Lead Project* interviews were conducted. Overall, it was established that just over 16 per cent of the original 350 businesses had ceased trading.[15] North East Suffolk showed the highest rate of firms who had ceased trading (21.1 per cent) whilst the urban areas figure overall was 15.1 per cent within which Islington was 17.4 per cent (second highest behind North East Suffolk). Thus, differences between the areas exist but are not significant.

Changes in turnover levels

A good deal of discussion of the current recession has suggested that more prosperous regions have been hit hard, particularly the South East, rather than the re-enforcing of the North-South divide which accompanied the 1979–83 recession. East Anglia was the fastest growing region in Britain between 1981 and 1990 (*Financial Times*, 1991) shown in part by the net increase in businesses registered for VAT which was second only to the level in the South East (Daly, 1991: table 3). More recent data on, for example, employment levels, suggests that recession has ended this period of rapid growth.

The data from the follow-up telephone survey of businesses shows marked differences in prosperity trends since the original interviews in 1990 (Table 6.5). North East Suffolk owner-managers had the highest proportion (40.4 per cent) reporting an increase in turnover since the original interviews and almost two out of three report turnover as up or the same as in 1990. In Islington, the most

Table 6.5 Business turnover change 1990–92

	All urban	Islington*	North East Suffolk
Lower	46.6	57.4	34.6
Higher	31.2	27.8	40.4
Same	20.4	14.8	25.0
No information	1.8	–	–
Total	221	54	52

Note: Data collected February 1992 for 274 businesses.
   * Chi-squared significance 0.0607 level for Islington–North East Suffolk differences.

prosperous area with the largest businesses in the original interviews, only a little over a quarter of the respondents reported turnover increases and well over a half reported falls.[16] Doncaster again emerges as most similar to North East Suffolk since its owner-managers were the next most likely to report increased turnover since 1990.

The necessity of not treating the urban grouping as a homogeneous category is emphasised yet again by the intra-grouping differences. Further, the experiences of the rural area owner-managers do not conform to stereotypical expectations of what happens in this kind of area during a recession, even when agriculture and agriculturally related activities are known to be showing falls in property values and income (Blackwell, 1991). The simplicities of any crude urban-rural dichotomy are again exposed.

Employment in rural and urban areas: a mixed picture

As might be assumed from Table 6.1, businesses in North East Suffolk were smaller in employment terms (See Curran *et al.*, 1991a: table 10). Almost 60 per cent of the businesses in North East Suffolk employed fewer than five people compared with just under half of all of the firms in the *Lead Project* sample.[17] They also employed more part-timers than businesses in all the other localities except Doncaster, suggesting that this similarity may also be related to levels of demand in the local economy. One effect of the population structure in North East Suffolk which shows up in the employment data, is that firms in this locality employ more retired or semi-retired people. Finally, they were also less likely to use self-employed workers than all the urban areas except Doncaster (Curran *et al.*, 1991a: table 14).

Over the two years to 1990, the proportion of firms in North East Suffolk expanding or decreasing their labour levels was in the middle of the range reported by owners in the other four localities. The greatest differences in employment changes for the 1988–90 period were between urban areas themselves, with Guildford suffering the largest contraction, apparently reflecting the onset of the current recession in the South East and Nottingham showing the largest proportion of firms reporting increases in levels of employment. Thus, the data indicates that the North East Suffolk firms had more stable employment levels than the urban areas in the late 1980s with fewer firms increasing or decreasing their labour forces. This stability was consistent with North East Suffolk's owners being less likely than owners in the other four localities to say that they had experienced difficulties in recruiting the right kinds of people for their businesses over this period.

The more recent 1992 telephone survey showed that in the surviving businesses average employment had risen to 8.7 people from 7 people in 1990 (Curran and Blackburn, 1992b: 11–13). North East Suffolk businesses showed buoyancy in employment change between 1990 and 1992 relative to the rest of the sample. In an analysis of 272 businesses in the telephone survey, the 53 firms in North East Suffolk had expanded employment by 172 jobs in comparison with 150 jobs in the 219 firms in urban areas. However, this should not be taken as an indicator of relative dynamism of all businesses in North East Suffolk since a more detailed analysis reveals that the overwhelming proportion of these new jobs are in one business which expanded by 127 people.[18] Nevertheless, the proportion of businesses staying the same size was the same in North East Suffolk (46.1 per cent) as in the urban areas (45.3 per cent) and proportionately fewer firms in North East Suffolk shed labour than in the composite urban area.

Table 6.6 Is it easier or harder to recruit the right people? Data from the surveys in 1990 and 1992

	All urban* 1990	All urban* 1992	Islington 1990	Islington 1992	North East Suffolk 1990	North East Suffolk 1992
Easier	16.4	61.5	18.0	68.5	11.8	45.3
More difficult	38.0	16.7	36.1	9.3	38.2	24.5
Same	29.6	13.1	34.4	14.8	22.1	17.0
Other	16.0	8.6	11.4	7.5	27.9	13.2
Total	250	221	61	54	68	53

Notes: For the 1992 data * chi-squared significance 0.055 for all urban–North East Suffolk differences.

In the telephone survey, although it was generally easier to recruit the right people than in 1990, it was the North East Suffolk's business owners who were the most likely to report difficulties in recruiting suitable people for their business (Table 6.6). The effects of the recession in the South East was shown by the very sharp increase in the proportion of owners in Islington finding it easier to recruit the kinds of people they wanted in 1992 than in 1990. Again, what emerges from this table is the smaller swings in opinion among North East Suffolk owner-managers: they agree with owner-managers in the other localities that it is easier to recruit suitable labour but the shift in views is less extreme. This data might suggest that one difference between the rural locality and the four urban localities is the greater stability over time of economic conditions in North East Suffolk. This stability is revealed in another way in the data on labour turnover from the *Lead Project* interviews. The overall comparison between the urban localities and North East Suffolk is shown in Table 6.7. Clearly, owner-managers in North East Suffolk find labour turnover less of a problem than their counterparts in the urban localities. This is probably explained by the fewer alternative jobs within a reasonable travelling distance from which to choose.

Table 6.7 Is employee turnover a problem?

	All urban*	Islington**	North East Suffolk
No	77.4	76.9	89.9
Yes	21.1	20.0	7.2
Other	1.5	3.1	2.9
Total	265	65	69

Notes: * Chi-squared significance 0.024 for all urban–North East Suffolk differences.
**Chi-squared significance 0.094 for Islington–North East Suffolk differences.

The sources of labour in the different localities are of interest since one central theme in the literature in the past was the alleged relative strength of the community in rural areas which was often associated with their agricultural, paternalistic past (Newby, 1979). In this study, however, few differences in sources of labour were found with one exception. Businesses in Islington were much more likely to use private employment agencies than those in North East Suffolk. Three reasons may be offered to explain this difference. First, Islington businesses were, on average, larger than those in North East Suffolk and may therefore have more formalised recruiting procedures. Secondly, the general difficulties of recruiting staff in the congested, cosmopolitan labour markets of urban areas may have led to a greater acceptance of private employment agencies. Finally, as noted above, businesses in North East Suffolk were much more likely to employ part-time staff than the urban areas (except Doncaster) a practice which may involve less use of private employment agencies.

However, caution is needed in interpreting the above differences as related to urban and rural locality characteristics. Some can plausibly be interpreted as products of such differences but it still has to be kept in mind that the differences within the urban category remain large and often greater than the differences between the composite urban group and North East Suffolk. In other words, it is probably safer to see some of the observed differences as the result of some characteristics being rather more pronounced in North East Suffolk compared with the urban areas but these should not be used to construct any fixed or sharply drawn urban-rural dichotomy.

Culturally, it is also reasonable to assume that there remains a spill-over or continuation of values and practices associated with agricultural and related activities into the new small service sector businesses in North East Suffolk. Some of the businesses had connections with agriculture through the backgrounds of owners and employees and even more directly through customers. For example, some of the small garages repaired and serviced agricultural machinery. But other norms which might be associated with a rural locality were not evident. For instance, owner-managers were no more likely to employ family members as staff or consider workers as close friends than in any of the other localities.

Some of these issues can be explored in greater depth with the aid of the data from the second project in the programme devoted to employment issues. The 81 owner-managers interviewed in this project were in Guildford, Doncaster and North East Suffolk and the range of types of enterprise was limited to those in advertising, marketing and design, computer services, employment, secretarial and training and free houses, wine bars and restaurants.

One area explored in depth was labour management practices and industrial relations issues which revealed some unexpected locality differences. Employers in North East Suffolk were more likely than those in Doncaster and Guildford to report that they had some formal or semi-formal means of discussing employees' grievances and were more likely to feel they would be affected by unfair dismissal legislation. These findings were unexpected in that they seem to go against any idea that firms in a rural locality would have lower levels of formality in employee–employer relations as compared with firms in urban localities. What was even more surprising was the finding that *employers* in North East Suffolk were more likely to be ex-trade union members than in either Doncaster or Guildford. Their *employees* were also more likely to be or have been trade union members. This might be explained by the history of trade union activism in Suffolk's agricultural sector which goes back at least as far as the beginning of this century and continued into the period after the Second World War (Newby, 1977: 256). In contrast, the relatively low proportion of Guildford's owners or their employees who are ex-trade union members may be explained by the historically low level of unions in that locality. Yet the relatively lower levels in Doncaster (and especially lower levels than recorded in North East Suffolk) given its long industrial and coal-mining past, were also unexpected (Curran *et al.*, 1993).

Finally, there appeared to be an association between locality and hostility to trade union recognition among owner-managers. Those in North East Suffolk expressed more resistance to the idea of employees being members of trade unions than those in Doncaster or Guildford. This appeared to be linked with employers' direct experience of trade unions which produced greater hostility towards unions. These issues have only been briefly mentioned here to demonstrate once again the way in which the findings warn against adopting stereotypical views of how rural localities are likely to compare with urban areas.

Overall, the data on employment and labour in the research programme suggest a mixed picture on the issue of whether it is possible to suggest clear differences between small service sector businesses in rural and urban localities. Firms in North East Suffolk are smaller measured by numbers employed and they display some distinctive aspects in terms of both the types of labour employed and the types of employment contracts they use, compared with businesses in the urban areas. But the differences are best seen as tendencies rather than sharp differences since, as with so much of the other data presented in this chapter, the differences between the businesses in the urban group are also often large. One characteristic supported by several findings was of the relative stability of employment patterns in North East Suffolk compared with the urban areas. Other differences such as those connected with industrial relations and trade union issues were unexpected in terms of stereotypical views of social relations in rural areas. They appeared to be explained by influences deriving from the historical background of the area's former major industry, agriculture, but it might be suggested that this underlines the point that there are no typical areas, rural or urban, revealed in the findings from the present projects.

LOCAL ECONOMIES AND NETWORKING: BUSINESS LINKS AND COMMUNITIES

A strong theme in many views of rural life is that of the closely integrated local community with a legacy of values associated with an agricultural based economy. Rural ways of life have become romanticised into an idyllic alternative to urban life which many aspire to even if only for weekend living. It is assumed that people still know their neighbours, still do business with each other as people rather than simply having market transactions devoid of sentiment. Small businesses have been similarly romanticised into alternatives to the alleged soulless, impersonality and hard-headed market rationalism of the large corporation.

Views of the above kind are easily criticised but how small firms are integrated into the economies of their localities, whether rural or urban, is itself an under-researched issue. It is widely assumed that small firms serve local needs and local markets and, hence, are important in any local economy although their importance declines as national and branches of international firms become omnipresent in every locality and larger enterprises, public and private, become major providers of jobs in almost every part of Britain.

This research programme addresses these issues with findings from three of its projects: the *Lead Project*; the project on *employment*; and, most directly, a project specifically investigating *networking* involving interviews with owners of 45 businesses. All provide locality comparisons of the businesses' economic relations with their immediate environment and on how business owners articulate with others in their locality ranging from relations with providers of professional services such as accountants and membership of chambers of commerce and the use of local bodies such as enterprise agencies. There is also data on the extent to which non-economic links such as family and kinship relations, impinge on the business.

Trading patterns and localities

Research on the trading patterns of small businesses in services is not easily come by. As noted above, it is usually assumed that sales are highly localised particularly where the business serves private consumers. In relation to any contrasts between urban and rural areas there is even less evidence. One hypothesis, however, is that lower labour and property costs and the other attractions of rural living have been attracting producer services firms such as advertising, marketing and design or computer services businesses but because of the limited local market, these businesses must sell their services largely outside the area. This is made easier by the ease and speed of modern communications which enable businesses to locate almost anywhere geographically without market disadvantage. In turn, these firms bring valuable income flows of money to stimulate poor rural economies and help equalise the distribution of wealth between urban and rural areas.

An analysis of the trading patterns of businesses in the localities revealed that North East Suffolk's businesses were more likely to be selling to a local market than the businesses in the urban areas and especially when the comparison is restricted to the most urban of the areas, Islington (Table 6.8). As reported elsewhere (Curran *et al.*, 1991a: table 7) there is a very strong relationship between type of business and trading patterns and a different mix of types of businesses would produce different overall patterns of trading in local and non-local markets. Here type of enterprise is being held constant and, hence, the differences may be related to locality. However, the explanation of the differences may or may not be related directly to the rural character of North East Suffolk. They might be related simply to narrowly economic influences rather than the effects of a rural culture. Businesses in North East Suffolk are smaller, on average, compared with those in the urban areas so they may find it more difficult to trade beyond their local markets. It might also be that there is less competition in North East Suffolk compared with, say, Islington and firms do not feel impelled to seek customers beyond the local area to keep in business. However, it was not the case that businesses in the more rural areas were more locally

Table 6.8 Geographical sales of firms

	All urban	*Islington*	*North East Suffolk*
75 per cent or more of sales to local market	59.1	53.6	66.2
75 per cent or more of sales to national market	21.9	20.3	11.3
75 per cent or more of sales are exports	0.7	1.4	0.0
Less than 75 per cent to any single geographical market	17.9	23.2	22.5
Total	278	68	71

dependent. If anything, firms in the more rural areas were reaching outside their locality for their sales.[19]

The notion of 'a local economy' is highly problematic (Curran and Blackburn, 1992a). Different types of businesses have differently shaped markets geographically. For example, the advertising, marketing and design businesses in the present study had very different markets geographically to the video hire outlets. Over half of the advertising, marketing and design businesses reported that three quarters or more of their business was with customers outside the locality. In other words, the view that *any* locality, urban or rural, has coterminous substantial and formal economic relations constituting an area designated 'the local economy' is questionable. Even North East Suffolk's businesses which come closest to the idea of small firms and locality being closely linked, display considerable tendencies to ignore local boundaries defined by, for example, local authority areas or the RDA.

Small business owners' networking

Whilst economic linkages may be a function of sector, what of the way in which business owners themselves articulate with their immediate environment? 'Networks' and 'networking' have recently been increasingly popular in discussing small business owner linkages with the wider environment. Although the extent of networking activities in the sample of 350 firms has been questioned elsewhere (Curran *et al.*, 1991a; Curran *et al.*, 1991b) it is reasonable to expect that small business owners in North East Suffolk would more actively network than owners in urban areas. They trade more within the locality than the urban owners and if rural communities are more integrated socially than urban areas, then networking should be easier. Alternatively, they may be a more insular because of the low density of population which means there are fewer outsiders to connect with in relation to specific, sectoral issues. For example, Meyer-Krahmer (1985) found a higher percentage of 'no outward orientedness' in firms located in rural regions and a stronger preference for internal problem solving.

Numerically, business owners in North East Suffolk were more active than owner-managers in urban areas through membership of the Rotary Club or round table or local political party but the proportions involved in these activities is still low overall (Table 6.9). In the case of chambers of commerce, they are less likely than the urban owners overall to be members. They are more likely to have joined than the owners in Islington but Islington's owners were the least likely of owner-managers in any locality to join their chamber of commerce. On the other hand, North East Suffolk's owners were also more likely to belong to a trade association or a national small business association such as the National Federation of Self-employed and Small Businesses[20] which are not local bodies. In some of their memberships, therefore, they were reaching out beyond the locality to a greater extent than owner-managers in the urban areas. This might indicate that they felt local sources were absent or offered too little help or support.

In terms of seeking outside advice, North East Suffolk's business owners appeared to be about as likely as those in urban areas to have sought the help of the *Small Firms Advisory Service.*[21] Islington's owners again stand out for their reluctance to use this source of advice but North East Suffolk's owners are similar to those in the other areas. They were, however, much less likely than owners in urban areas (including Islington) to have used their local enterprise agency. This may again be the result of the geographical spread of the businesses over the North East Suffolk area and their relative distance from an enterprise agency but, whatever the reason, there are no indications of greater use of community resources for promoting the business. Within the North East Suffolk businesses there were some significant differences in memberships and use of outside

Table 6.9 Selected indicators of networking activities

	All urban	Islington	North East Suffolk
Member of:			
Trade association	28.0	26.1	33.8
Chamber of commerce	25.1	10.1	18.3
Rotary Club, Round Table, etc.	1.4*	1.4	7.0
Political party	3.6*	5.8	11.3
National small business assocation	7.2**	2.9*	15.5
Has sought help or advice from:			
Small firms service	19.1	2.9**	15.7
Enterprise agency	20.3**	11.8	10.0
Total	278	69	71

Notes: * Chi-squared significance at 0.01 level for difference with North East Suffolk.
    ** Chi-squared significance at 0.05 level for difference with North East Suffolk.

agencies. Of those 41 businesses in more rural areas, 43.9 per cent were likely to be a member of a trade association in comparison with 20 per cent of those 30 firms in less rural North East Suffolk (a figure which is still lower than the urban composite group). This reinforces the notion of rural business owners reaching out of their locality for assistance or advice and further undermines their links with a community based on local connections.

Of course different localities have different levels and qualities of advice and support provision. These differences may be dependent on all kinds of influences which may have little to do with locality specifically. One chamber of commerce or enterprise agency may be much more energetically run or better resourced than another. Some areas will have special provisions not found generally elsewhere. For instance, Nottingham was a regional centre for the Small Firms Service and this apparently had the effect of encouraging more local businesses to use this source of advice than in other localities. North East Suffolk, of course, has the Rural Development Commission which had helped or been used as a source of help of advice by just under 17 per cent of businesses in the area on the most recent (February 1992) data.

One weakness in this method of analysis is that it involves mainly counting interactions business owners have with outside institutions. The *networks project* in the research programme sought to overcome this by seeking information on the level of intensity of any such relations and the motivations for business owners to seek outside help or advice.[22] The results from this study revealed that business owners' use of outside institutions cannot be interpreted simply as a reflection of the existence of local community institutions or support. The existence of such a set of institutions or aid bodies is independent of the desire or motivations of small business owners to take advantage of what they might offer. In talking through the various 'critical incidents' which formed the basis of the interviews in this project, what emerged very clearly was that owner-managers have strong views on seeking advice or help from outsiders including members of their own families. On the whole, they prefer to rely on others as little as possible even when resolving a critical incident which threatened the stability of the business. Rather, there was a pronounced 'fortress enterprise' mentality among owners in all the localities (Blackburn *et al.*, 1990; Curran *et al.*, 1991b). The overall strong preference was to go it alone rather than willingly participate in the exchange of problems and solutions with outsiders, irrespective of whether they were in a rural or urban area. None of the qualitative results showed North East Suffolk business owners to be distinctive from others in terms of their local community linkages.

This finding of a general lack among owners of seeking external assistance, even in rural areas, concurs with findings from a study in Ireland, where it might be assumed rural communities and their cultures have survived more strongly into the second half of the twentieth century than in England:

> Although most respondents commented on the benefits of working in a rural environment, they did not demonstrate a strong sense of community identity nor participation in that community. The active, diverse network created by some entrepreneurs suggests that the degree of external orientation is related more to individual circumstances than geographic location
>
> Petitt and Thompstone (1988: 32).

Overall, therefore, while there are some differences which might be seen as reflecting the characteristics of the urban and rural localities, the findings from the research programme do not offer a clear cut picture and certainly do not reveal the presence of rural values or cultures influencing the behaviour of the small business owners in North East Suffolk in any strong way. They trade more locally than the businesses in the urban areas although business sector appeared to explain more of the particular patterns of trading found than locality influences. They do not network any more vigorously than the businesses in the urban areas and had the same well-defined psychological outlook found in so many previous studies of small business owners which shows as a strong commitment to independence and a refusal to engage in activities which might be seen as threatening their autonomy or that of the business.

What should be stressed, however, is that these findings should not be taken as indicating there is no such thing as a rural way of life or rural cultures which mark localities such as North East Suffolk off from highly urban areas such as Islington. All that is being asserted here is that, in relation to small service sector businesses and their owners of the types studied in the research programme, there was little evidence of any strong rural influences on the businesses. They and their owners appeared to share much more in common with their counterparts in the urban areas and in their sector, than displaying any distinctive managerial and business strategies setting them apart.

CONCLUSIONS

Spatial considerations in the analysis of the role of small businesses in the UK economy have aroused increasing interest recently. Aggregate evidence has suggested an uneven performance in start-up rates of small businesses in the regions although the explanations offered for this remain debatable (Keeble and Wever, 1986; Mason, 1991). Most of the available data is from aggregate data sets at the level of the economy as a whole and concentrate on manufacturing to a greater extent than is warranted by the importance of manufacturing activities in the economy in the 1990s. The analyses of regional variations in small enterprise start-ups and importance for local economies derived from these kinds of data sets are almost invariably top down. There are severe limitations on what approaches of these kinds can offer as explanations of the way small enterprises perform under different spatial conditions or, indeed, what effects regional influences have at all on the small business.

The research programme upon which this chapter is based took a very different approach to the common types discussed above. It was based on a bottom up view of the small firm using direct evidence drawn from a close study of small businesses in services in different parts of Britain. The spatial element was provided by a careful selection of localities from which the firms were recruited. For this chapter, the main focus has been on the differences between businesses in a predominantly rural area, North East Suffolk, and businesses in four urban localities.

The findings do not reveal a clear contrast between the rural area's small services businesses and their counterparts in the urban areas. Instead, there are a number of differences, many of them relatively minor, which suggest that while local influences might have some impact on the character, managerial practices, trading patterns and employment strategies of the businesses studied, they need to be set against the mainly larger differences revealed as arising from other influences. For instance, the great majority of differences between North East Suffolk and the businesses in the different urban areas are no greater than the range of differences between the businesses in the urban areas. Similarly, the urban-rural differences (and the differences between the businesses within the urban areas) do not by any means outweigh the greater range of differences related to the economic sectors in which the businesses operate.

For example, businesses in North East Suffolk were significantly smaller on average than those in the urban areas but the disaggregation of the urban area data suggested that there was little difference between the firms in North East Suffolk and those in Doncaster. Thus, businesses in rural areas may be smaller than in many urban areas but there are, equally, urban areas where businesses are smaller than average and probably for much the same reason: the low levels of demand in the local economy. The latter is not a particularly rural characteristic. If independent businesses in rural areas are relatively small this cannot strictly be ascribed to something distinctive about rural cultures and their business patterns. The latter point is reinforced by the findings on managerial strategies in relation to the wider economy which suggested, for instance, that owner-managers in the rural local economy were no more likely to be engaged in networking activities than most of their urban counterparts.

It might be argued that the sample of small businesses studied in the research programme reported in this chapter were of a kind unlikely to reveal differences between rural and urban localities. The types of business activities chosen for investigation were, in several cases, from newer sectors of the economy – including computer services and advertising, marketing and design – and could not be expected to reveal differences between rural and urban economies since economic activities associated with rural economies were under-represented. Yet, in Britain's economy in the 1990s, a rural locality whose economy is strongly rooted in agriculture and agriculturally related activities, is likely to be hard to find. Agriculture is not an important industry in the UK in terms of contributions to employment or number of enterprises. Even in rural localities themselves, as the statistics for North East Suffolk's RDA show, it often far from dominates. Instead, rural localities are increasingly likely to have the kinds of businesses found elsewhere in Britain, regardless of locality. There has been an influx of manufacturing into rural areas but, even more, it is likely that newer businesses will be in the expanding services economy.

Searching for spatial differences which are more than simply statistical departures from the averages produced by national data sets, that is, differences which add up to different types of managerial strategies or employer–employee relations or trading patterns, appears difficult on the data collected from the present research programme. Where such differences do exist, they appear minor and are often difficult to link clearly with specific local influences, particularly of a non-economic kind, which show local cultures or associated behaviours at work.

References and notes

1 THE LOCATION OF SMALL AND MEDIUM ENTERPRISES: ARE THERE URBAN-RURAL DIFFERENCES?

References

Ball, M., Gray, F. and McDowell, L. (1989) *The Transformation of Britain, Contemporary Social and Economic Change*, London, Fontana.

Bayldon, R., Woods, A. and Zafaris, N. (1984) 'Inner city versus new towns: a comparison of manufacturing performance', *Oxford Bulletin of Economics and Statistics*, 46, 21–9.

Bolton Report (1971) *Small Firms, Report of the Committee of Inquiry on Small Firms*, Cmnd 4811, London, HMSO.

Champion, T. and Watkins, C. (eds) (1991) *People in the Countryside, Studies of Social Change in Rural Britain*, London, Paul Chapman.

Coombes, M.G., Storey, D.J., Watson, R. and Wynarczyk, P. (1991) 'The influence of location upon profitability and employment changes in small companies', *Urban Studies*, 28, 5, 723–4.

Daly, M. (1990) 'The 1980s – a decade of growth in enterprise', *Employment Gazette*, November, 553–65.

Daly, M. (1991) 'Vat registrations and deregistrations in 1990', *Employment Gazette*, November, 579–88.

Department of Employment (1992) *Small Firms in Britain*, London. HMSO,

Fothergill, S. and Gudgin, G. (1982) *Unequal Growth: Urban and Regional Employment Change in the United Kingdom*, London, Heinemann.

Graham, N., Beatson, M. and Wells, W. (1989), '1977–1987: a decade of service', *Employment Gazette*, January, 45–53.

Guardian (1992) 'Rich and poor feel chill as rural idyll turns sour', 28 November.

Jennings, K. (1991) 'How to make your start-up stay up', *Observer*, 17 March.

Keeble, D. (1976) *Industrial Location and Planning in the United Kingdom*, London, Methuen.

Keeble, D. (1986) 'The changing spatial structure of economic activity and metropolitan decline in the United Kingdom', in H.J. Ewers, J.B. Goddard and H. Matzerath (eds) *The Future of the Metropolis: Berlin*,

London, Paris, New York: The Economic Aspects, Berlin, Walter de Gruyter.

Keeble, D., Walker, S. and Robson, M. (1992) *Spatial and Temporal Variations in New Firm Formation, Small Business Growth and Firm Dissolution in the United Kingdom*, Report to the Employment Department and European Commission, Directorate General for Enterprise Policy.

Keeble, D., Tyler, P., Broom, G. and Lewis, J. (1992a) *Business Success in the Countryside: The Performance of Rural Enterprises*, HMSO, for the Department of the Environment.

Stanworth, J. and Gray, C. (eds) (1991) *Bolton Twenty Years On: The Small Firm in the 1990s*, London, Paul Chapman.

Storey, D.J., Keasey, K., Watson, R. and Wynarczyk, P. (1987) *The Performance of Small Firms*, London, Croom Helm.

Tyler, P., Moore, B.C. and Rhodes, J. (1988) 'Geographical variations in industrial costs', *Scottish Journal of Political Economy*, 35, 1, 22–50.

2 FOUNDING A NEW BUSINESS IN THE COUNTRYSIDE

Notes

1 Acknowledgement is due for funding support from the Economic and Social Research Council (Grant No. W.108251008), Barclays Bank, Commission of the European Communities (DG XXIII), the Department of Employment, and the rural Development Commission. Any views expressed do not necessarily reflect those of the sponsoring organisations. Acknowledgement is also made to the four county offices of the Rural Development Commission for assistance in providing a sample population of new small businesses. This chapter brings together the substance of four previously unpublished working papers: Townroe and Mallalieu (1990), Mallalieu and Townroe (1991), Townroe (1991) and Townroe (1992). Preliminary results of the survey were published in Townroe and Mallalieu (1991).

2 The survey was conducted in two parts; questionnaire 'A' and 'B', in the summer and autumn months of 1990. Both questionnaires were sent to four counties in England: Northumberland, Derbyshire, Norfolk and Devon. For each county 300 'A' questionnaires were sent out and 300 'Bs': a grand total of 2,400 questionnaires. The reason for splitting the survey like this was (i) to increase the response rate by cutting the number of questions that needed to be asked, and (ii) to compare results of responses to questions which emphasised different points. Thus questionnaire 'A' focused attention on training, business background, education, the rural market and the personal characteristics of the founder: questionnaire 'B' focused on the characteristics of the business itself and the problem areas such as entrepreneurial skills and the advantages and disadvantages of a rural location, etc.

The response rates at county level are as follows:

	Questionnaire 'A'	*Questionnaire 'B'*	*Total*
Northumberland	80 (26.6%)	59 (19.6%)	(23.0%)
Derbyshire	91 (30.3%)	40 (13.4%)	(21.8%)
Norfolk	70 (23.3%)	59 (19.6%)	(21.5%)
Devon	88 (29.3%)	72 (24.0%)	(26.6%)
Total	329 (27.4%)	230 (19.2%)	[23.3%]

In all there were 559 responses, yielding an overall response rate of 23.3 per cent.

The sample populations in each county were the contact lists of the county office in the Rural Development Commission.

3 The logit model assumes that the cumulative distribution of the error term is logistic and yields a probability of the dependent variable taking values of 1 or 0. A log-odds ratio is therefore a linear function of the explanatory variables. Estimates of the parameters of the models used here were obtained by the maximisation of a likelihood function, using Newton's iterative method, employing the Davison–Fletcher–Powell algorithm. The asterisks on the T-ratios of the coefficients indicate statistical significance at the 10 per cent level. The authors are indebted to Professor David Sapsford of the University of Lancaster for his assistance in their estimates used here.

4 In April 1991 there were over 300 enterprise agencies in the United Kingdom. They are locally funded by a mixture of public sector sources. The director of each agency has often been a secondee from a bank or an accounting firm or another larger company. Assistance to the advice role of the agency is often provided in kind by local professionals and established business managers. The focus is on the start-up problems of very small businesses.

5 By the end of 1991 there were 82 Training and Enterprise Councils in England and Wales. Each of these TECs now has a business plan running over three years and is controlled by a board of directors, largely appointed from local industry. The funding comes from central government. Strategic aims include:

(a) To create a new climate where training is accepted as an essential investment . . . as a means of enhancing not just skills but attitudes.

(b) To respond in terms of both training and enterprise to increased competition and the opportunities it will bring, together with those provided by the European Single Market.

(c) To maintain and develop existing training programmes in a way which is relevant and appropriate to the needs of individuals and those of the local economy.

References

Barkham, R. (1987) 'Regional variations in business size, financial structure and founder characteristics', *Discussion Paper No. 32*, Department of Economics, University of Reading.

Bolton Report (1971) *Report of the Committee of Inquiry on Small Firms*, Cmnd 4811, London, HMSO.

Casson, M. (1982) *The Entrepreneur. An Economic Theory*, Oxford, Blackwell.

Champion, A.G., Green, A.E., Owen, D.W., Ellin, D.J. and Coombes, M.G. (1987) *Changing Places: Britain's Demographic, Economic and Social Complexion*, London, Edward Arnold.

Cross, M. (1981) *New Firm Formation and Regional Development*, Farnborough, Hants, Gower.

Demarche, M.P. and Dupont, B. (1985) 'Characteristics of the new entrepreneur', *New Entrepreneurship*, December 1985.

Errington, A. (1986) The case for agriculture: an independent assessment, Centre for Agricultural Strategy Working Paper 10, University of Reading.

Gasson, R. (1988) *The Economics of Part-Time Farming*, London, Longman.

Hudson, J. (1989) 'Company births and deaths in Britain and the institutional environment', *International Small Business Journal*, 6(1), 37–70.

Keeble, D.E. (1990) 'New firms and regional economic development: experience and impacts in the 1980s', *Cambridge Regional Review*, 1, 26–37.

Keeble, D.E., Tyler, P., Broom, G. and Lewis, J. (1992) *Business Success in the Countryside: The Performance of Rural Enterprise*, London, HMSO for the Department of the Environment.

Kets de Vries, M.F.R. (1977) 'The entrepreneurial personality: a person at the crossroads', *Journal of Management Studies*, 14(1), 48–56.

Ganguly, P. (1985) *UK Small Business Statistics and International Comparisons*, London, Harper & Row.

Mallalieu, K. and Townroe, P.M. (1991) Entrepreneurship and the development of small business: competencies and training needs, Economics Research Centre, University of East Anglia (mimeo).

Moseley, M.J. (1979) *Accessibility: The Rural Challenge*, London, Methuen.

NEDO (1987) *Directions for Change: Land Use in the 1990s*, London, National Economic Development Office.

OPCS (1987) *Population Trends*, 48, London, HMSO.

Smallbone, D. (1990) 'Success and failure in new business start ups', *International Small Business Journal*, 8(2), 34–5.

Storey, D. and Johnson, P. (1987) *Job Generation and Labour Market Change*, Basingstoke, Macmillan.

Strak, J. (1989) *Rural Pluriactivity in the UK: A Report to the Rural Employment Group*, London, National Economic Development Office.

Townroe, P.M. and Mallalieu, K. (1990) Entrepreneurial roles and entrepreneurial competence in regional development. Economics Research Centre, University of East Anglia, Norwich (mimeo).

Townroe, P.M. (1991) New small businesses in the countryside, Paper for 14th national Small Firms Policy and Research Conference, Blackpool.

Townroe, P.M. and Mallalieu, K. (1991) 'Infrastructure for regional development: advice and support to new small businesses', in R.W. Vickerman (ed.), *Infrastructure and Regional Development*, London, Pion.

Townroe, P.M. (1992) Skills and strengths in new rural businesses, Paper for the ESRC Small Firms Initiative Workshop, University of Warwick.

3 SMALL FIRM CREATION, INNOVATION AND GROWTH AND THE URBAN-RURAL SHIFT

References

Bolton, N. and Chalkley, B. (1989) 'Counter-urbanisation – disposing of the myths', *Town and Country Planning*, 58, 9, 249–50.

Cambridge University Small Business Research Centre (1992) *The State of British Enterprise: Growth, Innovation and Competitive Advantage in Small and Medium-Sized Firms*. Small Business Research Centre, University of Cambridge.

Central Statistical Office (1992) *Social Trends 22*, London, HMSO.

Commission of the European Communities (1990) *Enterprises in the European Community*, Office for Official Publications of the European Communities, Luxembourg.

Costello, J. (1990) 'How far do people move house?' *Housing Finance*, 5, 13–17.

Department of the Environment (1977) *Inner London: Policies for Dispersal and Balance*. Final Report of the Lambeth Inner Area Study, London, HMSO.

Economist, The (1989) 'Demographic trends: rural rush', *The Economist*, 23 September, 43–44.

Fothergill, S. and Gudgin, G. (1982) *Unequal Growth: Urban and Regional Employment Change in the UK*, London, Heinemann.

Fothergill, S., Kitson, M. and Monk, S. (1985) *Urban Industrial Change: the Causes of the Urban-Rural Contrast in Manufacturing Employment Trends*, London, HMSO for the Departments of the Environment and Trade and Industry.

Jones, H., Caird, J. and Ford, N. (1984) 'A home in the highlands', *Town and Country Planning*, 53, 11, 326–7.

Jones, H., Caird, J., Berry, W. and Dewhurst, J. (1986) 'Peripheral counter-urbanization: findings from an integration of census and survey data in northern Scotland', *Regional Studies*, 20, 1, 15–26.

Keeble, D. (1976) *Industrial Location and Planning in the United Kingdom*, London, Methuen.

Keeble, D. (1980) 'Industrial decline, regional policy and the urban-rural manufacturing shift in the United Kingdom', *Environment and Planning A*, 12, 8, 945–62.

Keeble, D. (1984) 'The urban-rural manufacturing shift', *Geography*, 69, 2, 163–66.

Keeble, D. (1986) 'The changing spatial structure of economic activity and metropolitan decline in the United Kingdom', ch. 7, pp. 171–99, in H-J. Ewers, J.B. Goddard and H. Matzerath (eds), *The Future of Metropolis: Berlin, London, Paris, New York: The Economic Aspects*, Berlin, Walter de Gruyter.

Keeble, D. (1989) 'High-technology industry and regional development in Britain: the case of the Cambridge phenomenon', *Environment and Planning C, Government and Policy*, 7, 2, 153–72.

Keeble, D. (1990) 'Small firms, new firms and uneven regional development in the United Kingdom', *Area*, 22, 3, 234–45.

Keeble, D. (1992) 'High-technology industry and the restructuring of the UK space economy', ch. 8.1, pp. 172–181, in P. Townroe and R. Martin (eds), *Regional Development in the 1990s: The British Isles in Transition*, London, Jessica Kingsley.

Keeble, D., Bryson, J. and Wood, P. (1991) 'Small firms, business services growth and regional development in the United Kingdom: some empirical findings', *Regional Studies*, 25, 5, 439–457.

Keeble, D., Bryson, J. and Wood, P. (1992) 'Entrepreneurship and flexibility in business services: the rise of small management consultancy and market research firms in the United Kingdom', ch. 4, in K. Caley, E. Chell, F. Chittenden and C. Mason (eds), *Small Enterprise Development: Policy and Practice in Action*, London, Paul Chapman.

Keeble, D., Bryson, J. and Wood, P. (1993) 'The creation, location and growth of small business service firms in the United Kingdom', *Service Industries Journal*, April.

Keeble, D. and Gould, A. (1985) 'Entrepreneurship and manufacturing firm formation in rural regions: the East Anglian case', ch. 11, pp. 197–219, in M.J. Healey and B.W. Ilbery (eds), *The Industrialisation of the Countryside*, Norwich, Geo Books.

Keeble, D. and Kelly, T. (1986) 'New firms and high-technology industry in the United Kingdom: the case of computer electronics', ch. 4, pp. 75–104, in D. Keeble and E. Wever (eds), *New Firms and Regional Development in Europe*, London, Croom Helm.

Keeble, D., Owens, P.L. and Thompson, C. (1983) 'The urban-rural manufacturing shift in the European Community', *Urban Studies*, 20, 4, 405–18.

Keeble, D., Tyler, P., Broom, G. and Lewis, J. (1992) *Business Success in the Countryside: the Performance of Rural Enterprise*, London, HMSO for the Department of the Environment.

Keeble, D., Walker S. and Robson, M. (1993) *New Firm Formation and Small Business Growth in the United Kingdom: Spatial and Temporal Variations and Determinants*. Employment Department Research Series.

Martin, R. (1992) 'Financing regional enterprise: the role of the venture capital market', ch. 7.4, pp. 161–71, in P. Townroe and R. Martin (eds), *Regional Development in the 1990s: The British Isles in Transition*, London, Jessica Kingsley.

Oakey, R.P. and Cooper, S.Y. (1989) 'High technology industry, agglomeration and the potential for peripherally sited small firms', *Regional Studies*, 23, 4, 347–60.

Office of Population Censuses and Surveys (1981) *Key Statistics for Urban Areas, Census 1981*, 1–4, London, HMSO.

Pratten, C. (1991) *The Competitiveness of Small Firms*, Department of Applied Economics Occasional Paper 57, Cambridge, Cambridge University Press.

Townsend, A. (1993) 'The urban-rural cycle in the Thatcher growth years', *Transactions of the Institute of British Geographers*, New series, 18.

Tyler, P., Moore, B.C. and Rhodes J. (1988) 'Geographical variations in industrial costs', *Scottish Journal of Political Economy*, 35, 1, 22–50.

Wood, P., Bryson, J. and Keeble, D. (1993) 'Regional patterns of small firm development: evidence from the UK', forthcoming in *Environment and Planning A*, 25.

4 GROWTH AND SURVIVAL OF MATURE MANUFACTURING SMEs IN THE 1980s: AN URBAN-RURAL COMPARISON

Notes

The Economic and Social Research Council's Small Business Research Initiative includes financial contributions from Barclays Bank, Commission of the European Communities (DG XXIII), Department of Employment and the Rural Development Commission. The views expressed in this chapter do not necessarily reflect those of the sponsoring organisations.

The authors wish to acknowledge the contribution of Paul Lewin to the collection and analysis of the data on which this chapter is based.

References

Department of Trade and Industry (1991) *Constraints on the Growth of Small Firms*, London, HMSO.

Gibb, A. and Dyson, J. (1982) 'Stimulating the growth of the owner managed firm', Paper presented to the UK Small Business Research Conference, Glasgow.

Gibb, A. and Scott, M. (1985) 'Strategic awareness, personal commitment and the process of planning in the small business', *Journal of Management Studies*, 22, 6, 597–631.

Hughes, A. (1991) 'UK small businesses in the 1980s: continuity and change', *Regional Studies*, 25, 5, 471–9.

Keeble, D., Tyler, P., Broom, G. and Lewis, J. (1992) 'Business success in the countryside: the performance of rural enterprise', PA Cambridge Economic Consultants for the Department of the Environment, London, HMSO.

Leigh, R., North, D. and Smallbone, D.J. (1991) 'Adjustment processes in high growth small and medium sized enterprises: a study of mature manufacturing firms in London during the 1980s', ESRC Small Business Research Initiative, Middlesex Polytechnic Project, Working Paper No. 2.

Mason, C. (1991) 'Spatial variations in enterprise: the geography of new firm formation', in R. Burrows (ed.), *Deciphering the Enterprise Culture: Entrepreneurship, Petty Capitalism and the Restructuring of Britain*, London, Routledge.

North, D. and Smallbone, D.J. (1993) 'Employment and labour process changes in manufacturing SMEs during the 1980s', in J. Atkinson and D.J. Storey (eds), *The Small Firm and the Labour Market*, London, Routledge.

North, D., Smallbone, D.J. and Leigh, R. (1992) 'Employment and labour process changes in mature manufacturing SMEs in London during the

1980s', ESRC Small Business Research Initiative, Middlesex Polytechnic Project, Working Paper No. 5.

Smallbone, D.J., North, D. and Leigh, R. (1992) 'Managing change for growth and survival: a study of mature manufacturing firms in London during the 1980s', ESRC Small Business Research Initiative, Middlesex Polytechnic Project, Working Paper No. 3.

University of Cambridge (1992) *The State of British Enterprise*, Small Business Research Centre, University of Cambridge.

5 SPATIAL VARIATIONS IN THE ROLE OF EQUITY INVESTMENT IN THE FINANCING OF SMEs

Note

This chapter has been prepared under the research project 'Informal Risk Capital in the UK' which forms part of the Economic and Social Research Council's (ESRC) Small Business Research Initiative, and is funded by the ESRC in conjunction with Barclays Bank, the Department of Employment, the Rural Development Commission and DG XXIII of the Commission of the European Communities (Ref. W108 25 1017). We are very grateful to Jennifer Chaloner for her work on this project.

References

ACOST (Advisory Committee on Science and Technology) (1990) *The Enterprise Challenge: Overcoming Barriers to Growth in Small Firms*, London, HMSO.

Aston Business School (1991) *Constraints on the Growth of Small Firms*, London, HMSO.

Birley, S. and Westhead, P. (1989) *Private Advertised Sales in the United Kingdom*, Cranfield, Cranfield Entrepreneurship Research Centre, Cranfield School of Management.

Bryant, C.R., Russwurm, L.H. and McLellan, A.G. (1982) *The City's Countryside*, Harlow, Longman.

Buckland, R. and Davies, E.W. (1989) *The Unlisted Securities Market*, Oxford, Clarendon Press.

Burns, P., Burnett, A., Myers, A. and Cain, D. (1992) *Financing Enterprise in Europe*, Cranfield, Beds, 3i/Cranfield European Enterprise Centre, Cranfield School of Management.

Buss, T.F. and Popovitch, M.G. (1988) *Growth From Within: New Businesses and Rural Economic Development in North Dakota*, Washington, DC, Council of State Policy and Planning Agencies.

Buss, T.F., Popovitch, M.G. and Gemmel, D. (1991) 'Successful entrepreneurs and their problems in starting new businesses in rural America: a four state study', *Environment and Planning C: Government and Policy*, 9, 371–81.

Champion, A.G. and Townsend, A.R. (1990) *Contemporary Britain: A Geographical Perspective*, London, Edward Arnold.

Cloke, P.J. (1977) 'An index of rurality for England and Wales', *Regional Studies*, 11, 7–18.

Cloke, P. and Edwards, G. (1986) 'Rurality in England and Wales 1981: a replication of the 1971 index', *Regional Studies*, 20, 289–306.

Deutermann, E.P. (1966) 'Seeding science based industry', *New England Business Review*, December, 7–15.

Economic Council of Newfoundland and Labrador (ECNL) (1988) *Equity Capital and Economic Development in Newfoundland and Labrador*, St John's, Nfld, Economic Council of Newfoundland and Labrador.

Employment Department (1990) *A Survey of Owner-Managed Businesses*, HMSO, London.

Estall, R.C. (1972) 'Some observations on the internal mobility of investment capital', *Area*, 4, 193–8.

Estall, R.C. and Buchanan, R.O. (1980) *Industrial Activity and Economic Geography*, 4th edn, London, Hutchinson.

Florida, R.L. and Kenney, M. (1988) 'Venture capital, high technology and regional development', *Regional Studies*, 22, 33–48.

Florida, R. and Smith, D.F. (1990) Venture capital, innovation and economic development, *Economic Development Quarterly*, 4, 345–60.

Freear, J. and Wetzel, W.E. (1992) 'The informal venture capital market in the year 2000', in D.L. Sexton and J.D. Kasarda (eds), *Entrepreneurship in the 1990s*, Boston, PWS-Kent, pp. 462–86.

Gaston, R.J. (1989) *Finding Private Venture Capital Four Your Firm: A Complete Guide*, New York, Wiley.

Green, M.B. (1989) 'Patterns of preference for venture capital investment in the United States of America', *Environment and Planning C: Government and Policy*, 7, 205–22.

Guenther, H.P. (1991) The impact of deposit insurance reform proposals on small firm financing, Paper to the Third Annual International Research Symposium on Small Firm Finance, Florida State University, Tallahassee.

Harrison, R.T. and Mason, C.M. (eds) (1993) *Informal Venture Capital: Information, Networks and Public Policy*, Hemel Hempstead, Woodhead-Faulkner.

Hustedde, R.J. and Pulver, G.C. (1992) 'Factors affecting equity capital acquisition: the demand factor', *Journal of Business Venturing*, 7, 363–74.

Hutchinson, R. and McKillop, D. (1992) *The Financial Services Industry in Northern Ireland*, Belfast, Northern Ireland Economic Council, Report 91.

Jackson, E.T. and Peirce, J. (1990) *Mobilizing Capital for Regional Development*, Ottawa, Economic Council of Canada, Local Development Paper No. 21.

Keeble, D. (1976) *Industrial Location and Planning in the United Kingdom*, Methuen, London.

Keeble, D. (1990) 'Small firms, new firms and uneven development in the United Kingdom', *Area*, 22, 234–45.

Keeble, D. and Gould, A. (1985) 'Entrepreneurship and manufacturing firm formation in rural regions: the East Anglian case', in M.J. Healey and B.W. Ilbery (eds), *The Industrialization of the Countryside*, Norwich, Geo Books, pp. 197–219.

Keeble, D., Tyler, P., Broom, G. and Lewis, J. (1992) *Business Success in the Countryside: the Performance of Rural Enterprise*, London, HMSO.

Leigh, R., North, D. and Smallbone, D. (1991) *Adjustment Processes in High Growth Small and Medium Size Enterprises: A Study of Mature*

Manufacturing Firms in London During the 1980s, Enfield: Middlesex, Middlesex Polytechnic, Small Business Research Initiative Working Paper No. 2.

Leyshon, A. and Thrift, N. (1989) 'South goes North? The rise of the British provincial centres', in J. Lewis and A. Townsend (eds) *The North-South Divide*, London, Paul Chapman, pp. 114–56.

Malecki, E.J. (1991) *Technology and Economic Development*, Harlow, Essex, Longman.

Marsh, P. (1982) 'The choice between equity and debt: an empirical study, *Journal of Finance*, 37, 121–44.

Martin, R. (1989) 'The growth and geographical anatomy of venture capitalism in the United Kingdom', *Regional Studies*, 23, 389–403.

Mason, C.M. (1992) 'New firm formation and growth', in P. Townroe and R. Martin (eds), *Regional Development in the 1990s*, London, Jessica Kingsley, pp. 150–60.

Mason, C.M. and Harrison, R.T. (1989) 'Small firms policy and the "North-South divide" in the United Kingdom: the case of the Business Expansion Scheme', *Transactions, Institute of British Geographers*, 14, 37–58.

Mason, C.M. and Harrison, R.T. (1991) 'Venture capital, the equity gap and the north-south divide in the UK', in M. Green (ed.), *Venture Capital: International Comparisons*, London, Routledge, 202–47.

Mason, C.M., Harrison, R.T. and Chaloner, J. (1991) 'Informal risk capital in the UK: a study of investor characteristics, investment preferences and investment decision-making', *Venture Finance Research Project Working Paper No 2*, University of Southampton (Urban Policy Research Unit)/ University of Ulster (Ulster Business School).

Mason, C., Harrison, J. and Harrison, R. (1988) *Closing the Equity Gap? An Assessment of the Business Expansion Scheme*, London, Small Business Research Trust.

McKillop, D. and Barton, L. (1992) 'Small firms and their banks: a happy partnership?' *Banking Ireland*, Summer, 18–20.

McKillop, D.G. and Hutchinson, R.W. (1990) *Regional Financial Sectors in the British Isles*, Aldershot, Avebury.

McMullen, W.E., Long, R. and Tapp, J. (1984) 'Entrepreneurial share transaction strategies', in J.A. Hornaday, F. Tarpley, J.A. Timmons and K.H. Vesper (eds), *Frontiers of Entrepreneurship Research*, Wellesley: MA, Babson College, pp. 32–42.

McNaughton, R.B. and Green, M.B. (1988) 'Spatial patterns of Canadian venture capital investment', *Regional Studies*, 23, 9–18.

Myers, S. (1984) 'The capital structure puzzle', *Journal of Finance*, 39, 572–92.

Myers, S. and Majluf, N. (1984) 'Corporate financing and investment decisions when firms have information investors do not have', *Journal of Financial Economics*, 12, 187–222.

National Economic Development Committee (1986) *Finance for Growth: A study of Small and Medium-Sized Firms in the Electronics Sector*, London, NEDO.

Newfoundland Royal Commission on Employment and Unemployment (1986) *Building on our Strengths*, St John's: Nfld, Office of the Queen's Printer, Government of Newfoundland and Labrador.

O'Farrell, P.N. (1990) 'Small manufacturing firm competitiveness and performance: an analysis of matched pairs in Nova Scotia and New England', *Journal of Small Business and Entrepreneurship*, 8, 1, 15–40.

Perry, M. (1988a) 'Venture capital in New Zealand', *New Zealand Geographer*, 44, 2–7.

Perry, M. (1988b) 'The supply and demand of small business finance in a rural region', *Tijdschrift voor Econ. en Soc. Geografie*, 79, 188–98.

Pettit, R.R. and Singer, R.F. (1985) 'Small business finance: a research agenda', *Financial Management*, 14, 3, 47–60.

Phillips, D. and Williams, A. (1984) *Rural Britain: A Social Geography*, Oxford, Basil Blackwell.

Scherr, F.W., Sugrue, T.F. and Ward, J.B. (1990) 'Financing the small firm start-up: determinants of debt use', Paper to the Second Annual International Research Symposium on Small Firm Finance, California State University, Fresno.

Shaffer, R. and Pulver, G.C. (1985) 'Regional variations in capital structure of new small businesses: the Wisconsin case', in D.J. Storey (ed.), *Small Firms in Regional Economic Development: Britain, Ireland and the United States*, Cambridge, Cambridge University Press, pp. 166–92.

Shaw, J.M. (1979) (ed.) *Rural Deprivation and Planning*, Norwich, Geo Books.

Small Business Research Trust (1991) 'Small business finance', *NatWest Quarterly Survey of Small Business in Britain*, Milton Keynes, Small Business Research Trust, 19–21.

Smith, G.R. (1986) 'Profit sharing and employee share ownership in Britain', *Employment Gazette*, 94, 380–5.

Sweeney, G.P. (1987) *Innovation, Entrepreneurs and Regional Development*, London, Frances Pinter.

Turok, I. and Richardson, P. (1991) 'New firms and local economic development: evidence from West Lothian', *Regional Studies*, 25, 71–83.

University of Cambridge (1992) *The State of British Enterprise*, Cambridge, Small Business Research Centre.

Walker, D.A. (1989) 'Financing the small firm', *Small Business Economics*, 1, 285–96.

Westhead, P., (1989) 'A spatial analysis of new firm formation in Wales, 1979–1983', *International Small Business Journal*, 7, 2, 44–68.

Wickham, J., Fuchs, R. and Miller-Pitt, J. (1989) *Where Credit is Due: A Case Study of the Eagle River Credit Union*, Ottawa, Economic Council of Canada, Local Development Paper No. 4.

6 IN SEARCH OF SPATIAL DIFFERENCES: EVIDENCE FROM A STUDY OF SMALL SERVICE SECTOR ENTERPRISES

Notes

We wish to acknowledge the financial contributions from the Economic and Social Research Council, Barclays Bank, Commission of the European Communities (DGXXIII), Department of Employment and the Rural Development Commission. Any views expressed do not necessarily reflect those of the sponsoring organisations.

1 VAT data is not reliable for the purpose of estimating changes in the small business population because a large proportion of small business, perhaps as many as a half according to one informed estimate (Jennings, 1991) are not registered for VAT. The sharp rise in the 1992 Budget in the threshold for registration will render VAT data even less helpful for this purpose.

2 Within this structural shift, again using VAT data, smaller scale activities have mushroomed in services although there are some large differences within this grouping. For example, 'other services' and 'finance, property and professional services' experienced net increases of 7.3 per cent and 6.8 per cent per annum respectively between 1979 and 1990 compared with 2.6 per cent for all industries and services (Daly, 1991).

3 A full description of the strategies used to construct sampling frames and samples together with definitions of the kinds of enterprise covered and response rates is provided in Curran, Blackburn and Woods (1991a, Appendix).

4 Champion and Green's index divides Britain into 280 local Labour Market areas ranked (on the amalgamated index) from the most prosperous (1) to the least prosperous (280). Four of the localities selected scored as follows on the index: Guildford 15, Nottingham 141 and Doncaster 274. Lowestoft and Woodbridge, the nearest local Labour Markets corresponding to North East Suffolk, ranked 213 and 189 respectively. London Boroughs such as Islington were not included separately in the index in a form to allow a strict comparison with the above rankings but it was selected using local data for the area which showed a very mixed inner city economy.

5 The employment effect of Sizewell B nuclear power station was expected to peak at about 3500 jobs in 1991. The bulk of these were temporary, filled by people from outside the area but it was expected to have a wider impact through the drawing of labour from local industries and the impact on local spending (Rural Development Commission, 1988: Appendix A).

6 One example of fixed costs being higher in urban areas is shown by a comparison of office accommodation costs in Suffolk and Islington. Data collected by Suffolk County Council (1988) suggests that in 1990 office accommodation cost an average of £3.00 per square feet per year in comparison with a range from £8.00 to £20.00 in Islington in the same year (Islington Borough Council, 1992).

7 These differences mean that it would be unwise to assume that because small businesses in rural areas are smaller measured by turnover than in more prosperous urban areas, they are also less profitable. Collecting data on small business profits is extremely difficult because respondents are usually reluctant to provide such information and, indeed, may not know themselves or may calculate profit in different ways, some of which would be regarded by professionals such as accountants as eccentric.

8 For example, in a postal survey of 62 businesses in Waveney in 1987, nearly half of the respondents expressed some dissatisfaction with their present premises (Economic Research Centre, 1987).

9 As argued in Curran *et al.*, 1991a: 32, the exploration of motivations is probably best analysed using a qualitative approach. However, for the purposes of this chapter, a simple quantitative categorisation has been employed

because the original interviews asked only one or two questions on owner-managers' relations to locality and, therefore, a qualitative analysis of this dimension cannot be taken very far.

10 Of the four business owners in North East Suffolk mentioning money making as a key motivation for starting a business, only one came from the more remote rural areas, possibly reflecting the even more limited market opportunities in these areas.

11 This relative geographical immobility of owners in North East Suffolk was reinforced by the finding (not statistically significant but nevertheless suggestive) that the overwhelming majority (69 or 97.2 per cent) were white British in comparison with 86.0 per cent in the urban areas as a whole.

12 Chi-square significance 0.065.

13 Chi-square significance 0.004.

14 The re-interviews were with 274 of the *Lead Project* owner-managers although it was established that, in fact, 293 firms were still trading in some form. It proved impossible to arrange interviews with eight owner-managers in the time available to carry out the interviews, ten of the firms had changed hands and the new owners were not interviewed, and one of the original owners declined to be interviewed.

15 The phrase 'ceased trading' is used here rather than terms such as 'failed' or 'died' since there are a wide range of possible reasons why a business may cease. Failure, in the sense of the business being unable to generate sufficient turnover to cover all costs and provide an income for the owner, is not the only possible reason for closure. For example, the owner may have seen an opportunity elsewhere and closed one business simply to open another even though the first business was still operating satisfactorily or the owner may have retired and closed the business rather than selling it on.

16 These points are supported by data from the February 1992 survey on difficulties of attracting enough customers. Of urban business owners, 50.5 per cent had experienced difficulty in attracting enough customers in comparison with 63.8 per cent in Islington and 36.6 per cent in North East Suffolk (for the Islington–North East Suffolk difference chi-square sig. 0.005).

17 The number of people employed was calculated including all those working for the enterprise, full-time permanent employees, part-timers, casuals and those who worked for the enterprise as self-employed. The reasons for this approach are given in Curran *et al.* (1991a: 13–20).

18 Even leaving this business out, however, surviving North East Suffolk firms created 0.85 jobs per firm in comparison with 0.68 in the urban firms between 1990 and 1992.

19 Of the firms in more rural areas, 14.6 per cent were selling 75 per cent or more of their services outside the locality in comparison with 6.7 per cent in the less rural areas of North East Suffolk, although this difference was not statistically significant.

20 Now called the *National Federation of Small Businesses*.

21 Now defunct and these activities have been delegated to local TECs.

22 For a full discussion of this project and the detailed results see Blackburn, Curran and Jarvis (1990) and Curran *et al.* (1991b).

References

Allen, J. and Massey, D. (1988) (eds) *The Economy in Question*, London, Sage.

Armstrong, H. and Taylor, J. (1983) *Regional Economic Policy and its Analysis*, Oxford, Philip Allan.

Ashcroft, B., Love, J.H. and Malloy, E. (1991) 'New firm formation in the British counties with special reference to Scotland', *Regional Studies*, 25, 395–410.

Ball, M., Grey, F. and McDowell, L. (1989) *The Transformation of Britain, Contemporary Social and Economic Change*, London, Fontana.

Blackburn, R.A., Curran, J. and Jarvis, R. (1990) 'Small firms and local networks: some theoretical and conceptual explorations' Paper presented at the 13th National Small Firms Policy and Research Conference, Cardiff.

Blackwell, D. (1991) 'Winds of change', *Financial Times*, 30 October.

Burrows, R. and Curran, J. (1989) 'Sociological research on service sector small businesses: some conceptual considerations', *Work, Employment and Society*, 3, 4, 527–39.

Champion, T. and Green, A. (1988) 'Local prosperity and the north-south divide: winners and losers in 1990s Britain', Department of Town Planning, University College of Cardiff.

Champion, T. and Watkins, C. (1991) (eds) *People in the Countryside: Studies of Social Change in Rural Britain*, London, Paul Chapman.

Chell, E., Haworth, J. and Brearley, E. (1991) *The Entrepreneurial Personality, Concepts, Cases and Categories*, London, Routledge.

Cooke, P. (1990) (ed.) *Localities*, London, Unwin Hyman.

Curran, J. (1986) *Bolton Fifteen Years On*, Milton Keynes, Small Business Research Trust.

Curran, J. and Blackburn, R.A. (1991) 'Small firms and local economic networks, a report to the Midland Bank', Small Business Research Centre, Kingston Business School, Kingston University, Kingston upon Thames.

Curran, J. and Blackburn, R.A. (1992a) 'Small firms and local economies: a view from the ground', Paper presented to a seminar at the Small Business Research Centre, Cambridge University, June.

Curran, J. and Blackburn, R.A. (1992b). 'Small business survey, February 1992', ESRC Centre for Research on Small Service Sector Enterprises, Kingston Business School, Kingston University, Kingston upon Thames.

Curran, J., Kitching, J., Abbott, B. and Mills, V. (1993) 'Employment and employee relations in the small service sector firm', Kingston upon Thames, Kingston Business School, Kingston University.

Curran, J., Blackburn, R.A. and Woods, A. (1991a) 'Profiles of the small enterprise in the service sector', Kingston upon Thames, ESRC Centre for Research on Small Service Sector Enterprises, Kingston Business School, Kingston University.

Curran, J., Jarvis, R., Blackburn, R.A. and Black, S. (1991b) 'Small firms and networks: constructs, methodological strategies and preliminary findings', Paper presented to the 14th National Small Firms Policy and Research Conference, Blackpool, November.

Curwen, P. (ed.) (1990) *Understanding the UK Economy*, London, Macmillan.

Daly, M. (1991) 'VAT registrations and deregistrations in 1990', *Employment Gazette*, November, 579–88.

208   *References and notes*

Department of Employment (1992) *The 1991 Labour Force Survey*, Press Notice, London, Department of Employment, March.

Economic Research Centre (1987) *Economic Development Study for Waveney District Council*, University of East Anglia School of Economic and Social Studies, October.

Employment Gazette (1992) Table 2.3, April.

Financial Times (1991) 'Suffolk Profile', 30 October, pp. 33–5.

Fothergill, S. and Gudgin, G. (1982) *Unequal Growth: Urban and Regional Employment Change in the UK*, London, Heinemann.

Giaoutzi, M., Nijkamp, P. and Storey, D.J. (1988) (eds) *Small and Medium Size Enterprises and Regional Development*, London, Routledge.

Gould, A. and Keeble, D. (1984) 'New firms and rural industrialisation in East Anglia', *Regional Studies*, 18, 189–202.

Guildford Borough Council (1989) *Digest of Population, Housing and Employment Statistics*, Monitoring Report 2/89, Guildford Borough Council Technical Services Department, January.

Islington Borough Council (1992) Information Provided by the Commercial Valuations and Estates Management Section.

Jennings, K. (1991; 'How to make your start-up stay up', *Observer*, 17 March.

Keeble, D. (1980) 'Industrial decline, regional policy and the urban-rural manufacturing shift in the United Kingdom', *Environment and Planning A*, 12, 945–62.

Keeble, D. (1990) 'Small firms, new firms and uneven regional development in the United Kingdom', *Area*, 22, 234–45.

Keeble, D. and Wever, E. (1986) (eds) *New Firms and Regional Development in Europe*, Beckenham, Croom Helm.

Keeble, D., Bryson, J. and Wood, P. (1991) 'Small firms, businesses growth and regional development in the United Kingdom: some empirical findings', *Regional Studies*, 25, 5, 439–57.

Lee, D. and Newby, H. (1983) *The Problem of Sociology, An Introduction to the Discipline*, London, Hutchinson.

Lloyd, P. and Mason, C. (1984) 'Spatial variations in new firm formation in the United Kingdom: comparative evidence from Merseyside, Greater Manchester and South Hampshire, *Regional Studies*, 18, 207–20.

Mason, C.M. (1989) 'Explaining trends in new firm formation in the UK', *Regional Studies*, 23, 331–46.

Mason, C.M. (1991) 'Spatial variations in enterprise: the Geography of New Firm Formation' in Burrows, R. (ed.), *Deciphering the Enterprise Culture, Entrepreneurship, Petty Capitalism and the Restructuring of Britain*, London, Routledge.

Massey, D. and Allen, J. (1988) (eds) *Uneven Re-Development, Cities and Regions in Transition*, London, Hodder & Stoughton.

Mclaughlin, B. (1986) 'The rhetoric and the reality of rural deprivation', *Journal of Rural Studies*, 2, 4, 291–307.

Meyer-Krahmer, F. (1985) 'Innovation Behaviour and Regional Indigenous Potential' *Regional Studies*, 19, 523–34.

New Earnings Survey (1991) *New Earnings Survey 1991*, Part E, Analyses by Region, London, HMSO.

Newby, H. (1977) *The Deferential Worker*, Harmondsworth, Penguin.

Newby, H. (1979) *Green and Pleasant Land? Social Change in Rural England*, Harmondsworth, Penguin.

Nottingham City Council (1989) *Economic Profile of Nottingham*, Nottingham, Nottingham City Council.

Office of Population Censuses and Surveys (1984) *Key Statistics for Urban Areas: The Midlands Cities and Towns 1981*, Table 1, London, HMSO.

Petitt, S. and Thompstone, K. (1988) 'Entrepreneurial networking within rural Ireland', Paper presented to International Conference on Rural Entrepreneurship, Silsoe College, Cranfield Institute of Technology, September.

Pyke, F., Beccattini, G. and Sengenberger, W. (1990) (eds) *Industrial Districts and Inter-Firm Co-operation*, Geneva, International Labour Organisation.

Regional Trends (1991) London, HMSO.

Rural Development Commission (1988) 'Suffolk Rural Development Area', *Rural Development Programme 1989–1990*, London.

Rural Development Commission (1992) Information provided by the RDC, Ipswich.

Savage, M. (1989) 'Spatial Differences in Modern Britain', in C. Hamnett, MacDowell, L. and Sarre, P. (eds), *Restructuring Britain, The Changing Social Structure*, London, Sage with the Open University.

Savage, M., Barlow, J., Duncan, S. and Saunders, P. (1987) 'Locality Research: The Sussex Programme on Economic Restructuring, Social Change and the Locality', *Quarterly Journal of Social Affairs*, 3, 1, 27–51.

Sayer, A. (1984) *Method in Social Science: A Realist Approach*, London, Hutchinson.

Stanworth, J. and Gray, C. (1991) (eds), *Bolton Twenty Years On: The Small Business in the 1990s*, London, Paul Chapman.

Suffolk County Council (1988) 'Be . . . County Wise Suffolk Key Facts', Suffolk County Council, Ipswich.

Townsend, P. (1979) *Poverty in the United Kingdom*, Harmondsworth, Penguin.

Townsend, A.R. (1991) 'New forms of employment in rural areas: a national perspective', in Champion and Watkins (eds), *People in the Countryside*, ch. 6.

Utting, D. (1991) 'Merely a question of time', in *Financial Times*, 30 October.

Index